Validation in Language Testing

MODERN LANGUAGES in PRACTICE

Series Editor
Michael Grenfell, *School of Education,University of Southampton*

Editorial Board
Do Coyle, *School of Education, University of Nottingham*
Simon Green, *Trinity & All Saints College, Leeds*

Editorial Consultant
Christopher Brumfit, Centre for Language in Education, University of Southampton

Other Books in the Series
Le ou La? The Gender of French Nouns
    MARIE SURRIDGE

Other Books of Interest
Approaches to Second Language Acquisition
    R. TOWELL and R. HAWKINS
Culture and Language Learning in Higher Education
    MICHAEL BYRAM (ed.)
Distance Education for Language Teachers
    RON HOWARD and IAN McGRATH (eds)
French for Communication 1979-1990
    ROY DUNNING
Quantifying Language
    PHIL SCHOLFIELD
Reflections on Language Learning
    L. BARBARA and M. SCOTT (eds)
Tasks and Language Learning
    GRAHAM CROOKES and SUSAN M. GASS (eds)
Tasks in a Pedagogical Context
    GRAHAM CROOKES and SUSAN M. GASS (eds)
Teaching-and-Learning Language-and-Culture
    MICHAEL BYRAM, CAROL MORGAN and colleagues

Please contact us for the latest book information:
Multilingual Matters Ltd, Frankfurt Lodge, Clevedon Hall,
Victoria Road, Clevedon, Avon BS21 7SJ, England

MODERN LANGUAGES IN PRACTICE 2
Series Editor: Michael Grenfell

Validation in Language Testing

Edited by
Alister Cumming
and Richard Berwick

MULTILINGUAL MATTERS LTD
Clevedon • Philadelphia • Adelaide

Library of Congress Cataloging in Publication Data

Validation in Language Testing/Edited by Alister Cumming and Richard Berwick
(Modern Languages in Practice: 2)
Papers originally presented at the 14th Annual Language Testing Research
Colloquium which was held Feb. 27 – Mar. 1, 1992, University of British
Columbia, Vancouver.
Includes bibliographical references and index.
1. Language and languages–Examinations–Validity–Congresses.
I. Cumming, Alister, H. II. Berwick, Richard. III. Language Testing Research
Colloquium (14th: 1992: University of British Columbia). IV. Series.
P53.4.V35   1995
418′.0076–dc20   95-6556

British Library Cataloguing in Publication Data

A CIP catalogue record for this book is available from the British Library.

ISBN 1-85359-296-X (hbk)
ISBN 1-85359-295-1 (pbk)

Multilingual Matters Ltd

UK: Frankfurt Lodge, Clevedon Hall, Victoria Road, Clevedon, Avon BS21 7SJ.
USA: 1900 Frost Road, Suite 101, Bristol, PA 19007, USA.
Australia: P.O. Box 6025, 83 Gilles Street, Adelaide, SA 5000, Australia.

Typeset by Wayside Books, Clevedon.
Printed and bound in Great Britain by the Cromwell Press.

Contents

Introduction: The Concept of Validation in Language Testing
Alister Cumming 1

SECTION I. EVIDENTIAL BASES OF TEST INTERPRETATION

*I.i. Validation of New Instruments and Procedures: Feasibility,
Reliability, and Model-Fitting*

1   Developing Rating Scales for CASE: Theoretical Concerns and
    Analyses
    *Michael Milanovic, Nick Saville, Alastair Pollitt and
    Annette Cook* 15
2   Validation of a New Holistic Rating Scale Using Rasch
    Multi-faceted Analysis
    Belle Tyndall and Dorry Mann Kenyon 39

*I.ii. Criterion Evidence in Test Interpretation: Hypothesis Testing for
Construct Validation*

3   Hypothesis Testing in Construct Validation
    Sara Cushing Weigle and Brian Lynch 58
4   An Investigation into the Validity of Written Indicators of
    Second Language Proficiency
    Alister Cumming and Dean Mellow 72

I.iii. Concurrent Validation: Comparing Alternative Test Methods

5   Multiple-choice Summary: A Measure of Text Comprehension
    Ari Huhta and Elina Randell 94
6   Using the Information Curve to Assess Language CAT Efficiency
    Michel Laurier 111

SECTION II. EVIDENTIAL BASES OF LANGUAGE TEST USE

II.i. Criterion Evidence in Test Use: Expert Judgments

7   Comparing the Scaling of Speaking Tasks by Language Teachers
    and by the ACTFL Guidelines
    Charles W. Stansfield and Dorry Mann Kenyon 124

II.ii. Tracing Learners' Cognitive Processes and Domain-Specific
Knowledge in Test Use
8   A Communicative Test in Analysis: Strategies in Reading
    Authentic Texts
    Ingrid F. Wijgh 154
9   What Makes an ESP Reading Test Appropriate for its
    Candidates?
    Caroline Clapham 171

SECTION III. CONSEQUENTIAL BASES OF LANGUAGE
TESTING: IMPACTS ON EDUCATIONAL AND
PROFESSIONAL SYSTEMS

10 Examining Washback: The Sri Lankan Impact Study
    Dianne Wall and J. Charles Alderson 194
11 The Role of the Segmental Dictionary in Professional Validation:
    Constructing a Dictionary of Language Testing
    Alan Davies 222
12 Language Testing Courses: What Are They?
    Kathleen M. Bailey and James Dean Brown 236

Introduction: The Concept of Validation in Language Testing

ALISTER CUMMING

Validity is an ominous word. The *Oxford English Dictionary* assigns it several meanings, deriving from Latin origins of 'powerful, effective': 'possessing legal authority or force', 'technically perfect or efficacious', as well as 'sound and to the point; against which no objections can fairly be brought'. These senses are all relevant to current uses of the term *validity* in language testing. But as the chapters in the present volume make clear, various practices, modes of argumentation, sources of information, and complex conceptual issues exist for establishing the validity of language testing instruments, procedures, and their uses in educational settings. Moreover, many valuable analytic approaches and theoretical considerations have only recently been explored, applying innovative measurement techniques, corresponding to the complex nature of language proficiency itself, and accounting for the diverse purposes for which languages are learned as well as settings in which languages are used.

Validation in language assessment *is* ominously important, arbitrating educational and linguistic policies, institutional decisions, pedagogical practices, as well as tenets of language theory and research. But establishing validity in language assessment is by all accounts problematic, conceptually challenging, and difficult to achieve – probably more so than is recognized outside the specialized spheres of those few persons who make this endeavor their particular business, and perhaps even more so than most specialists in language education, research, or policy have acknowledged (Bachman, 1990; Groot, 1990).

The present book is unique in offering a single volume that displays the wide range of current approaches to the technical methods, conceptual issues, and broader implications of establishing validity in language assessment. Its 12 chapters were all originally presented as refereed papers at

1

the Fourteenth Annual Language Testing Research Colloquium held at the University of British Columbia in Vancouver, Canada from February 27 to March 1, 1992, organized by Mari Wesche, Grant Henning, and John H. A. L. De Jong. Each chapter presents a carefully-designed, systematically-researched effort to validate a particular instrument, procedure, or aspect of language assessment. The chapters represent researchers and assessment situations from diverse parts of the globe as well as different types of educational contexts. As such, each chapter serves as a unique case study of validation in language testing.

Collectively, the chapters contrast with one another in fundamental ways, revealing a multiplicity of perspectives on the information, analyses and arguments that bear on validation in language assessment. This contrast moves the present volume beyond simple, textbook definitions of language test validation, providing a single reference book on the current *state of the art* suitable for advanced study by graduate students, administrators, evaluators, researchers, and scholars of language assessment.

What Validates a Test?

Test validation has long been recognized as an exacting process that requires many types of evidence, analyses, and interpretation:

> all data yielded by the administration of a test could serve as legitimate evidence of validity – not only predictive data, but correlational studies generally, factorial studies, studies of differences with respect to groups, situations, tasks, and times, observational studies of change, and studies of experimentally induced change. (Angoff, 1988, p. 30)

Indeed, Angoff's (1988) historical review of conceptions of test validity describes no fewer than 16 types of validity that have featured prominently in the psychometric literature since the 1930s:

- **concurrent validity:** 'correlation of test against criterion; but here the predictor scores and the criterion scores [are] observed at the same point in time . . . evidence that a newly proposed test, or a brief version of an existing test, was measuring a given trait', p. 21
- **construct validity:** 'a mutual verification of the measuring instrument and the theory of the construct it is meant to measure', p. 29; 'we examine the psychological trait, or construct, presumed to be measured by the test and we cause a continuing, research interplay to take place between the scores earned on the test and the theory underlying the construct', p. 26

- **content validity:** 'review of the test by subject-matter experts and a verification that its content represents a satisfactory sampling of the domain', p. 22
- **convergent validity:** 'correlations among different methods of measuring the same construct', p. 26
- **criterion-related validity:** 'combined concurrent and predictive validity and referred to . . . as a class', p. 25
- **discriminant validity:** 'correlations among different constructs that are measured by the same methods', pp. 26–27
- **ecological validity:** 'variation in validity coefficients across different . . . situations', p. 28
- **face validity:** 'the appearance of validity . . . for example that the language and contexts of test items be expressed in ways that would *look* valid and be acceptable to the test taker and to the public generally', pp. 23–24
- **factorial validity:** 'the loading of a particular factor on the test in question', p. 25
- **intrinsic validity:** 'any given measure of a construct should show strong relationships with other measures of the same construct, but weak relationships with measures of other constructs', p. 26
- **operational validity:** 'that which the test measures', p. 20
- **population validity:** 'variation in validity coefficients across different populations', p. 28
- **predictive validity:** 'the correlation between observed scores on the test with observed scores on the criterion', p. 20
- **task validity:** 'variation in validity coefficients across different . . . tasks', p. 28
- **temporal validity:** 'variation in validity coefficients across different . . . points in time', p. 28
- **validity generalization:** 'studies of [various] effects . . . yielding . . . important data and theory that have value not only in testing and modifying the construct, but in the strictly utilitarian sense of extending the contexts in which a predictor may be useful', p. 28

As if this daunting list were not sufficient, numerous new conceptions of validity have been proposed in recent years by ethnographic or interpretive researchers seeking to extend the notions of truth practised in educational inquiry and the value of its results (Cherryholmes, 1988; Guba & Lincoln, 1989; Maxwell, 1992; Wolcott, 1990). For example, Lather (1986) adds two additional terms to the list of 'validities' above, and a new twist on the idea of *face validity*, basing her neologisms on examples of what she calls 'openly ideological research':

- *reflexive subjectivity* (some documentation of how the researcher's assumptions have been affected by the logic of the data)
- *face validity* (established by recycling categories, emerging analysis, and conclusions through at least a subsample of respondents)
- *catalytic validity* (some documentation that the research process has led to insight and, ideally, activism on the part of the respondents), (Lather, 1986, p. 78)

Moreover, many others have suggested replacing psychometric notions of test validity with ethical, psychological, institutional, or policy criteria capable of prompting more desirable types of student learning and educational practices than conventional testing has produced. For example, Linn, Baker & Dunbar (1991) appeal to validation criteria of:

- *consequences* on the 'ways teachers and students spend their time and think about the goals of education' (p. 17);
- *fairness*;
- *transfer and generalizability*;
- *cognitive complexity*;
- *content quality*;
- *content coverage*;
- *meaningfulness*; and
- *cost and efficiency*.

The existing array of technical definitions and their mechanical applications in test development have in fact prompted many analysts of test validation to declaim the 'crude and oversimplified grouping of many data gathering procedures that contribute to an understanding of what a test measures' (Anastasi, 1986, p. 2), to question the limited value of single, partial approaches to test validation, and even to challenge the prospects of test developers feasibly achieving all types of technical validity in practice:

> Who would maintain as a *general* proposition, for example, that validity is solely good criterion prediction? Or, validity is representative coverage of relevant content? Or, validity is the attainment of intended functional consequences with minimal or tolerable adverse side-effects? Or, validity is trustworthy score interpretation? . . . Or, validity is all of the foregoing? And if that is the case, how can it be made tangible in testing practice? (Messick, 1988, p. 35)

It is one thing to say that test validity is confidence that a test assesses what it is intended to assess. But it is another, more challenging thing to know, with confidence, what that intention precisely is or should be, what any one test actually does under different conditions, how the conditions themselves are affected by the test, how well the intentions and functions of the test correspond, and ultimately to be able to explain all of that definitively.

The Centrality of Construct Validation

In recent years, most theorists have reconsidered the status of the multiple definitions of validity that have populated textbooks on testing for most of this century. Rather than enumerating various types of validity as appear above, the concept of *construct validity* has been widely agreed upon as *the* single, fundamental principle that subsumes various other aspects of validation (i.e. those listed above), relegating their status to research strategies or categories of empirical evidence by which construct validity might be assessed or asserted.

Moss' (1992) review of this emerging consensus refers to it as the current 'philosophy of validity' (p. 229), tracing its recent emergence through: widespread concerns for the societal or educational impacts of testing; inter-related positions taken by key psychometricians such as Anastasi (1986), Cronbach (1988) and Messick (1988, 1989); as well as the arguments of interpretive critics who have reassessed the epistemological bases of validity previously asserted in the scientific terms of behavioral science, questioning the privileged values and exercises of power associated with standardized evaluation (Cherryholmes, 1988; Guba & Lincoln, 1989). The most visible, professional statement of the current prominence of *construct validity* appears in joint revisions between 1966 and 1985 by the American Educational Research Association, American Psychological Association, and National Council on Measurements Used in Education to their *Standards for educational and psychological testing*, where construct validity is now termed 'the most important consideration in test evaluation' (AERA *et al.*, 1985, p. 2) and validity is considered 'a unitary concept requiring multiple types of evidence to support specific inferences made from test scores' (Moss, 1992, p. 232).

Numerous scholars have observed that construct validation is a long-term 'process, not a procedure' (Agnoff, 1988, p. 26) directed at explanation of specific test results in relation to a theoretically-defined conception of human behavior. As Moss (1992, pp. 233–234) explains, an extensive program of construct validation research is necessary to 'define an explicit conceptual framework', deduce 'testable hypotheses from it' and prepare 'multiple lines of evidence to test the hypotheses' as well as rival hypotheses, leading to ongoing modifications of test instruments, the construct, and the conceptual framework. One widely-cited model for considering the full manifestations of such conceptions of construct validity is that proposed by Messick (1988, 1989).

Messick (1989, p. 5) suggests that a single, central question exists for test validation in practice and theory, but this question has various aspects related to evidence about, rationales for, interpretations of, and uses of a particular test in a specific social context:

> To what degree – if at all – on the basis of evidence and rationales, should the test scores be interpreted and used in the manner proposed?

Messick (1988) proposes that logical distinctions exist between empirical evidence for construct validation, that is, its (1) *evidential basis*, and its (2) *consequential basis* or functional impacts on social systems and values, including unintended, negative effects. Messick similarly distinguishes arguments for construct validation based on analyses of (3) *test interpretation* and of (4) *test use*.

Together, these four facets form a 'progressive matrix' (see Figure 1) in which efforts to establish construct validation can be determined and systematically appraised. Most basically, arguments for construct validity of a test may be based on *evidence* on *test interpretation*, such as conventional correlational analyses or assessment against criterion measures. Progressing through the cells of Messick's matrix, additional *evidence* for construct validation may be sought through consideration of *test use*, particularly its relevance and utility, for example with specific populations, situations, or periods of time, as well as evidence of variations these elements may produce.

	Test Interpretation	Test Use
Evidential Basis	Construct Validity	Construct Validity + Relevance/Utility
Consequential Basis	Construct Validity + Value Implications	Construct Validation + Relevance/Utility + Value Implications + Social Consequences

Figure 1 Messick's (1989) 'Progressive Matrix' of construct validation

Considering the additional dimension of *consequences* in *test interpretation*, Messick points out the need to analyze further the values, ideologies, and broader theories related to the conceptual framework guiding the program of construct validation – once evidence has been obtained from the interpretation of test scores. Ultimately, Messick proposes that the social *consequences* of *test use* must be appraised, combining the considerations raised in all three previous cells of his matrix, to assess the long-term effects that actually occur from implementation of a test, for example, the *washback* of tests on educational practices or more broadly the realization of specific values related to the construct of interest on whole societal systems.

Current Conceptions, Ongoing Issues and Past Trends

The implications of Messick's concepts of test validation have been outlined for language testing by Bachman (1990, pp. 236–295), who has identified the serious challenges it poses for current practices in language assessment, while reviewing exemplary studies of language test validation that have begun to address the conceptual and analytic complexities that systematic construct validation demands. Other theorists of language assessment have, in recent publications, similarly asserted the centrality of construct validation and the importance of social consequences in language testing. For instance, Davies (1990, pp. 38–50) grounded his definitions of language test validity in the practical requirements of specific educational systems while placing *construct validity* firmly in the foreground of such contextual and pragmatic considerations. Likewise, Groot (1990) argued for the fundamental importance of *construct validation* in research, theory-building, and achievement testing in second or foreign language education, while appealing for greater standardization in the methods, evidence, and quality of assessment instruments in this domain. Alderson and Wall (1993) analyzed the idea of *washback* in language testing, pointing out how little evaluation and few empirical studies have actually assessed this integral aspect of the consequences of language tests.

The past decade has seen many systematic research studies devoted to the construct validation of the concept of *communicative competence* in terms relevant to second language education and theory. These efforts span a period marked by various studies reported in Palmer, Groot & Trosper's (1981) *Construct Validation of Tests of Communicative Competence* up to Harley, Cummins, Swain & Allen's (1990) analyses in their project, *Development of Bilingual Proficiency*. This concerted, international focus in language testing research has not yet produced definitive test instruments nor thorough explanations of the nature of second language proficiency. But the impact of widespread efforts to validate a single, fundamental construct has been enormously helpful in building theories of second language knowledge, defining relevant goals for educational curricula, as well as specifying the performance domains, measurement methods, and analytic techniques required to assess second language proficiency (Bachman, 1990; Harley, Cummins, Swain & Allen, 1990).

Issues of construct validation have also featured prominently in recent debates over the popular use of rating scales to assess the oral proficiency of second language learners. Developers of oral proficiency rating scales like Clark & Clifford (1988) have acknowledged the need to further improve assessment procedures like the FSI interview or ACTFL guidelines using conventional validation methods, such as criterion evidence, concurrent comparisons with various testing instruments, comparative analyses across different populations, reliability assessments across different rater groups, and refinement of descriptive criteria (pp. 141–145). But critics of this testing approach have appealed to broader views of construct validation, for example, to argue against this testing approach's theoretical premises, conceptual logic, social purposes, and educational value (Bachman & Savignon, 1986; Kramsch, 1986; Lantolf & Frawley, 1988). Moreover, recent empirical studies describing the conditions of actual test use with these instruments have identified glaring discrepancies between the behaviors demonstrated in testing situations and the construct of natural language performance the instruments claim to elicit (Ross & Berwick, 1992; Young & Milanovic, 1992; Van Lier, 1989). Related concerns have been voiced over the constructs and practices guiding the widespread adoption of holistic schemes for rating second language written compositions (Cumming, 1990; Raimes, 1990).

Emphases on construct validation in language testing have emerged in recent decades as knowledge about the nature of language proficiency and assessment has accumulated, the institutional structures of public policy have placed greater demands on accountability and regulation, and increasing scrutiny has been given to the authority of established testing practices. Extended discussions of construct validation in language assessment did appear in publications several decades ago, for example in Carroll (1958), Davies (1968) or Spolsky (1968). But many authoritative sources informing language education practices at that time paid little attention to construct validation *per se*, instead following trends in general psychology or education to emphasize test reliability, feasibility, or content analyses.

For example, Pilliner's (1968) review of differing types of language tests discussed *predictive*, *concurrent*, and *content* validity at length but failed to raise the idea of construct validation. Similarly, Harris' (1969, pp. 13–23) definitions of the 'characteristics of good language tests' attributed considerable value to issues of reliability and administrative practicality but restricted his definition of 'empirical validity' to only *predictive* or *concurrent* validity. Lado (1961, p. 30) even declared that the validity of a new test could be determined solely on the basis of one instance of concurrent, criterion-related evidence:

> If the two sets of scores correlate highly, that is, if the students who make high scores on the valid criterion test also score high on the experimental test and if those who score low on one also score low on the other, we say that the test is valid.

Facets of Test Validation in the Present Volume

Chapters in the present volume demonstrate, in reference to issues of language assessment, the full range of issues in construct validation outlined by Messick (1988, 1989). As Figure 2 shows, individual chapters pursue unique facets of test validity, reporting particular phases in long-term programs of test validation research. The greatest attention in these chapters is, in Messick's terms, devoted to interpreting test results as evidence for validation, as has conventionally been the practice in psychological and educational assessment; and various, alternative approaches are exemplified. But three chapters also consider important aspects of the *consequential bases* of test validation, particularly the impacts of specific tests on educational systems and of key concepts and professional training programs on the nature of language testing internationally.

The first six chapters in the book put forward, in Messick's terms, evidence for validation by interpreting scores from specific test instruments and student populations in reference to *analytic methods and conceptual frameworks* that help to explain patterns in the test data gathered. Three different approaches are exemplified. Chapters by Milanovic, Saville, Pollitt & Cook and by Tyndall & Kenyon assess the *feasibility and reliability* of new rating scales, demonstrating how correlational analyses and Rasch model-fitting can assess the consistency of ratings performed, as well as relations between components of tests, while suggesting improvements to the instruments and assessment procedures. Milanivoc *et al.* show how such test development needs to be situated within relevant theoretical conceptions, whereas Tyndall & Kenyon emphasize the pragmatic considerations and issues of relevance to be accounted for among participants in a single educational institution.

Chapters by Cushing, Weigle & Lynch and by Cumming & Mellow take an approach that is more akin to experimental design, *setting specific*

	Test Interpretation	*Test Use*
Evidential Basis	*Construct Validity* Model Fitting: – Milanovic *et al.* – Tyndall & Kenyon Criterion Evidence: – Cushing & Lynch – Cumming & Mellow Concurrent Evidence: – Huhta & Randell – Laurier	*Construct Validity* *+ Relevance/Utility* Expert Judgments: – Stansfield & Kenyon Process-tracing & Knowledge Relevance: – Wijgh – Clapham
Consequential Basis	*Value Implications* Terminological Consensus: – Davies	*Social Consequences* Impact Assessment: – Alderson & Wall Induction Systems: – Brown & Bailey

Figure 2 Facets of test validity in the present volume, following Messick's (1989) *Progressive Matrix*

hypotheses about student performance in reference to *criterion measures* and relevant theoretical frameworks, then interpreting aspects of students' language performance as a basis for construct validation focused on anticipated patterns of language development. Cushing & Lynch apply this approach to assess a newly-revised test instrument and expectations for learning related to a university curriculum. Cumming & Mellow seek more general evidence about the qualities of second language development that holistic assessments of students' written compositions might expect to identify as valid indicators of language acquisition.

Huhta & Randell's and Laurier's chapters use methods of *concurrent validation* and various analytic techniques to compare scores arising from applications of different test methods on the same populations. Huhta & Randell use regression and correlational analyses, as well as student surveys, to establish tentative support for the reliability and validity of a summary task format as a measure of English reading comprehension among Finnish university students. Laurier establishes evidence for the feasibility of computer-adaptive assessment for a placement test for French language courses, using analytic techniques from Item Response Theory to compare scores resulting from pencil and paper and from computer-adaptive versions of the same test.

Three chapters analyze, in Messick's (1988, 1989) terms, evidence on how specific language tests are used, assessing the *relevance and utility* of these tests from the perspectives of subject-matter specialists and of student test-takers. One chapter seeks validation evidence from *expert judgments*: Stansfield & Kenyon assess content-related and convergent evidence for difficulty ratings in ACTFL oral proficiency tasks in comparison to the judgments of practicing language teachers, identifying points of commonalty and discrepancy between these two criterion sources as well as their underlying constructs or value systems.

Two other chapters focus on the knowledge students use while taking specific tests, assessing test validity in terms of relevance and utility to the *content domain specifications* of these tests. Wijgh analyzes students' think-aloud protocols from English-language reading comprehension tests in The Netherlands to determine whether the reading strategies demonstrated in the test environment validly corresponded to the strategies ideally envisioned by designers of the test. Clapham assesses the knowledge demands made in a test of reading for academic purposes in different subject areas, analyzing trends in student performance related to their fields of study as well as subject-matter specialists' ratings of key features of the reading passages.

The final three chapters in the book address, in Messick's (1988, 1989) terms, the consequential bases of construct validation. Wall & Alderson's study, however, is the only example here that fulfils Messick's criteria for systematic, long-term analyses of the *consequences of language test use* on educational systems. Indeed, Wall & Alderson's study is unique in the existing literature on language testing, providing a multi-year observational and interview study focused on Sri Lankan teachers' and students' classroom behaviors in reference to an innovative curriculum and national examination. The idea of test *washback* has been widely discussed, but it has not previously received much empirical scrutiny in language education (Alderson & Wall, 1993). The detailed results here identify numerous curriculum variables and processes related to language test use, providing a landmark for future validation and impact studies, but raising important questions about the extent to which a language test may alter conventional teaching practices.

The two other chapters addressing social consequences take a broad perspective on the concepts, values, and practices characterizing the overall field of language testing. Davies documents his initial efforts to compile a specialist dictionary of standard terminology used in language testing, citing logical steps needed to prepare *definitions for key terms*, while arguing that a transparent consensus on such terms is necessary to achieve a broad construct validation for language testing practices among cooperating professionals. Bailey and Brown similarly consider issues affecting the *induction and orientation of professionals* to the field of language testing, reporting results of an international survey on the conditions of university courses on the topic of language testing. Although the chapters by Davies and by Bailey & Brown do not, like other chapters in this book, aim to validate specific tests, they do point toward fundamental issues related to the consequential bases of construct validation, considered broadly as the ongoing assessment of ideologies, value systems, and normative practices informing language testing. Their studies raise such concerns as, How does one determine what counts as fundamental concepts informing constructs of language testing? Under what conditions are professionals trained for language testing, and what might affect their conceptions of test validation? How are the specialized techniques and practices of language testing conveyed to other professionals in language education, such as classroom teachers?

Future efforts in language test validation will need to continue to experiment with the various methodologies and issues raised by the 12 studies offered in the present volume. As such, this book will hopefully serve as a foundation point to illuminate the range of considerations and approaches that language testers need to pursue to achieve goals of construct validation, curtailing practitioners' reliance on limited or single forms of evidence for test validation. The chapters collectively suggest that more thorough, systematic attention will need to be given in the future, not only to combining rigorous, multiple approaches to assess the evidential bases of test interpretation and test use, but more especially for evaluating the long-term consequential bases of test use on particular educational and societal systems, as suggested in the chapter by Alderson & Wall. Moreover, as Davies, Brown & Bailey propose, the overall field of language testing needs to evaluate systematically the terms, values and practices currently institutionalized around language testing in order to establish standards and qualifications explicitly compatible with the ideals of construct validation, as well as to increase public and professional awareness of central tenets and specialized practices in this domain.

References

Alderson, C. and Wall, D. (1993) Does washback exist? *Applied Linguistics* 14, 115–129.

American Psychological Association (1966) *Standards for educational and psychological tests and manuals*. Washington, DC: Authors.

American Educational Research Association, American Psychological Association, & National Council on Measurements Used in Education (1985) *Standards for Educational and Psychological Testing*. Washington, DC: Authors.

Anastasi, A. (1986) Evolving conceptions of test validation. *Annual Review of Psychology* 37, 1–15.

Angoff, W. (1988) Validity: An evolving concept. In H. Wainer and H. Braun (eds) *Test Validity* (pp. 19–32). Hillsdale, NJ: Erlbaum.

Bachman, L. (1990) *Fundamental Considerations in Language Testing*. Oxford: Oxford University Press.

Bachman, L. and Savignon, S. (1986) The evaluation of communicative language proficiency: A critique of the ACTFL Oral Interview. *Modern Language Journal* 70, 380–1.

Carroll, J. B. (1958) A factor analysis of two foreign language aptitude batteries. *Journal of General Psychology* 59, 3–19.

Cherryholmes, C. (1988) Construct validity and discourses of research. *American Journal of Education* 96, 421–57.

Clark, J. and Clifford, R. (1988) The FSI/ILR/ACTFL proficiency scales and testing techniques: Development, current status, and needed research. *Studies in Second Language Acquisition* 10, 129–47.

Cronbach, L. (1988) Five perspectives on validity argument. In H. Wainer and H. Braun (eds) *Test Validity* (pp. 3–17). Hillsdale, NJ: Erlbaum.

Cumming, A. (1990) Expertise in evaluating second language compositions. *Language Testing* 7, 31–51.

Davies, A. (1968) Introduction. In A. Davies (ed.) *Language Testing Symposium: A psycholinguistic approach* (pp. 1–18). London: Oxford University Press.

— (1990) *Principles of language testing*. Oxford: Basil Blackwell.

Groot, P. (1990) Language testing in research and education: The need for standards. In J. De Jong (ed.) (1990) *Standardization in Language Testing, AILA Review* 7, 9–23.

Guba, E. and Lincoln, Y. (1989) *Fourth Generation Evaluation*. Newbury Park, CA: Sage.

Harley, B., Cummins, J., Swain, M. and Allen, P. (eds) (1990) *The Development of Second Language Proficiency*. Cambridge: Cambridge University Press.

Harris, D. (1969) *Testing English as a Second Language*. New York, NY: McGraw-Hill.

Kramsch, C. (1986) From language proficiency to interactional competence. *Modern Language Journal* 70, 366–72.

Lado, R. (1961) *Language Testing: The construction and use of foreign language tests*. London: Longman.

Lather, P. (1986) Issues of validity in openly ideological research: Between a rock and a soft place. *Interchange* 17, 63–84.

Lantolf, J. and Frawley, W. (1988) Proficiency: Understanding the construct. *Studies in Second Language Acquisition* 10, 181–95.

Linn, R., Baker, E. and Dunbar, S. (1991) Complex, performance-based assessment: Expectations and validation criteria. *Educational Researcher* 20, 5–21.

Maxwell, J. (1992) Understanding and validity in qualitative research. *Harvard Educational Review* 62, 279–300.

Messick, S. (1988) The once and future issues of validity: Assessing the meaning and consequences of measurement. In H. Wainer and H. Braun (eds) *Test Validity* (pp. 33–45). Hillsdale, NJ: Erlbaum.

— (1989) Meaning and values in test validation: The science and ethics of assessment. *Educational Researcher* 18, 5–11.

Moss, P. (1992) Shifting conceptions of validity in educational measurement: Implications for performance assessment. *Review of Educational Research* 62, 229–58.

Palmer, A., Groot, P. and Trosper, G. (eds) (1981) *The Construct Validation of Tests of Communicative Competence*. Washington, DC: TESOL.

Pilliner, A. (1968). Subjective and objective testing. In A. Davies (ed.) *Language Testing Symposium: A psycholinguistic approach* (pp. 19–35). London: Oxford University Press.

Raimes, A. (1990) The TOEFL test of written English: Causes for concern. *TESOL Quarterly* 24, 427–42.

Ross, S. and Berwick, R. (1992) The discourse of accommodation in oral proficiency interviews. *Studies in Second Language Acquisition* 14, 159–76.

Spolsky, B. (1968) Language testing: The problem of validation. *TESOL Quarterly* 2, 88–94.

van Lier, L. (1989) Reeling, writhing, drawling, stretching and fainting in coils: Oral proficiency interviews as conversation. *TESOL Quarterly* 23, 489–508.

Wolcott, H. (1990). On seeking – and rejecting – validity in qualitative research. In E. Eisner and A. Peshkin (eds) *Qualitative Inquiry in Education: The continuing debate* (pp. 121–52). New York: Teachers College Press.

Young, R. and Milanovic, M. (1992) Discourse variation in oral proficiency interviews. *Studies in Second Language Acquisition* 14, 403–24.

1 Developing Rating Scales for CASE: Theoretical Concerns and Analyses

MICHAEL MILANOVIC, NICK SAVILLE,
ALASTAIR POLLITT and ANNETTE COOK

This paper reviews the development of the Cambridge Assessment of Spoken English (CASE), with particular reference to the trialling and validation of the rating scales (1989–91). CASE was originally envisaged as an oral test for in-house company use. However, it soon became apparent that it could be used in a wider context and three objectives were established.

These were to produce a test that would assess an individual's ability to:

- produce and process spoken English;

- demonstrate the ability to communicate in English through the use of grammatical, discourse and interactive skills;

- maintain fluent and accurate discourse as appropriate.

From the inception of the project it was decided to base the test on a model of language proficiency. This was termed the model-based approach. Throughout the 1980s, testing theory has been moving steadily towards defining and validating models of communicative competence. This is demonstrated by the work of Canale & Swain (1980, 1981), and most recently Bachman (1990, 1991). CASE was initially based on the Canale & Swain model but account was taken during the development project of Bachman's work.

The *model-based approach* provided an explicit conceptual framework and thus the potential for test validation, particularly construct validation. In other words, by beginning with a model of spoken language ability it was possible to hypothesize what would be tested and to explore ways to test out these hypotheses. In the assessment of spoken language, the number and type of rating scales used must clearly reflect the traits of ability in the candidate's performance that can be observed and judged. This paper, therefore, concerns the theoretical basis for the rating scales in CASE and the attempts which the researchers have made to analyse and validate them.

The model of spoken language ability that was used has grown out of the debate on the issue of conceptual frameworks to describe language ability and thus to inform test design. It attempts to characterise the interrelatedness of the components of language ability and the processes which are to be elicited. The Canale & Swain (1980) version of this model defines communicative competence as the underlying systems of *knowledge* and *skills* required for communication (e.g. knowledge of vocabulary and skill in using the sociolinguistic conventions for a given language) as well as *strategic competence*. Bachman (1990, 1991) has further developed this model. His version of the model focuses on the interactions among the *components and processes* of language ability and how these interact with characteristics of the target language use context and test task. The target language use context includes such factors as the relationship between the two participants, the topic and the purpose or intentions of the language users. This processing aspect of the model allows him to deal with the area of strategic competence in the Canale & Swain model. Bachman also notes that, as well as context, language use is affected by knowledge schemata (real world knowledge) and affective schemata (emotional memories).

A version of the Canale & Swain model was used operationally at the outset of the CASE project in 1989–90 and was adapted to reflect spoken language ability in particular. It can be summarised as follows:

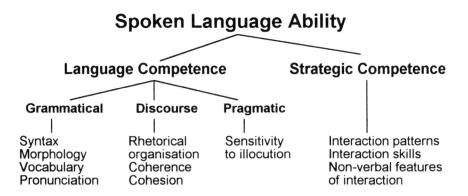

Figure 1.1 Model of spoken language ability used in the CASE project

In addition to the model-based approach, another key element in the methodology used in developing CASE, was the close attention which was paid to the development *process* itself (see Milanovic & Saville, 1992). There has been a tendency for test development to be linear in approach. From the outset, it proved impossible to follow a linear approach in the development of CASE, since this implies that, once decisions are made, they dictate future progress and cannot be readily changed in light of later findings. With the development of CASE it proved necessary to use an approach which was both cyclical and iterative. Decisions were evaluated in the light of experience and trialling evidence and changes of direction applied as appropriate. Materials were developed in parallel with rating scales, training and administrative procedures.

The Structure of CASE

CASE consists of three phases. The first is a structured conversation, which is a 1–1 interaction between an interlocutor, normally a native speaker (NS), and a non-native speaker (NNS) candidate. While the interlocutor acts as an assessor, there is also a second, passive assessor present. In this phase, which is dominated primarily by the interlocutor, a fairly fixed range of topics, related to everyday life, is covered in a period of about five minutes. This phase is called the **interview**. The interlocutor is provided with a frame of topics and questions to be dealt with – the interlocutor frame. S/he is expected to follow this frame closely for all candidates, although, clearly the nature of the interaction is influenced by several factors such as background, personality and competence of the candidate. The range of topics covered in this phase include:

greetings and introductions;
giving information about self related to:
current job or status;
work and travel;
a built in topic switch;
future career prospects;
interests;
closing exchanges.

The second phase is called the **presentation**. In this phase, two candidates are asked to prepare a short presentation on a topic selected from a choice of three each. They are allowed about five minutes for the preparation phase. Each candidate then gives a 1–2 minute presentation. After each presentation, there is a short question and answer session, in which the candidate who is not giving the presentation is required to ask questions of the presenter. While there is some NS involvement in this phase, the interaction is largely NNS/NNS. In this phase, the candidate is expected to:

structure discourse;
organise information;
illustrate and exemplify;
show awareness of an audience;
respond to comments questions and objections;
demonstrate linguistic control.

The third and final phase is called **discussion**. In this phase, candidates are engaged in an activity that involves the discussion of a problem, negotiation and then arriving at consensus. The phase lasts 3–4 minutes. It is largely a NNS/NNS interaction although the scene is set by the NS interlocutor, who may intervene in the discussion if required. In this phase, the candidate is expected to:

negotiate meaning;
manage conversational direction;
take turns;
summarise own and partner's position;
assess responses in real time;
monitor and adjust linguistic performance.

The overall structure and timing of CASE is illustrated graphically in Appendix 1.

CASE differs in important ways from many other oral interviews. Firstly, it is a paired interview that allows for a variety of interactions – NS/NNS, NS/NNS–NNS, NNS/NNS. Secondly, candidates engage in a range of activities that allow for a broad sampling of overall ability. Thirdly, the pairings in phases two and three are based on an initial impression of compatibility and ability arrived at in phase 1. Briefly, candidates take CASE in groups of six. After phase 1, which is a series of six 1–1 interactions, the raters pair the candidates for phases two and three. As mentioned above, this pairing is based on an initial impression of compatibility and ability.

The Rating Scales

The rating scales were developed along side the structure of CASE and in light of the model of spoken language ability that is being assessed. Essentially the scales break down into three main areas. These are grammatical, discourse and strategic competence. Initial trialling of the CASE procedure showed that it would be difficult to elicit and test certain aspects of pragmatic competence such as switches in register. Therefore, this type of pragmatic competence was not included in the operational model. It could be argued, however, that the scale which was labelled *Communication Strategies and Interaction* includes some other elements of pragmatic competence (such as sensitivity to illocution) as well as elements of strategic competence.

There are three grammatical scales: grammar, vocabulary and pronunciation. Each of these has five points. One scale is related to discourse competence (organisation) and another to strategic competence (communication skills and strategies). These scales have five points. Four scales focus on the success with which the four major tasks in CASE are achieved. These main tasks are the interview, the presentation, the questions and the discussion. These scales have four points. Another scale, called interlocutor support, is also included. This was intended to quantify the amount of support a candidate might require from the interlocutor during CASE. This scale has four points. The notion of interlocutor support is similar to that of accommodation defined by Ross (1992).

While the scales described above attempt to focus on the components of spoken language ability, it was also decided to develop a scale related to overall competence. It must be pointed out that this scale is not a summation of the component scales. Rather it is an independent assessment of overall spoken language ability. The overall ability scale has six points. In conclusion, CASE employs 11 rating scales in all. Ten are related to components of spoken language ability and the 11th is a measure of overall ability. The scales are summarised in Appendix 2.

It should be noted that the scales are of different lengths. When CASE was first developed not only were all the scales of the same length, they also covered nine points. It soon became apparent that raters were not able to differentiate effectively over all the scales. The scale lengths were therefore adjusted in light of feedback from raters. In addition, the overall scale was made substantially different from the component scales in order to avoid contamination of either scale by the other. This is illustrated by reference to Appendix 2. The extent to which raters would be able to differentiate effectively using the revised scales was considered to be an empirical question. This will be discussed below.

The Validation of the CASE Rating Scales

Three major trialling exercises have taken place to date. The first in Hong Kong, the second in Thailand and the third in the UK.

The Hong Kong and Thailand trials focused primarily on administrative feasibility and face validity. The question of rating scales was addressed, but largely from the point of view of subjective feedback from raters and analysis of video recordings. On the basis of this feedback and analysis, the type and length of the scales was established. In some cases the scales were too long and in others they were irrelevant and, therefore, corrective action was taken. In addition, analysis of the video recordings, including transcript analysis, was used to guide the production of scale descriptors which reflected the nature of the language produced.

The UK trials, on the other hand, focused mainly on training activities and scale validation. It is these trials which will be reported on here.

The UK trials

Between January and September 1991 a total of 70 candidates were assessed in Norwich, Cambridge, Cardiff and Newcastle. They came from a variety of backgrounds but were mostly working in a business context or students. All interviews were either audio or video recorded. Approximately half the interviews were transcribed. In all 10 raters were trained and participated in the study. All of them came from an EFL background and were practising teachers at the time of the study. All received at least one full day of training and standardisation before they engaged in rating. Four of them rated on more than one occasion, while the remaining six rated on one occasion only.

Each interview requires the presence of two raters, one acting as interlocutor, the other acting as an independent assessor. Five of the raters engaged in both roles at various times. Scores were recorded in specially prepared score booklets and then transferred to a database system developed using a programme called Crystal, which is a PC-based expert system. Rules were created that enabled the scores of the two assessors to be reconciled to create profile statements. The scores that the scale validation is based on have not been adjusted in any way.

Inter-rater reliability

The first question addressed was the degree of inter-rater agreement. Correlations between the first and second ratings on the 11 scales were computed using SPSSPC. The correlation between the overall ratings of first and second rater was established at 0.93. The inter correlations of the component scales varied between 0.47 and 0.90. Appendix 3 provides a complete correlation matrix of the scales across raters. The correlations are high for the most part. There are several possible reasons for this:

- phase 1 pairing serves as an initial assessment and allows the raters to discuss candidates prior to arriving at a final assessment;
- an opportunity is supplied for the pairing in phases 2 and 3 to provide a conducive inter personal environment;
- training and standardisation procedures are effective and rigorous;
- the presence of two raters allows for an ongoing standardisation process;
- the length of the scales reflects the degree to which raters can make accurate decisions;
- the procedure is actually highly reliable;
- the range and nature of the language sampled can be assessed using the scales.

Scales and construct

Initial investigation of the extent to which the scales reflect the model of spoken language ability upon which they are based has employed correlational analysis. The analyses focused on average between rater covariances.

Between rater analysis

The scales were based on three basic elements of the model of spoken language ability – grammatical, discourse and strategic competence – and a series of four task achievement scales. In order to investigate the extent to which the scales associated with these elements converged, the average, inter-rater correlations were computed for the various scales. For example, grammar on the first rating correlated at 0.88, 0.74 and 0.69 with the three separate components of grammatical competence on the second rating; the mean of these was 0.77 (see Appendix 3, column headed Gram1). The correlation of grammar on the first rating with discourse competence on the second rating was 0.70; the correlation with strategic competence was 0.65 and the correlation with the tasks was 0.61. The same procedure was conducted for each of the scales in turn. A Fisher Z transformation was not employed since it makes virtually no difference with mid-range correlations. In order to represent these results in terms of the proportion of variance the two ratings shared, these mean correlations were squared (r^2).

Table 1.1 below shows the r^2's of the grammar, vocabulary and pronunciation scales with the elements of spoken language ability and the task scales.

Table 1.1 Inter-rater r^2 and components of spoken language ability

	Grammar	*Vocabulary*	*Pronunciation*
Grammatical	0.59	0.55	0.55
Discourse	0.49	0.61	0.30
Strategic	0.41	0.52	0.22
Task	0.37	0.44	0.22

The vocabulary scale converges more with discourse competence than it does with grammatical competence. Figure 1.2 illustrates the relationships very clearly.

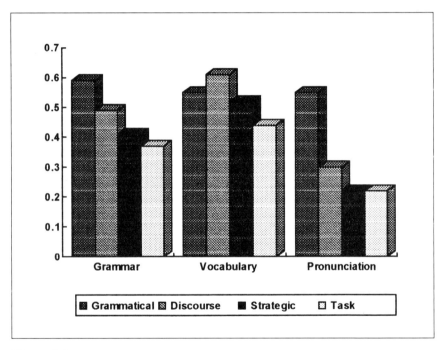

Figure 1.2

It is interesting the extent to which pronunciation relates better to grammatical competence than it does to either strategic, discourse or task achievement. On this evidence, it would seem that pronunciation does not need to be closely associated with an individual's ability to function effectively in a foreign language.

Table 1.2 illustrates the relationship between discourse and strategic competence, the components of spoken language ability and task achievement. There appears to be a stronger relationship between discourse and strategic competence than between grammatical and strategic.

Table 1.2 Inter-rater r^2 and components of spoken language ability

	Organisation	Communication
Grammatical	0.42	0.41
Discourse	0.76	0.62
Strategic	0.61	0.81
Task	0.46	0.55

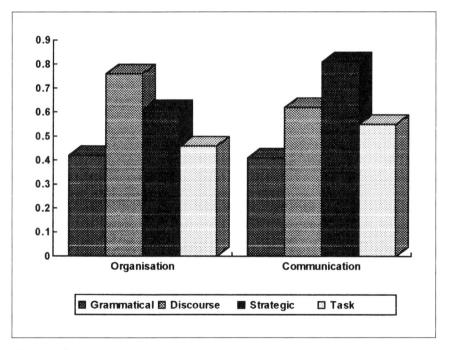

Figure 1.3

Grammatical competence relates in much the same way to both the organisation and communication scales. However, the communication scale has a stronger relationship with task achievement than does organisation.

Table 1.3 below illustrates the relationship between the four task related scales and the components of spoken language ability. In all cases the weakest relationship is with grammatical competence particularly with the questions and discussion. These are the most spontaneous of the tasks and this may well be a reason for the weaker relationship.

Table 1.3 Inter-rater r^2 and components of spoken language ability

	Interview	*Presentation*	*Questions*	*Discussion*
Grammatical	0.38	0.44	0.30	0.31
Discourse	0.42	0.58	0.52	0.46
Strategic	0.52	0.66	0.64	0.67
Task	0.55	0.62	0.64	0.74

The communication scale, which represents strategic competence, consistently has a stronger relationship with the achievement of tasks than does the organisation scale. In the presentation task, the organisation scale correlates more highly than it does elsewhere. It makes sense that organisation should be best evaluated during the presentation. Indeed, the presentation task was designed to allow for a view of discourse skills to be best achieved.

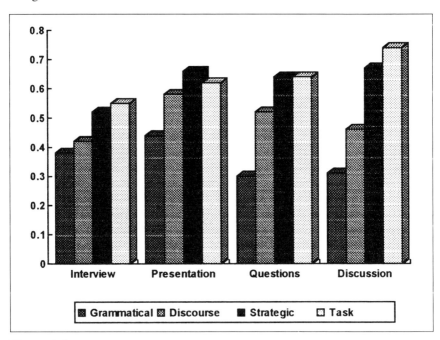

Figure 1.4

While inter scale correlations are consistently high, which might indicate some sort of halo effect, it is also apparent that raters are able to distinguish between the various scales.

The integrity of the scales

There are many difficulties associated with the construction of rating scales. For example, there is the issue of what to describe. In this project, the nature of the scales was dictated to a large extent by the model of spoken language ability employed. One way of validating the integrity of the scales in this sense is through some form of correlational analysis. This was attempted in the previous section. Once what to describe has been established, the degree to which raters are able to differentiate between the points on the scale needs to be investigated. As mentioned above, this can be done through feedback from raters. This method was employed in the first instance after the trials in Hong Kong and Thailand.

Partial credit analysis (Wright & Masters, 1982) provides a means for the empirical validation of rating scales in a way that feedback from raters does not. The partial credit model allows for the scoring of test items in any number of ordered categories and is an appropriate analysis tool for rating scales (Adams *et al.*, 1987, Pollitt & Hutchinson, 1987). The model describes the relationship between a person's ability and the difficulty of the task or scale in terms of the probability of an individual providing an adequate language sample to get a certain score.

For the purposes of this study, the rating scales were analysed in three ways using BIGSTEPS (Wright & Linacre, 1991): first rating, the second rating and the combined ratings. The results are most clearly illustrated through the item characteristic curves, which will be discussed below. However, it is first necessary to look at the degree to which the model fits the data. Table 1.4 below is a measure of person fit. In this case the table refers to the first rating. The results are similar for the second rating and combined ratings. The results of these analyses are not discussed here.

Several points can be noted from this table. First, the mean score of the persons in the study across all the scales is reported in the 'SCORE' column. The score is 35.6 (60%) out of a possible total score of 59. The standard deviation is reported just below at 7.9 (13%). The 'COUNT' column refers to the number of items or in this case scales analysed.

The 'MEASURE' column refers to the average ability of the group of candidates in logits, 0.11 and the ability spread or standard deviation of the group in logits, 3.26. The spread of ability is quite broad. The 'ERROR' column reports the mean error in logits, 0.64, and its standard deviation, 0.12. The weighted fit statistics are reported in the 'MNSQ' (mean square) and 'INFIT' columns. Perfect fit would result in a 'MEAN' of 0 and a 'SD' of 1 in the 'INFIT' column. As can be noted from the table the data fit the model well. The 'MNSQ' and 'OUTFIT' columns are unweighted measures. There is a slight degree of misfit, though this is not significant. The 'RMSE' (root mean standard error) measure is equivalent to a traditional standard error of measurement and the 'ADJ.S.D.' (adjusted standard deviation) is the standard deviation corrected for measurement error. The 'PERSON SEP' measure shows how many times wider the ability scale is than the error in that scale. It is calculated as a ratio of ADJ.S.D. over RMQS (3.19/0.65). The 'PERSON SEP REL' measure is an indication of the reliability of the test. It is similar to a coefficient alpha. In all we can be fairly satisfied with the scales in this data.

Table 1.4 Summary of 68 measured persons

```
        CASE Analysis : Feb 1992        R MODEL   "BIGSTEPS" RASCH

INPUT:    70 PERSONS   11 ITEMS  ANALYSED:  68 PERSONS   11 ITEMS  47 CATEGORIES

      SUMMARY OF    68 MEASURED (NON-EXTREME) PERSONS
      ---------------------------------------------------------------------
                 SCORE     COUNT     MEASURE    ERROR      MNSQ   INFIT   MNSQ OUTFIT
      ---------------------------------------------------------------------
        MEAN      35.6      11.0        .11      .64        .98    -.2     .98    -.1
        S.D.       7.9       .0        3.26      .12        .59    1.2     .71    1.2
      ---------------------------------------------------------------------
        RMSE      .65  ADJ.S.D.       3.19   PERSON SEP    4.90   PERSON SEP REL.    .96
      ---------------------------------------------------------------------
      MAXIMUM EXTREME SCORE:     2 PERSONS
```

Table 1.5 is a representation of the quality of measurement. The two horizontal dotted lines at 2 and -2 are at the 5% significance band. The numbers on the table represent people.

It will be noted that nobody misfits at the bottom. Misfit at this end might well indicate a flat profile and suggest that a halo effect were coming into play. This is not the case. There is some slight misfit at the top. This is likely to be due to a particularly jagged profile. It will be noted that there is only a limited amount of misfit. From this table we are able to conclude that the people fit the model well.

Table 1.5 Person fit

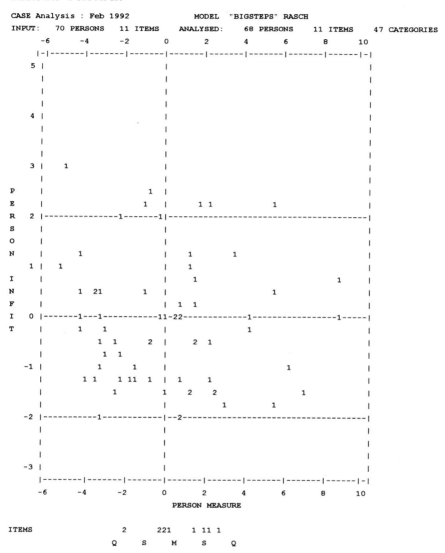

```
CASE Analysis : Feb 1992                    MODEL  "BIGSTEPS" RASCH
INPUT:    70 PERSONS    11 ITEMS    ANALYSED:    68 PERSONS    11 ITEMS    47 CATEGORIES
          -6       -4       -2       0       2       4       6       8       10
        |-|-------|-------|-------|-------|-------|-------|-------|------|-|
      5 |                         |                                          |
        |                         |                                          |
        |                         |                                          |
        |                         |                                          |
      4 |                         |                                          |
        |                         |                                          |
        |                         |                                          |
        |                         |                                          |
      3 |      1                  |                                          |
        |                         |                                          |
  P     |                     1   |                                          |
  E     |                     1   |       1 1           1                    |
  R   2 |----------------1-------1|------------------------------------------|
  S     |                         |                                          |
  O     |                         |                                          |
  N     |       1                 |   1         1                            |
      1 |  1                      |   1                                      |
  I     |                         |   1                              1       |
  N     |       1   21        1   |               1                          |
  F     |                         | 1 1                                      |
  I   0 |-------1---1-----------11-22-------------1-----------------1-----|
  T     |      1    1             |               1                          |
        |          1  1       2   |   2  1                                   |
        |          1  1           |                                          |
    -1  |          1      1       |                              1           |
        |       1 1    1 11  1   | 1       1                                 |
        |             1           | 1   2   2              1                 |
        |                         |       1         1                        |
    -2  |-----------1------------|--2--------------------------------------|
        |                         |                                          |
        |                         |                                          |
        |                         |                                          |
    -3  |                         |                                          |
        |-------|-------|-------|-------|-------|-------|-------|------|-|
          -6       -4       -2       0       2       4       6       8       10
                              PERSON MEASURE

    ITEMS              2       221   1 11 1
                       Q       S   M   S   Q
```

Table 1.6 is a representation of the raters' sensitivity to the scales. For ease of reference the 3 point on the scales have been changed to an asterisk. The table shows where raters are prepared to give credit for ability or not as the case may be. For example it can be noted that a person is most likely to get a band 2 on the grammar and vocabulary scales at any ability level of −3 logits or below. It appears easier to get a band 3 on the pronunciation scale, and the length of the 3 band in the pronunciation scale is rather long. This may indicate that raters are hedging their bets to some extent when it comes to pronunciation. This is not a counter-intuitive finding, however. We all know from experience that there is a tendency for pronunciation to fossilise. Perhaps the scale is a representation of this tendency. Interestingly, the bottom point on the grammar, vocabulary and pronunciation scales does not come into play. This may be an indication that the scales are too long, and that raters cannot differentiate at five points. It may mean that no one was at the one point in terms of these particular scales. Or it may mean that the scale descriptions need clarification at the lowest ability levels. In any case, this question will be addressed as the validation of the scales continues.

Table 1.6 Most probable responses

```
CASE Analysis : Feb 1992          R MODEL  "BIGSTEPS" RASCH

INPUT:  70 PERSONS   11 ITEMS   ANALYSED:   68 PERSONS   11 ITEMS   47 CATEGORIES


MOST PROBABLE RESPONSES  (BETWEEN "0" AND "1" IS "0", ETC.)


      ITEM          -7    -5    -3    -1    1    3    5    7    9
                    |------|------|------|------|------|------|------|------|

GRAMMAR             22222222222222222****************4444444444444444444444444555
VOCABULARY          22222222222222222************444444444444444444444555555555
PRONUNCIATION       22222222***********************44444444444444444444445555

ORGANISATION        1111112222222222****************4444444444444444444555555555
COMMUNICATION       1111111222222222***************44444444444444455555555555555


SUPPORT             111112222222222222***************44444444444444444444444444
INTERVIEW           112222222222222222222**********4444444444444444444444444444
PRESENTATION        111111112222222222222222***************44444444444444444
QUESTIONS           11111111111112222222222222**********44444444444444444444
DISCUSSION          11111111111122222222222222***********444444444444444444444


OVERALL             33333333333344444444444444455555555556666666666666666667777777

                    |------|------|------|------|------|------|------|------|
                    -7    -5    -3    -1    1    3    5    7    9

PERSON                      11  41352 231 224 22264 413 21 1 2    3 1  1      22
                        Q        S          M         S          Q
```

The bottom point on the scales is used in the organisation and communication scales. This finding is a further indication that raters are able to differentiate between the grammatical and discourse components of spoken language ability. Effective organisation skills are as much a feature of NS discourse as they are of NNS discourse.

The task related scales function only on four points as opposed to the five point scales for grammar, vocabulary, pronunciation, organisation and communication. It appears to be the case that it is easiest to get the top point on the scale in the interview task. The degree of interpersonal interaction between a rater and candidate is greatest during this task. The rater might be positively influenced by personality factors or the familiarity of this type of task to candidates may come into play. On other hand, it might just be easier to talk to someone in a 1–1 interaction than it is to give a short presentation.

In the validation of rating scales it is also important to establish the extent to which the points on a scale can be effectively differentiated by raters. A very graphic way of doing this is to study the ICC tables for the scales (see Appendix 4 – overall ability, grammar, pronunciation, organisation and interview task achievement). ICCs show how the modelled probability of getting a particular point on the scale varies with the ability of the people in question.

The first table in Appendix 4 illustrates the overall ability scale. The five points, from 3–7 are fairly clearly differentiated. The 8th point was used but the two candidates it applied to were excluded from the analysis due to fit. We can clearly see from the overall ability scale that there is always a range of ability where a particular scale point is the most probable score. The degree of overlap between the five points is quite limited and the overlap is rarely more than one point on the scale. Points 4 and 5 on the scale are the least discrete, while points 3, 6 and 7 are reasonably distinct. Point 6 seems to have the greatest spread, however, the probability of an individual getting a 4 instead of a 6 is low. This particular ICC is reassuring in that it demonstrates raters' ability to distinguish the ability levels fairly clearly. We can feel confident that the scale is about the right length. It will be noted however, that the bottom points on the grammar and pronunciation scales have not been used at all. It may well be the case that only four meaningful differentiations can be made on these scales.

The peakedness of the curves is also an important feature of ICCs. The greater the peakedness, the higher the probability that an individual with an ability in line with the peak is being correctly assessed. In conjunction with the peakedness, it is important to consider the spread of the ICCs. The wider the spread, the greater the possibility of inappropriate scoring. The two

ICCs related to grammar and pronunciation seem to indicate that the scale points are well differentiated. However, the organisation scale shows that the probability of achieving the second point on the scale is relatively low. This may be due to a lack of differentiation in the scale descriptor, it may indicate that a five point scale is too long, or it may suggest that the abilities measured by this scale has a rather strange step action. By this we mean that the ability may be either not present (1) or present to some reasonable degree (3) with little in between.

The task achievement scales are all similar to the extent that the probability of scoring the mid points is lower than that of scoring the extreme points it may be that the descriptors for the mid points need some work, or that raters find it more straightforward to judge good and bad performances than they do mediocre. In any case, some attention to these scales will be required in light of this validation study and prior to further trialling.

Conclusion

The principled development and validation of the CASE rating scales has proven to be a valuable exercise. It has supplied the test developers with many useful insights and ammunition for continued work. It has not been the tradition in language testing to devote much time to the empirical validation of rating scales prior to tests being widely used. This project is placing substantial emphasis on validation prior to use. As a result we feel confident that CASE will represent a better and more valid measurement tool.

The next stage of validation will be to establish the relative harshness of the raters and scales. This will be done through multi-faceted Rasch analysis. In addition, it will be necessary to carry out a detailed analysis of the intrinsic difficulty of the tasks themselves. Only at this point will we feel confident enough to make use of this test on a wide scale.

References

Adams, R., Griffin, P. and Martin, L. (1987) A latent trait method for measuring a dimension in second language proficiency. *Language Testing* 4, 9–27.
Canale, M. and Swain, M. (1980) Theoretical bases of communicative approaches to second language teaching and testing. *Applied Linguistics* 1, 1–47.
Bachman, L. (1990) *Fundamental Considerations in Language Testing*. Oxford: Oxford University Press.

— (1991) Manuscript.

Milanovic, M. and Saville, N. (1992) Action research in EFL examination development. *Research notes* 1. EFL Division, University of Cambridge Local Examinations Syndicate.

Pollitt, A. and Hutchinson, C. (1987) Calibrating graded assessments: Rasch partial credit analysis of performance in writing. *Language Testing* 4, 72–92.

Ross, S. (1992) Accommodative questions in oral proficiency interviews. Paper presented at the 14th annual Language Testing Research Colloquium, Vancouver.

Wright, B. and Linacre, M. (1991) *A User's Guide to BIGSTEPS.* Chicago: Mesa Press.

Wright, B. and Masters, G. (1982) *Rating Scale Analysis: Rasch Measurement.* Chicago: Mesa Press.

Appendix 1. The structure of CASE

5 mins.	5 mins.	1 min.	8 mins.	4 mins.
Stage One		Stage Two		
		Section One	Section Two	Section Three
Interview	Deciding on Pairings	Warm-up	Presentation	Discussion

Appendix 2: CASE scales

CASE Scales

Rating	Grammar	Vocabulary	Pronunciation	Organisation	Communication Strategies and Interaction	Interlocutor Support	Task Achievement
A	Wide range of structures including complex structures used accurately; very few errors.	Extensive range; accurate and appropriate use; wide topic range; little hesitation in selection.	Accurate and consistent use of all aspects of pronunciation.	Excellent - logically developed discourse; precise use of cohesive features.	Intended meaning communicated in all contexts; interaction initiated and maintained; topic changes responded to with ease.	Not required.	Task fully achieved and communicated successfully.
B	Full range of basic structures used with few errors; errors with complex structures.	Large range of everyday vocabulary though not always sufficient for discussion; little hesitation in selection.	Broadly accurate and consistent use of most aspects of pronunciation; foreign influence does not interfere.	Well organised - main points distinguished and appropriately sequenced; most discourse relationships well marked.	Intended meaning communicated in most contexts; interaction initiated and maintained; occasional difficulty in responding to changes of topic.	Occasionally required.	Task is achieved but one or more task requirements lacking.
C	Accurate use of basic structures; inaccurate use of complex structures causing occasional misunderstandings.	Moderate range for everyday use; some hesitation in selection.	Occasional inaccuracies but still intelligible; noticeable foreign accent but comprehensible.	Limited effectiveness; some discourse relationships inadequately marked; occasional need for clarification and repetition.	Main ideas communicated; repair strategies used; some difficulty in initiating interaction and responding to shifts of topic.	Frequently required.	Task only partly achieved; several task requirements are not fulfilled.
D	Inaccurate use of many basic structures; rare and inaccurate use of complex structures; frequent problems with intelligibility.	Restricted range sufficient for basic communication only; much hesitation in selection.	Inaccuracies sometimes result in unintelligible utterances; frequent serious errors interfere with communication.	Badly organised - discourse relationships not marked; frequent inappropriate sequencing; only basic discourse or conversational routines.	Main idea communicated in limited contexts; repair strategies rarely used; interaction seldom initiated; difficulty in responding to shifts of topic.	Continually required.	Task not achieved; task requirements not fulfilled.
E	Inaccurate use of most basic structures; no use of complex structures; largely unintelligible.	A few words and phrases only; usually inadequate for communication.	Inaccurate and inconsistent. Largely unintelligible.	No evidence of extended discourse or conversational rules; impossible to follow.	Great difficulty in communicating; unable to use repair strategies; needs others to maintain interaction.		

There is no columnar connections between this bar and the table above

Overall ability	800 Very good user	700 Good user	600 Competent user	500 Independent user	400 Threshold level user	300 Waystage level user

Appendix 3: Intercorrelations between raters

Correlation	Overall	GRAM1	VOCAB1	PRON1	ORG1	COMM1	SUPP1	INT1	PRES1	QUES1	DISC1
OVERALL1	1.0000	.7352	.7524	.6413	.7262	.7461	.5817	.7170	.7569	.7232	.7240
GRAM1	.7352	1.0000	.8277	.7142	.7382	.7252	.6027	.6931	.6909	.6095	.6107
VOCAB1	.7524	.8277	1.0000	.6401	.7557	.7191	.6099	.6802	.7334	.6623	.6420
PRON1	.6413	.7142	.6401	1.0000	.5829	.5779	.5419	.4706	.6232	.5028	.4670
ORG1	.7262	.7382	.7557	.5829	1.0000	.8142	.4425	.7058	.7573	.7485	.6976
COMM1	.7461	.7252	.7191	.5779	.8142	1.0000	.4476	.7490	.7999	.7634	.7939
SUPP1	.5817	.6027	.6099	.5419	.4425	.4476	1.0000	.6186	.4626	.4090	.3945
INT1	.7170	.6931	.6802	.4706	.7058	.7490	.6186	1.0000	.7486	.7348	.7879
PRES1	.7569	.6909	.7334	.6232	.7573	.7999	.4626	.7486	1.0000	.8246	.8563
QUES1	.7232	.6095	.6623	.5028	.7485	.7634	.4090	.7348	.8246	1.0000	.8756
DISC1	.7240	.6107	.6420	.4670	.6976	.7939	.3945	.7879	.8563	.8756	1.0000
OVERALL2	.9324	.7064	.7312	.6125	.7317	.7502	.6066	.7175	.7373	.7174	.7391
GRAM2	.7208	.8765	.7895	.7142	.6819	.7084	.6457	.7341	.6708	.5739	.5925
VOCAB2	.7267	.7441	.8285	.6541	.6986	.6378	.5625	.6450	.7058	.5843	.5958
PRON2	.6745	.6850	.6045	.7630	.5940	.5714	.5208	.4760	.5904	.4911	.4965
ORG2	.7907	.6967	.7783	.5496	.8665	.7858	.4895	.6590	.7598	.7166	.6785
COMM2	.7457	.6482	.7200	.4738	.7847	.9049	.4621	.7177	.8142	.8048	.8179
SUPP2	—	—	—	—	—	—	—	—	—	—	—
INT2	.7282	.6029	.6615	.4273	.6500	.7222	.4925	.8098	.7222	.7705	.8471
PRES2	.7444	.6898	.7196	.5576	.7072	.7618	.4672	.7379	.8756	.7499	.8253
QUES2	.7190	.5606	.6616	.4630	.7145	.7315	.4200	.7082	.7949	.8937	.8605
DISC2	.6840	.5818	.5957	.4233	.6332	.7310	.4086	.7041	.7827	.7924	.8881
N of cases	70										

Appendix 4: Response category probability curves

OVERALL ABILITY

```
INPUT:      70 PERSONS     11 ITEMS

ANALYSED:     68 PERSONS       10 ITEMS      47 CATEGORIES

PLOT CENTERED ON    ITEM DIFFICULTY OF    1.08

P       ++-----+-----+-----+-----+-----+-----+-----+-----+-----++
R   1.0 +333                                                     +
O       |    333                                             777|
B       |     33                                          77    |
A       |       3                           666             7   |
B    .8 +        3                        66    6          7     +
I       |         3                     6         6       7      |
L       |         3                    6           6     7       |
I       |         3     4444       555 6           6   7         |
T    .6 +          3  4      4    5    5  6          6  7         +
Y       |          3 4      4    5     5 6              67        |
        |           *         45        56             *         |
O       |           *        54        65             76         |
F    .4 +           4 3      5 4       6 5            7  6         +
        |           4   3    5   4     6  5          7  6         |
R       |           4   3  5    4   6    5        7    6          |
E       |            4    3  5    4  6      5     7      6         |
S    .2 +           4         35        46      5    7      6     +
P       |           4        53        64       5  77        6    |
O       |         44        5  3    6   4         57          66  |
N       |     444        555      3*66     444  777555        666|
S    .0 +*******************7********************************+
E       ++-----+-----+-----+-----+-----+-----+-----+-----+-----++
          -9    -7    -5    -3    -1     1     3     5     7     9
                              MEASURE
```

Appendix 4: Response category probability curves *cont.*

GRAMMAR

INPUT: 70 PERSONS   11 ITEMS

ANALYSED: 68 PERSONS   10 ITEMS   47 CATEGORIES

FOR GROUP "0",   MODEL TYPE "R",   ITEM NUMBERS: 2

PLOT CENTERED ON   ITEM DIFFICULTY OF   2.38

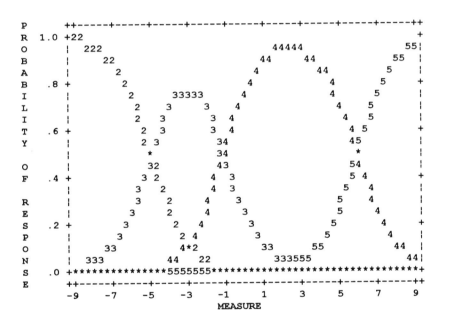

Appendix 4: Response category probability curves *cont.*

PRONUNCIATION

INPUT: 70 PERSONS   11 ITEMS

ANALYSED: 68 PERSONS   10 ITEMS   47 CATEGORIES

FOR GROUP "0", MODEL TYPE "R",   ITEM NUMBERS: 4

PLOT CENTERED ON   ITEM DIFFICULTY OF   1.60

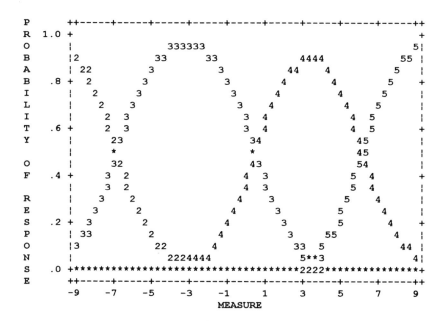

Appendix 4: Response category probability curves *cont*.

ORGANISATION

INPUT: 70 PERSONS   11 ITEMS

ANALYSED: 68 PERSONS   10 ITEMS   47 CATEGORIES

FOR GROUP "0", MODEL TYPE "R", ITEM NUMBERS: 5

PLOT CENTERED ON   ITEM DIFFICULTY OF   -.33

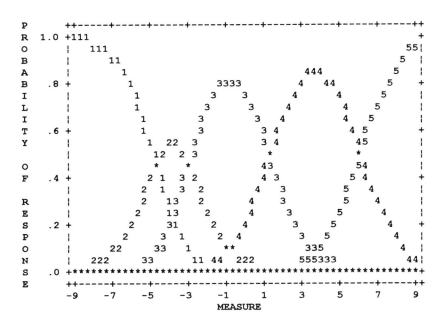

Appendix 4: Response category probability curves *cont.*

INTERVIEW

```
INPUT:    70 PERSONS    11 ITEMS

ANALYSED:    68 PERSONS    10 ITEMS    47 CATEGORIES

FOR GROUP "0",  MODEL TYPE "R",   ITEM  NUMBERS:    8

PLOT CENTERED ON   ITEM DIFFICULTY OF  -2.18
```

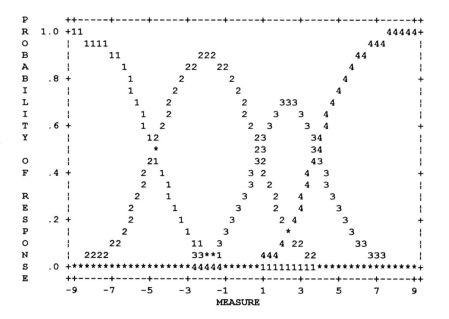

```
P       ++----+----+-----+-----+-----+-----+-----+-----+----++
R  1.0 +11                                              44444+
O       | 1111                                        444     |
B       |    11              222                     44       |
A       |     1           22    22                  4         |
B   .8 +      1         2        2                 4         +
I       |     1        2          2               4          |
L       |      1      2            2      333     4           |
I       |       1     2            2    3   3    4            |
T   .6 +        1   2            2   3      3   4            +
Y       |        12              23           34             |
        |         *              23           34             |
O       |        21              32           43             |
F   .4 +        2  1            3  2        4  3            +
        |       2   1            3   2        4  3           |
R       |      2     1           3     2    4     3           |
E       |     2      1          3      2    4      3          |
S   .2 +     2        1        3        2 4        3         +
P       |    2          1     3          *          3         |
O       |   22              11  3           4 22        33     |
N       | 2222             33**1        444      22        333 |
S   .0 +*******************44444******111111111***************+
E       ++----+----+-----+-----+-----+-----+-----+-----+----++
        -9      -7    -5    -3    -1     1     3     5     7     9
                                  MEASURE
```

2 Validation of a New Holistic Rating Scale Using Rasch Multi-faceted Analysis

BELLE TYNDALL and DORRY MANN KENYON

The purpose of this study is to examine the validity of a newly developed holistic scale for grading English essays using a Rasch multi-faceted approach. The first section of the paper describes how the new scale was developed and its first operational use. The second section describes the analysis of the data collected in the first operational use of the scale using Rasch multi-faceted analysis. One of the secondary goals of this paper is to illustrate the use of this approach to analyzing rating data by drawing attention to the wealth of data that it supplies.

For the purposes of this paper, a restricted definition of validity is used, one that is common in Rasch analysis. In the context of Rasch analysis, the construct validity of a measurement may be established by investigating the model fit (Wright & Stone, 1979; Wright & Masters, 1982). When little misfit is present, there is evidence for the construct validity of the variable that is being measured. In this paper, the measurement variable is essay writing ability. The measurement of this ability is subject to the elicitation of the essay by a single prompt in a timed writing context. Of more importance in this study, it is also subject to the scale used to judge the essay writing quality and the judges used in the operational scoring of the essays. If the Rasch analysis shows little misfit, there is evidence for the construct validity of this measurement procedure. The authors acknowledge that this definition falls short of Messick's definition of validity based on the empirical and theoretical rationales that support the adequacy and appropriateness of inferences and actions based on the test scores (Messick, 1989).

Background

Placing students accurately into homogeneous ability groups for the purpose of instruction is one of the important functions of EFL/ESL programs. The

39

George Washington University EFL Program continually grapples with this challenge of placement as it performs its two-fold function of advising the university as to the language preparedness of foreign students for university courses and of teaching those EFL courses offered in the department.

All international students entering The George Washington University to pursue undergraduate or graduate degrees in the various colleges of the university are required to take the English as a Foreign Language Placement Test administered by the EFL Department. The test consists of two components: the commercially available multiple choice type Michigan English Placement Test (MEPT), and an in-house written composition test.

The results of these tests give an indication of the students' general proficiency in English and determine whether these students can proceed to their academic courses without any further instruction in English, or whether they need to improve their English while taking a reduced academic load, or even before beginning academic courses.

Students who fall into the latter categories, that is, those who must take a reduced course load, and those who are not permitted to take any academic course at all because of their inadequate control of English, may be assigned to one of the six levels of EFL courses offered by the department. These courses range from EFL 50, the Advanced composition course, the equivalent of regular Freshman composition (English 9) offered by the English department, to EFL 15, the lowest level course. The other courses are EFL 45, EFL 40, EFL 30, and EFL 20. The lower down the student places, the longer that student must remain in the program, and the more costly his education becomes. Accurate placement is therefore important.

In addition to those students pursuing undergraduate and graduate programs, some students are admitted to do English only. These students must also take the Placement Test in order to ensure that they are placed at the level of instruction appropriate to their proficiency level. Although there exist within the program procedures for replacement if the initial placement proves inappropriate, the concern is always to ensure that the initial placement is as accurate as possible.

Procedures for placement

Prior to the fall of 1991, three placement scores were reported for each student, the MEPT score, the composition score, and a combined average score which was a combination of the MEPT score and the composition score. Students were usually placed on the basis of the combined average score. Cut off points for the MEPT, the composition and the combined scores were established for each level. Thus, for example, an MEPT score of 70 would fall within the EFL 40 range (66–79), while a composition score of 50 would fall within the EFL 20 range (45–53). However, the two scores combined (70 + 60) yielding an average score of 50 would fall within the EFL 30 range (52–65). Thus a student with such a profile would be placed in EFL 30. (See Appendix 1 for MEPT, Composition, and Combined Score Placement Guides.)

The practice of reporting scores in this way made it possible to compare the performances of students on each component of the test. Such comparisons very often highlighted a mismatch between the MEPT score and the composition score. Students would obtain high scores on the multiple choice test but surprisingly low scores on the composition test. Such a situation became problematic for the faculty responsible for placement allocation. Needless to say, the students were dissatisfied with the placement allocation since their combined average score would often place them at a level that did not meet their high expectations. In order to deal with possible misplacements, diagnostic tests were routinely given during the first week of semester, and on the basis of the results students were moved up or down within the program as necessary.

Need for a change

At the same time as this observation regarding the mismatch in performance on the two components of the placement test was manifesting itself, the test population was not only increasing dramatically, but also changing demographically. The department recognized the need to address the problem which these changing circumstances created. Clearly, something had to be done about the placement test. In light of the conventional wisdom regarding placement tests (that the most successful ones are those created for the specific situations), and recognizing that the creation of a reliable and valid multiple choice test to replace the MEPT would be a mammoth undertaking, the department began to give greater weight to the written composition component of the test. Thus the need to improve the validity of this aspect of the placement test became important.

Development of the Holistic Scale

The first decision taken was to develop a holistic scoring guide to replace the more analytic ESL Composition Profile (Hughey *et al.*, 1983), the instrument for assessing the composition component of the Placement Test which had been in use for many years. This Profile, while an excellent tool for evaluating writing, seemed for our purposes best suited to the evaluation of diagnostic tests – the purpose for which it is now used.

In place of the analytic Profile, the department developed a new holistic rating scale, similar in format to a holistic scoring guide developed by Glenn *et al.* (1990) and to the scoring guide for the Test of Written English (TWE) used by the Educational Testing Service (Educational Testing Service, 1990). Unlike these scales, however, the new scale had a range of 1 to 7 and was specifically designed to correspond to the required entry level writing skills of the courses in the department's program.

Entry level writing skills for a specific level were defined as the writing skills characteristic of students exiting the level below. For example, compositions with a score of 7, the highest score, should evidence characteristics of the writing of students who have completed EFL 50, the most advanced course offered by the department. Students with a composition score of 7 would require no special English. Similarly, a composition with a score of 4, and thus qualifying for placement in EFL 40, should reflect the characteristics of writing done by students exiting the level below, that is EFL 30. A composition with a score of 1 would indicate placement in the lowest level course in the program, EFL 15.

The descriptors of the scale were thus based on the writing outcomes of each level as stated in the syllabus. The first draft of the new scale was circulated to faculty for comment regarding the accuracy of the descriptors for each level and modified in accordance with faculty input.

A further attempt at honing the descriptors involved collecting compositions representative of each level and matching them with the corresponding level descriptors. Accordingly, towards the end of the 1991 spring semester, students at each level were required to write a composition on the same given topic in a 45 minute period. Instructors were asked to rank the compositions as High, Average, or Low, before turning them in. One month later, faculty were asked to rate a randomized sample of the compositions using the new holistic rating scale in an effort to see whether the descriptors accurately described each level. As a result of this exercise, some descriptors were again modified. The modified scale was then piloted in the summer of 1991, and used for the 1991 fall semester admissions with minor modifications. (See Appendix 2 for the Holistic Rating Scale)

The New Placement Policy

Since the composition component was now measured on a 1–7 scale, and the MEPT component on a 0–100 scale, a combined average score (MEPT and

Composition) was no longer feasible. The policy was therefore established that whenever there was a mismatch between the level placement derived from the MEPT score and that derived from the composition rating, students should be placed according to the composition rating.

The First Testing Period

Approximately 400 students were tested over a period of five days from 19 August to 23 August, 1991. The tests were held at the same time every day, with the composition component administered first. The students were required to write a composition on the single topic set, a different one for each day. The time allocated for this component of the Placement Test was 45 minutes. The compositions were read and rated by faculty directly following the administration. A total of eleven faculty participated in this exercise.

A workshop for all faculty was conducted on the first day of the testing period to calibrate raters to the use of the scale. Additionally, before every marking session, the coordinator of the session would pull three or four scripts for initial scoring and discussion to further establish a sense of unanimity with regard to the allocation of scores. Each script was rated by two readers who independently assigned a score of 1 to 7 based on the rating scale. If the two scores were dissimilar, a third reader was asked to rate the script. The score allocated would be that given by two of the three readers. If there was still no agreement among the three readers, a fourth reader would rate the script.

Analysis of the Data

The data analyzed in this study is derived from 246 students. These represent students who were assigned to courses within the department's program and completed the fall semester. The scores for students who did not enroll in the university, who enrolled or did not complete the semester, or who passed the English language placement test requiring no special English instruction, were not included in this analysis. Since all essays receiving a score of 7 ('No special English') were excluded from this data set, the scale analyzed contained six points (1, 2, 3, 4, 5, 6).

The rating data was analyzed using FACETS (Linacre, 1991), a Rasch-based rating scale analysis program which allows a number of different facets of the data to be examined on the same scale yet independently of one another. In this study, only two facets were examined: essays and raters. The Rasch model employed was:

$$\log (P_{njk} / P_{njk-1}) = B_n - C_j - F_k$$

where P_{njk} is the probability of Essay n being rated k by Rater j; and P_{njk-1} is the probability of Essay n being rated k–1 by Rater j. B_n is thus the quality of the essay while C_j is the severity of the rater, and F_k is the difficulty of the rating scale step relative to the previous scale step.

The number of essays that received two ratings was 172 (70% of the total). These are the essays that needed no double scoring. Seventy essays (28%) required a third rating before a final rating could be assigned, while four (2%) received four ratings. Thus, the total number of individual essay ratings in this analysis was 570. The reliability of the scoring procedure in terms of Rasch analysis was 0.85.

Analysis of the raters

Our analysis will first examine the raters. Table 2.1 indicates the distribution of the ratings across both the raters and the rating scale points. The last column presents the average rating assigned by each rater.

Table 2.1 Distribution of ratings across raters and rating scale points

Rater	Scale points						Total	Average rating
	1	*2*	*3*	*4*	*5*	*6*		
AA	1	0	7	14	5	5	32	4.0
BB	0	4	5	21	18	6	54	4.2
CC	2	2	14	29	21	7	75	4.1
DD	0	3	6	19	15	4	47	4.2
EE	1	2	10	15	24	10	62	4.3
FF	3	2	3	14	21	4	47	4.5
GG	1	1	3	11	26	11	53	4.7
HH	3	1	5	15	14	1	39	4.2
II	0	2	6	27	14	5	54	4.1
JJ	1	3	12	11	14	4	45	4.0
KK	2	2	9	20	25	4	62	4.1
(Total)	14	22	80	196	197	61	570	(Average) 4.2

With the FACETS program, it is not necessary that every rater rate every essay, nor that each rater score the same number of essays. Table 2.1 indicates that AA scored the least number of essays (32), while rater CC scored the most (75). Although in terms of the points on the rating scale the average rating on an essay was 4.2, raters ranged from an average score of 4.0 (raters AA and JJ) to a high of 4.7 for rater GG. This dispersion of average ratings in raw scores is due to two factors: the ability of the writers of the group of essays which any individual rater scored, and the differences in the trends of severity among the raters. A comparison of the average raw score is inadequate to account for both of these factors simultaneously. The FACETS analysis, however, accounts for both of these factors.

Table 2.2 presents the FACETS calibration for each rater, with the average rating in raw scores for comparison purposes and the measurement error associated with each rater's calibration.

Table 2.2 Calibration of the raters compared with average ratings

Rater	Average rating	Calibration logit
AA	4.0	1.03
BB	4.2	0.68
CC	4.1	0.15
DD	4.2	0.81
EE	4.3	−0.91
FF	4.5	−0.97
GG	4.7	−2.83
HH	4.2	2.03
II	4.1	−0.90
JJ	4.0	0.65
KK	4.1	−0.04
Average	4.2	0.00

The calibration of each rater indicates that although HH's average calibration is the same as the group average, this rater is actually the most severe rater (2.03). Rater GG is the least severe (−2.83). Note that most of the raters clump together around the mean rating of 0.00. This is shown more graphically in Figure 2.1, in which the raters are aligned to the nearest 0.50 logit along the left-hand scale.

We next want to look at the fit of these raters. If there is much misfit, then the validity of the scoring procedure is in question. This, in turn, may be due to the inability of the raters to apply the new scoring guide. Table 2.3 presents the fit statistics for the raters in this study, together with the rater calibration information.

Logit	Rater	Location	
3.50			Most severe
3.00			
2.50			
2.00	HH		
1.50			
1.00	AA	DD	
0.50	BB	JJ	
0.00	CC	KK	
−0.50	FF		
−1.00	II	EE	
−1.50			
−2.00			
−2.50			
−3.00	GG		
−3.50			Least severe

Figure 2.1 Graphical location of the raters in terms of serverity

Table 2.3 Calibration and fit statistics for the raters (ordered by rater calibration)

	Calibration	Infit	Outfit	
Raters	Logit	Std	Std	
HH	2.03	−2	−2	Most severe
AA	1.03	0	0	
DD	0.81	0	0	
BB	0.68	0	0	
JJ	0.65	0	0	
CC	0.15	−2	−1	
KK	−0.04	0	0	
FF	−0.67	−2	−2	
II	−0.90	−2	−2	
EE	−0.91	0	0	
GG	−2.83	2	1	Least severe

The measures of fit in Table 2.3 are an indication of inconsistency. In traditional rating terms, they are an indication of intra-rater reliability. Two measures of fit for the standardized fit statistic are given. This statistic has an expectation of 0 and a standard deviation of 1. Traditionally in Rasch analysis, the mean squared outfit statistic has been used as the primary indication of fit. This statistic reflects unexpected scores (in our case, ratings assigned). The infit statistic is similar, but is more sensitive to unexpected ratings close to the rater's calibration, since it weights how far away the unexpected rating occurs.

Interpreting these may be more of an art than a science. As a rule of thumb, standardized fit statistics greater than 2 or less than -2 may indicate problems. None of the raters have fit statistics outside this range. Thus, we can say that these raters appear to be able to consistently apply the new scoring scale to the essays.

To understand these fit statistics further, we need to mention that they have different meanings whether the standardized fit statistic is positive or negative. Positive fit statistics indicate 'noise' while the negative statistics indicate 'dependency' in the data. For raters, negative fit statistics means unexpected consistency. Since we desire raters to be consistent, we do not view, in this analysis, the ratings with negative standardized fit statistics as problematic. This leaves us with only one rater, GG, whose fit statistics, relatively speaking, indicate that we may want to take a closer look at this person's rating behavior.

Analysis of the essays

We will now look at the essay calibrations themselves. Table 2.4 indicates the number of essays that had misfit statistics in each category. Table 2.4 indicates that none of the essays were misfitting. This also gives evidence of the consistency with which the new scoring scale may be applied.

Analysis of the scale

We next examine how well the ratings procedures distinguished between levels. Estimable essays ranged in a calibration from 14.08 to -11.61. Table 2.5 shows the mean logit of the essays by the initial level placements based on the essays. The level shows the course level assignment. Scale shows the rating scale point assigned to that level. Number indicates the number of essays that were assigned to that level. The mean logit shows the average logit score for the essays assigned to that level. The standard deviation gives an indication of the dispersion of the essay scores within a level. The mean error of the logit indicates the average error associated with each logit

Table 2.4 Summary of misfitting essays

Standardized outfit statistic	Number of essays	
above 2	0	
2	13	(5%)
1	9	(4%)
0	223	(91%)
−1	1	(0%)
−2	0	
below −2	0	

Standardized infit statistic	Number of essays	
above 2	0	
2	9	(4%)
1	16	(7%)
0	220	(89%)
−1	1	(0%)
−2	0	
below −2	0	

estimation. The final two columns compare the results with a scalar analysis. The first column shows the logit value at which that scalar point is the most probable to be assigned. The midpoint column shows the point on the logit scale at which that rating has the same probability of being awarded as the next point on the scale.

Table 2.5 Mean logit scores by initial level placements

			Essay scores			Scale analysis	
Level	Scale	Number	Mean logit	Std dev.	Mean error of logit	Most probable	Mid point
10	1	7	−11.20	0.41	1.25	∞	−11.42
20	2	8	−8.87	0.82	1.67	−8.91	−6.46
30	3	29	−2.79	1.99	1.85	−3.36	−0.41
40	4	71	2.01	1.94	1.98	2.52	5.61
45	5	101	7.83	2.54	2.20	9.03	12.73
50	6	30	11.30	1.86	1.99	∞	

From Table 2.5 we see that the levels were rather clearly classified. Levels 40 and 45, into which 70% of the essays were initially placed, was clearly separated by almost 6 logits. The scalar analysis indicates that the scale points were well separated and well defined. No points on the scale were in danger of overlapping or being mistaken. The operational scoring procedure categorized the examinees well.

Figure 2.2 illustrates the response category probability curves. This figure depicts the likelihood for any score to be chosen at any ability level (along the bottom axis). Of note in this figure are the clear peaks and the separation between the categories. This indicates the clarity with which the scale was applied.

The mean error logit for these ratings, which is quite high (the root mean square error of all the essay calibrations was 2.12 logits), gives a standard against which to interpret the significance of the differences in rater severity in this operational rating setting. We note from Table 2.3 and Figure 2.1 that 9 of the 11 raters lay within 2 logits of each other in severity, and within one logit of the average. Since this is within the root mean square error, these differences in rater severity are of little practical consequence. However, rater GG would be expected to rate essays somewhat higher than the average rater, while rater HH would be expected to rate essays somewhat lower.

In summary, the FACETS analysis provides strong evidence for the construct validity of the new rating scale, as applied in the operational procedures of the program. No misfit for raters indicates that raters are applying it consistently to the essays they read. No misfit for essays indicates that the essays are scorable according to the new guide. Scalar analysis indicates that, as applied, the new scoring guide can classify the incoming students into rather clear groupings.

Information for rater training

In the last section of our paper, we want to illustrate the information that a FACETS analysis can provide for feedback in rater training. The FACETS analysis indicates which of the individual ratings were misfitting according to standards set by the user. In this application, all individual ratings with a standardized residual greater than 2 or less than −2 were to be reported at misfitting. It should be noted that this test is more severe than the suggested default value of +3 and −3.

Given this criterion, there were only 28 individual misfitting ratings (5.3% of all the ratings). The next analysis was to look for patterns within the problematic ratings. First, we looked at the distribution of these misfitting

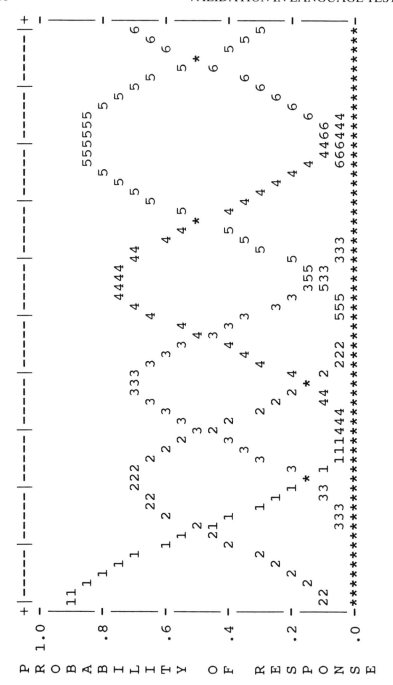

Figure 2.2 Response category probability curves

ratings over essays. This revealed that 10 essays had two misfitting ratings, while eight had one. Of these 18 essays, only two were essays that in the operational program received only two ratings. In other words, 16 of the 18 required more than two ratings. Thus, the operational program was working to correct problems. The two essays for which both ratings were misfitting should probably be examined to see what characteristics may have made them difficult to rate on the given scale.

Next we looked for any patterns of misfits over the raters. Table 2.6 presents the number of individual misfitting ratings per rater and then that number as a percentage of all ratings awarded.

Table 2.6 Distribution of misfitting ratings over raters

Rater	Number	Percent of individual's ratings
AA	2	6.3
BB	3	5.5
CC	2	2.3
DD	2	4.3
EE	4	6.5
FF	0	0.0
GG	7	13.2
HH	1	2.6
II	1	1.9
JJ	3	6.7
KK	3	4.8

Table 2.6 clearly indicates that there was not a pattern of misfitting ratings for most raters. However, rater GG had a relatively high proportion of her ratings involved in misfitting ratings. This corroborates the data in Table 2.3 and indicates that rater GG may need more training.

To determine whether rater GG had problems at all points the scale or at only certain scale points, we looked at her individual ratings that were marked as misfitting in comparison with those of the other raters. Table 2.7 presents the profiles of the ratings received for all essays that had at least one misfitting rating. An analysis of the 7 misfitting ratings for rater GG shows that all of them occurred between the awarding of 5 and 6 on the rating scale. This rater seems to be confused on these two score points. Further training with her should focus on these two score points.

Table 2.7 Profiles of misfitting ratings

Essay Number	A	B	C	D	E	F	G	H	I	J	K
	A	B	C	D	E	F	G	H	I	J	K
21		2(+)	3						4(−)	3	
25	3				2(+)					3	
57			4	4				3(+)			5(−)
73					5(−)						3(+)
95	4				3(+)		5				
99	3				3	4	5(−)				
100	3				3		5(−)				
116	3				3		5(−)				
158			4	3(+)	5						5
167		4(+)					6(−)			5	
181		6(−)				5				4(−)	
201	6(−)						5(+)				
203			6(−)				5(+)				
210			4(+)	5							
215				6(−)						6(−)	
226	4(+)				6(−)		5				4(+)
237					6	6	5				
245			5				5(+)			6(−)	

Key (+) = Misfitting rating whose expected value was higher than the rating assigned.
     (−) = Misfitting rating whose expected value was lower than the rating assigned.

Summary

In this paper we have attempted to examine the validity of a new holistic rating scale developed for a very specific purpose. From the FACETS analysis, it appears that there is a single construct of writing ability that is being measured with this scale in the operational procedure used.

It is interesting to speculate on why the scale appeared to work so well. We propose that the reason lies within the harmony between the descriptors of the rating scale and the raters own internalized experience. All of the raters had experience within the EFL Program of The George Washington University. The descriptors for the new scale were directly related to courses they taught. They reflected papers they had often read and were experienced with. The raters themselves had input during the development of the scale and its descriptors.

As support for our speculation, we offer the following results from a questionnaire that informally collected feedback from the raters. In order to ascertain whether these raters actually used the scale or relied on their knowledge of the levels established over time, they were asked to indicate how they used the scale when rating the compositions.

Four of the 10 raters polled responded. One rater indicated that she 'did not use the scale'. Another indicated that she read the scale only at the beginning of the marking session but did not refer to it again. She made a guess at a level then adjusted based on evidence from rereading. The final two indicated that, having studied the scale beforehand, they read the composition and formed a general impression about the level. They referred to the scale only when they needed to 'verify the impression', or 'when making a level decision'. It appears that these raters were acting on strongly internalized criteria.

There is one final piece of evidence in support of our speculation. One of the participating raters was on sabbatical during the year the new scale was developed and could not comment on it. She also entered the scoring session 'cold', away from a year of teaching. Which rater was she? Rater GG.

References

Educational Testing Service (1990) *TWE Scoring Guide*. Princeton, NJ: Educational Testing Service.

Glenn, C., Graves, R., Nelms, R. G. and Guon, D. (1989) *St. Martin's Handbook: Annotated Instructor's Edition*. New York, NY: St. Martin's Press.

Hughey, J. B., Wormuth, D. R., Hartfiel, V. F. and Jacobs, H. L. (1983) *Teaching ESL Composition: Principles and Techniques*. Rowley, MA: Newbury House Publishers.

Linacre, J. M. (1989) *Many-faceted Rasch Measurement*. Chicago, IL: MESA Press.
— (1991) *FACETS* [Computer program] Chicago, IL: MESA Press.
Messick, S. (1989) Validity. In R. L. Linn *Educational Measurement* 3rd ed. New York: Macmillan Publishing Company.
White, E. (1990) *The Diagnostic Essay: Holistic Scoring Guide*. New York, NY: St. Martin's Press.
Wright, B. D. and Masters, G. N. (1982) *Rating Scale Analysis*. Chicago, IL: MESA Press.
Wright, B. D. and Stone, M. H. (1979) *Best Test Design*. Chicago, IL: MESA Press.

Appendix 1: English as a foreign language. EFL placement grid

MULTIPLE CHOICE

MEPT	LEVEL
0–34	15
35–49	20
50–65	30
66–79	40
80–89	45
90–95	50
96–100	NSE

WRITING

WRITING	LEVEL
34–44	15
45–53	20
54–64	30
65–76	40
77–87	45
88–95	50
96–100	NSE

COMBINED AVERAGE

AVERAGE	LEVEL
Less than 40	15
40–51	20
52–65	30
66–78	40
79–88	45
89–95	50
96–100	NSE

Appendix 2: EFL placement test. Proposed holistic scoring guide (revised 8/91)

A SCORE OF 7 (No special English)

Suggests superior competence in writing on both the rhetorical and the syntactic levels, though it may have occasional errors.

A paper in this category:

- addresses the topic fully, explores several relevant aspects, conveys a sense of completeness
- is well organized: thesis fully developed, ideas clearly stated, fully supported and logically ordered, introductory and concluding paragraphs, smooth transitions between paragraphs
- uses varied sentence structure appropriately: effective complex constructions, parallel structures, appropriate word choice and idiomatic use of language
- has virtually no errors of agreement, tense, number
- shows mastery of spelling, capitalization, and punctuation.

A SCORE OF 6 (Level 50)

Demonstrates competence in writing on both the rhetorical and the syntactic levels, though it may have occasional errors.

A paper in this category:

- addresses the topic, explores some relevant aspects
- is organized: thesis developed, ideas supported, paragraphs logically ordered, a sense of introduction and conclusion, transitions between paragraphs may be ineffective
- uses generally well-formed sentences; subordination may be effective
- may have problems with appropriate word choice and idiomatic use of language
- has few errors of agreement, tense, number
- shows control over spelling, capitalization, and punctuation.

Appendix 2: EFL placement test. Proposed holistic scoring guide *cont.*

A SCORE OF 5 (Level 45)

Demonstrates some competence in writing on both the rhetorical and syntactic levels, though it will have many errors.

A paper in this category:

- addresses some aspects of the topic more fully than others: content relevant to the topic, but thesis development somewhat limited or uneven
- shows evidence of organization, a sense of introduction and conclusion
- shows evidence of paragraph development: main ideas stated and supported though not fully, transitions between paragraphs may be weak
- uses effective but simple constructions, problems with complex structure, some errors of word choice or idiom, but meaning clear
- may contain errors in agreement, tense, word order, spelling, punctuation and capitalization.

A SCORE OF 4 (Level 40)

Demonstrates minimal competence in writing on both the rhetorical and syntactic levels.

A paper in this category:

- addresses the topic: content relevant, but thesis not fully developed
- displays some evidence of paragraph structure: topic sentence and some support, may lack logical order
- uses simple and coordinate constructions, problems with complex constructions, fragment sentences, run-ons
- contains errors of word choice, frequent errors of idiomatic usage, meaning sometimes unclear
- contains several errors of agreement, tense, word order, several errors in spelling, punctuation, capitalization.

Appendix 2: EFL placement test. Proposed holistic scoring guide *cont.*

A SCORE OF 3 (Level 30)

Demonstrates developing competence, but may show deficiency at either the rhetorical or the syntactic level, or both.

A paper in this category:

- may/may not address the topic
- may contain inappropriate or insufficient detail to support ideas
- may reveal major problems with simple and compound sentences, shows little subordination
- may reveal noticeably incorrect word forms, problems with cohesive devices, few or no transitions, omissions
- may have serious problems with agreement, tense, word order, fragments, run-ons.

A SCORE OF 2 (Level 20)

Suggests incompetence in writing.

A paper in this category:

- may contain content not appropriate to the topic
- shows little evidence of paragraph structure, lacks topic sentence, lacks detail, is seriously disorganized
- shows little knowledge of sentence construction, vocabulary, difficult to follow
- displays severe errors of agreement, tense, word order/function, little mastery of the conventions of spelling, and punctuation.

A SCORE OF 1

Demonstrates incompetence in writing.

A paper in this category:

- may not contain enough material to evaluate
- may be incoherent
- may display no mastery of sentence construction
- may display no mastery of the conventions of spelling, punctuation, capitalization.

3 Hypothesis Testing in Construct Validation

SARA CUSHING WEIGLE and BRIAN LYNCH

This chapter describes an investigation of the construct validity of the recently revised English as a Second Language Placement Examination (ESLPE) at the University of California, Los Angeles (UCLA). The new test was designed to measure the English skills needed for university course work, whereas the old test was designed primarily to measure knowledge of formal features of English. Two groups of test takers – recently arrived international graduate students and immigrant under-graduate students – both took the new test and grammar subsection of the old test. Based on the attributes of these groups of test takers, principally their previous exposure to formal grammar instruction and to academic work in English, several hypotheses about group differences in performance on the two tests were generated and tested in an ex post facto design. The results partially supported the research hypotheses and provided valuable information about the skills being tested by the new ESLPE.

Construct validation in language testing has frequently been investigated by testing hypotheses about the relationship between theoretical models of language ability and test scores. Most frequently, this has involved the use of correlational techniques such as factor analysis and multidimensional scaling. For example, Davidson (1988) investigated a form of the UCLA English as a Second Language Placement Exam (ESLPE) with exploratory factor analysis and multidimensional scaling (MDS). His findings indicated that, despite the existence of multiple subtests designed to measure different language subskills such as listening and reading, the data were best accounted for by a single factor solution. In terms of construct validity, these results argued that the ESLPE was measuring a unidimensional trait, or, more properly, that the ESLPE dataset was statistically unidimensional. Davidson noted that this was not the same as concluding that the language ability being measured by the ESLPE was a single mental trait.

Oltman & Stricker (1990) also used MDS to examine the trait structure of the Test of English as a Foreign Language (TOEFL). In examining the relationship between the dimensions (clusters) identified by MDS and the sections (subtests) of the TOEFL, they concluded that there were 'distinguishable but related clusters of items that are congruent with the constructs that the sections are intended to assess' (p. 11), thereby providing evidence in support of the test's construct validity. It should be noted, however, that they found different relationships between statistical dimension and test section for different ability groups (i.e. high and low scoring test takers).

Approach to Construct Validation Employed in the Study

These techniques of factor analysis and MDS tested the hypothesis that the existence of one or more statistical dimensions account for the test data. From this evidence, conclusions regarding the construct validity of the test – its ability to measure the underlying theoretical model of language proficiency – are drawn. Rather than testing whether or not a single statistical dimension can account for the observed test scores as in the previous studies, another approach, adopted in the present research, is to posit a hypothesis with the following form:

if Test X is measuring Construct Y, then examinees with Attributes Z1, Z2 will be expected to score higher/lower than examinees with Attributes Z3, Z4

The hypothesis can then be tested with the appropriate statistical technique (e.g. t-test or ANOVA). This approach amounts to an ex post facto experimental design in which the dependent variable is the test being validated and the independent variable is a set of examinee characteristics. A notable example of this approach to construct validation can be found in Klein-Braley (1985). In her study of the C-test, she applied various theoretical notions from the second language acquisition literature to form hypotheses concerning performance on the C-test. For example, she tested and was able to confirm the hypothesis that if the C-test was a measure of language competence, subjects at later stages of language development would perform better than those at earlier stages of development.

We were interested in applying this type of hypothesis testing to the construct validation of the revised UCLA English as a Second Language Placement Exam (New ESLPE), particularly after significant revisions were undertaken to the ESLPE over the period Fall 1989 to Fall 1990. The motivation for revising the test came from criticisms by instructors in the UCLA ESL program that the language tasks used on the previous forms of the ESLPE (Old ESLPE) did not match the tasks that were used in the ESL curriculum (i.e. that the test needed to be more criterion-referenced). The Old ESLPE included a number of tasks that were designed primarily to measure a construct we will call Formal Knowledge of English Grammar (FKEG). However, the ESL curriculum at UCLA focuses primarily on the development of academic English skills rather than FKEG, and it was felt that the ESLPE should reflect this curriculum orientation. Another motivation for revising the Old ESLPE came from evidence in the literature that traditional ESL proficiency tests are not good predictors of academic success, in part because they do not provide good measurement of communicative language use (Savignon, 1986; Graham, 1987).

The New ESLPE, then, was designed to measure a student's ability to use English for academic purposes (the basic philosophy of the UCLA ESL curriculum) through tasks that mirrored academic language use and the types of tasks used in the instructional curriculum. As such, we might label the underlying construct as English Academic Language Proficiency (EALP). The definition of this construct goes beyond grammatical and textual competencies (see Bachman, 1990) to include academic skills such as:

(1) the ability to write with fluency on an academic topic;

(2) the ability to understand academic lectures;

(3) the ability to understand written academic texts;

(4) the ability to write on academic topics with well developed ideas;

(5) the ability to organize written text in accordance with academic rhetorical conventions.

The New ESLPE operationalized this construct with three subtests: composition; listening and notetaking; and reading and vocabulary. In the composition subtest the students write on one of two essay topics. Information in the form of a chart or graph accompanies the topic. The students have 50 minutes to write a formal, academic essay, which is evaluated with a rating scale comprising three subscales: content, rhetorical control, and language. In the listening and notetaking subtest the students listen to and take notes on two passages (one approximately 15 minutes in length, the other seven minutes) which simulate academic lectures. After each passage, students use their notes to answer multiple-choice and true-false questions based on the lecture. In the reading and vocabulary subtest students read two passages (each 800 to 1,500 words in length), one of which comes from an academic textbook and the other from a popular news magazine. After each passage the students answer multiple-choice and true–false questions concerning main ideas, specific details, inferences drawn from the text, and vocabulary items found in the text.

Attributes and Hypotheses

There were two subpopulations of interest to us in relation to the construct of EALP: recently-arrived international graduate students (GRADS) and immigrant undergraduate students (UGRADS). Our experience with these subpopulations led us to believe that they had the following attributes:

(1) GRADS will have studied formal English grammar more than UGRADS and will have had more experience preparing for and taking discrete-point grammar exams.

(2) UGRADS will have had more experience using English in academic work (US schools) and will have acquired more fluent writing skills as a result of being in an ESL environment.

(3) UGRADS will have had greater exposure to English in an academic environment (US schools) and will have acquired greater listening skills as a result of being in an ESL environment.

(4) UGRADS will have had greater exposure to reading English in an academic environment, but this exposure will be balanced by the GRADS having had more overall academic experience and more sophisticated academic content schemata. (GRADS will have had greater opportunity to read than they will have to listen to academic texts in their EFL environment.)

(5) GRADS will have had more experience with academic content and will thus have acquired more sophisticated academic content schemata to draw upon in their writing than will UGRADS.

(6) GRADS will have had greater experience with academic discourse and its organization, but this will be balanced by the UGRADS having had more exposure to the conventions of English rhetoric and more experience writing in English.

In general, we expected that, based on these attributes, predictions could be made concerning the relative performance of the two subpopulations on the ESLPE that could serve as hypotheses to test the construct validity of the exam. The specific attributes would, of course, be mediated by the amount of time that GRADS, in the EFL context, and UGRADS, in the ESL context, were exposed to English.

In order to initiate this process of construct validation for the ESLPE, we began with the following hypotheses (drawn from the attributes presented above):

(1) GRADS will perform better than UGRADS on the Old ESLPE grammar subtest.

(2) UGRADS will perform better than GRADS on the New ESLPE language subscale (composition subtest).

(3) UGRADS will perform better than GRADS on the New ESLPE listening & notetaking subtest.

(4) UGRADS and GRADS will perform equally on the New ESLPE reading & vocabulary subtest.

(5) GRADS will perform better than UGRADS on the New ESLPE content subscale (composition subtest).

(6) UGRADS and GRADS will perform equally on the New ESLPE organization subscale (composition subtest).

These hypotheses are shown in Table 3.1.

Table 3.1 Hypotheses

	Subtest	*Prediction*
1.	Grammar	GRAD > UGRAD
2.	Language	UGRAD > GRAD
3.	Listening	UGRAD > GRAD
4.	Reading	GRAD = UGRAD
5.	Content	GRAD > UGRAD
6.	Organization	GRAD = UGRAD

An additional, perhaps obvious hypothesis is that students (both GRADS and UGRADS) with more exposure to English would perform better than those with less. If these hypotheses were supported by the test performance data from the Fall 1991 administration of the New ESLPE, such a finding could be taken as partial evidence that the test is measuring the construct of EALP (and, with respect to hypothesis #1, that the Old ESLPE, in particular the grammar subtest, was measuring FKEG). Although we assumed FKEG is a component of EALP, hypotheses #2 through #6 were designed to test whether the New ESLPE was measuring more than just FKEG.

Procedures

To test these hypotheses, test data for graduate and undergraduate students who took the Fall 1991 ESLPE Form C were analyzed using a multivariate analysis of variance (MANOVA). The dependent variables were the Old ESLPE grammar subtest and the New ESLPE subtests: composition (language, content, and organization subscales), listening & notetaking, and reading & vocabulary. The independent variables were academic *Status* (GRADS vs. UGRADS), where only GRADS who had been in the US for less than one year (N = 82) and only UGRADS who had lived in the US for more than one year were considered (N = 70), and *Time* (one to five years, six to 10 years, and greater than 10 years), which was the number of years of English study for GRADS and the amount of time in the US for UGRADS. The distribution of the students who served as our population in the various categories of *Status* and *Time* is found in Table 3.2.

Table 3.2 Participating students

	Time			
Status	*Short (1–5 yrs)*	*Medium (6–10 yrs)*	*Long (>10 yrs)*	*Total*
GRAD	15	47	20	82
UGRAD	33	29	9	71
Total	48	76	29	153

Results

Tables 3.3 and 3.4 present the descriptive statistics for the GRADS and UGRADS, respectively. The MANOVA test for overall effect of the independent variables was significant for both populations at the alpha level set for this experiment ($a = 0.05$; Pillai's Trace: $p = 0.0001$ for *Status*; $p = 0.0019$ for *Time*). The interaction of *Status* and *Time* was not statistically significant. We then examined the univariate results for the dependent variables associated with the specific hypotheses.

Hypothesis #1 was not supported by the test data. There was a significant interaction between *Status* and *Time* on the grammar subtest ($F(2,147) = 3.46$, $p = 0.034$), suggesting that grammar performance depended on certain combinations of the two independent variables. The Scheffé multiple-comparison procedure (for all *Status* by *Time* means) revealed that the GRADS who had studied English for one to five years performed significantly poorer on the grammar subtest than all other subgroups. Overall, however, it could not be claimed that GRADS performed better than UGRADS, as hypothesized (see Figure 3.1, for graph of the interaction of *Status* and *Time* on the grammar subtest).

Table 3.3 Descriptive statistics, graduate students

Subtest	n	mean	s.d.	min.	max.
Grads, 1–5 years					
Listening	15	20.27	6.30	12	30
Reading	15	29.40	7.13	16	37
Content	15	6.17	1.06	4.5	8.5
Organization	15	5.73	0.88	4.5	8
Language	15	11.73	3.65	3	16
Grammar	15	14.33	3.18	6	19
Grads, 6–10 years					
Listening	47	21.79	4.71	13	30
Reading	47	31.06	3.95	21	39
Content	47	6.55	0.92	4	8.5
Organization	47	6.19	1.14	4	8.5
Language	47	11.73	3.65	3	16
Grammar	47	16.68	1.95	12	20
Grads, > 10 years					
Listening	20	26.25	2.36	22	30
Reading	20	33.60	2.87	27	40
Content	20	7.78	1.03	6	9
Organization	20	7.25	1.23	4.5	9
Language	20	18.30	1.72	14	20
Grammar	20	18.30	1.72	14	20

Hypothesis #2 was supported by the test data. The main effects for *Status* and *Time* on the language subtest were both significant ($F(1,147) = 5.40$, $p = 0.022$ and $F(2,147) = 6.84$, $p = 0.001$, respectively) and the interaction effect was not significant (see Figure 3.2 for graph of the interaction). This indicated that UGRADS performed significantly better than GRADS on the language subscale of the composition subtest. The Scheffé comparisons for the main effect of *Time* showed that those students (both GRADS and UGRADS) who had studied or lived for more than 10 years in the US performed significantly better than those who had studied or lived less in the US for lesser periods. However, there were no significant differences between those who had studied or lived six to 10 years in the US and those who had studied or lived one to five years in the US.

Table 3.4 Descriptive statistics, undergraduate students

Subtest	n	mean	s.d.	min.	max.
UGrads, 1–5 years					
Listening	33	24.24	3.32	15	29
Reading	33	29.21	3.90	19	35
Content	33	6.64	0.98	4.5	8.5
Organization	33	6.50	1.02	4	9
Language	33	13.50	2.29	10	19.5
Grammar	33	16.67	2.19	12	20
UGrads, 6–10 years					
Listening	29	24.90	2.66	20	29
Reading	29	31.38	5.19	14	38
Content	29	6.64	1.45	2	9
Organization	29	6.52	1.35	2.5	9
Language	29	13.97	1.84	10	17
Grammar	29	17.76	1.72	13	20
UGrads, > 10 years					
Listening	9	24.33	3.00	20	29
Reading	9	29.89	3.69	24	35
Content	9	6.61	1.90	3	9
Organization	9	6.83	1.62	3.5	9
Language	9	14.89	3.22	8	19
Grammar	9	17.78	2.95	10	19

Hypothesis #3 was partially supported by the test data. There was a significant interaction (see Figure 3.3) between *Status* and *Time* on the listening & notetaking subtest ($F(2,147) = 4.78, p = 0.010$). The Scheffé comparisons (for all *Status* by *Time* means) revealed that UGRADS who had lived in the US for six to 10 years performed better than GRADS who had only studied English for one to five years. GRADS who had studied for more than 10 years also outperformed GRADS who had studied less than that. Whereas the UGRADS were expected to outperform the GRADS at all levels of experience, it appears that the greater academic experience of the GRADS who had studied for more than five years balanced their weaker listening skills in relation to the UGRADS. Also, those UGRADS who had lived in the US for more than 10 years did not perform significantly better from the other subgroups.

Hypothesis #4 was supported by the test data. The main effect for *Status* $(F(1,147) = 2.05, p = 0.155)$ and the interaction $(F(2,147) = 1.92, p = 0.150)$ were not significant for the reading subtest and there was a significant main effect for *Time* $(F(2,147) = 3.16, p = 0.045)$. (See Figure 3.4.) The Scheffé comparisons revealed that those students (GRADS and UGRADS) with more than 10 years of contact with English through studying or living in the USA performed significantly better than those who had less contact, which is consistent with the general hypothesis of a positive effect for amount of exposure to English. As expected, the GRADS were able to perform equally as well as the UGRADS, regardless of the amount of exposure.

Hypothesis #5 was partially supported by the test data. There was a significant interaction $(F(2,147) = 4.10, p = 0.019)$ on the content subscale of the composition subtest (see Figure 3.5). The Scheffé comparisons (for all *Status* by *Time* means) indicated that the GRADS who had studied English for more than 10 years were significantly better than the other GRADS and the UGRADS who had lived in the US for less than 10 years. Although these GRADS (more than 10 years of study) were not able to outperform the UGRADS on the language subscale, they were able to outperform the UGRADS with less experience on content, as expected. However, the hypothesis was not supported for all subgroups of GRADS versus UGRADS.

Hypothesis #6 was supported by the test data. The main effect for *Status* $(F(1,147) = 1.04, p = 0.309)$ and the interaction (see Figure 3.6) were not significant $(F(2,147) = 1.94, p = 0.147)$ and there was a significant main effect for *Time* on the organization subscale of the composition subtest $(F(1,147) = 4.90, p = 0.009)$. The Scheffé comparisons revealed that those students (GRADS and UGRADS) who had had more than 10 years of exposure to English were significantly better than those in the other groups. As predicted, GRADS were able to perform equally well with the UGRADS, regardless of the amount of exposure.

Table 3.5 presents a summary of the hypothesis testing results.

Table 3.5 Summary of results

	Subtest	Prediction	Supported?
1.	Grammar	G > U	no
2.	Language	U > G	yes
3.	Listening	U > G	partially
4.	Reading	G = U	yes
5.	Content	G > U	partially
6.	Organization	G = U	partially

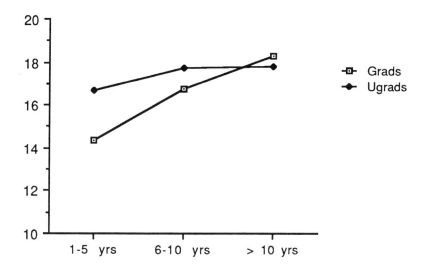

Figure 3.1 Grammar means by status and time

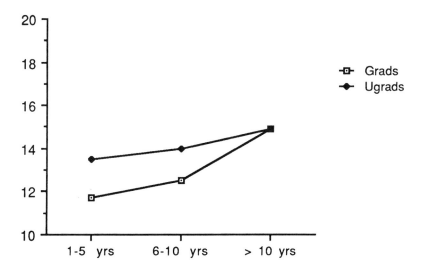

Figure 3.2 Language means by status and time

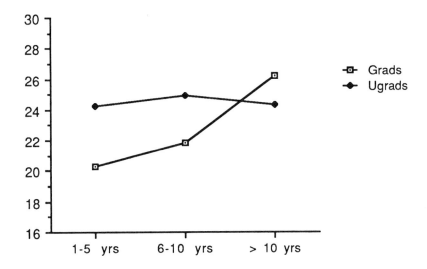

Figure 3.3 Listening means by status and time

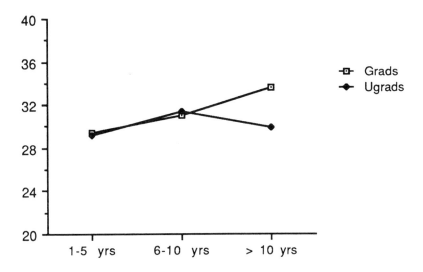

Figure 3.4 Reading means by status and time

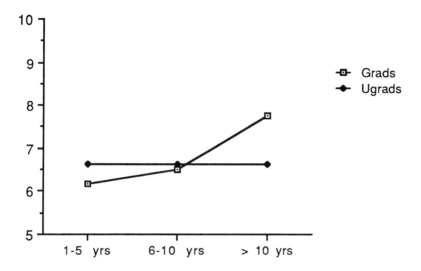

Figure 3.5 Content means by status and time

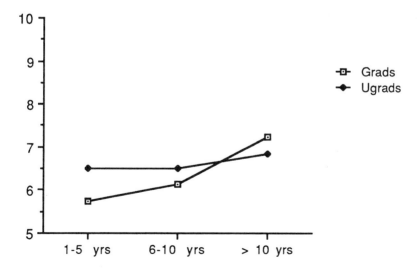

Figure 3.6 Organization means by status and time

Discussion

Overall, our results provide partial evidence for the construct validity of the New ESLPE as a measure of EALP. With one exception (hypothesis #1), the hypotheses were supported or partially supported by the test data. One interpretation of the failure of the data to support hypothesis #1 is that formal study of grammar and experience with discrete-point tests does not have an effect different from that of naturalistic language learning on the underlying construct (FKEG). Another interpretation is that the Old ESLPE grammar subtest is measuring something other than FKEG; for example, it may be that the subtest is a measure of general ESL proficiency (including FKEG). It may also be that the grammar subtest had a ceiling effect and was insensitive to differences at the upper end of the ability range. A preliminary IRT analysis suggests this was most likely the case. Finally, it is possible that the construct of EALP is defined differently at different levels of ability (Lyle Bachman, personal communication).

Future research will need to specify the nature of the *Time* variable in order for the results of this study to be more interpretable. To what degree are the GRADS and UGRADS experiencing similar exposure to English in the EFL and ESL contexts, respectively? Are there differences in test performance based on type of exposure to English? It would also be interesting to investigate the listening and reading subtests from the previous forms of the ESLPE to determine if test performance on those measures would fail to support the hypotheses tested in this study. Implicit in the hypotheses tested in this study is the notion that there are important differences between the two subpopulations, GRADS and UGRADS, in the UCLA ESL Service Courses. These differences were used to approach the construct validation of the ESLPE as the placement exam that places both groups into a single curriculum. The results of this hypothesis testing, then, do more than provide partial evidence for the validity of the test – they also suggest that different curricula need to be developed to respond to the differing needs of the two groups. In fact, the ESL Service Courses faculty has been aware of this GRAD versus UGRAD (also referred to as the *foreign-immigrant split*) problem for some time. In response, sections limited to GRAD students have been created where multiple sections of the course level exist, and specific curricula for GRAD student versions of these course levels have begun to be developed.

We consider that the use of this hypothesis testing approach to construct validation has been quite informative. It has provided us with a sense of the construct that underlies the New ESLPE that is expressed in terms of specific attributes and language abilities relevant to our students and our curricula. This seems to us much more interpretable than validation techniques that express the construct only as a statistical *factor*, or *dimension*. Furthermore, such specific hypothesis testing can result in recommendations for adjustments in the curricula (and the placement test) that are more clearly operationalized in terms of the actual instructional setting.

References

Bachman, L. F. (1990) *Fundamental Considerations in Language Testing*. Oxford: Oxford University Press.

Davidson, F. G. (1988) An exploratory modeling survey of the trait structure of some existing language test datasets. Unpublished Doctoral Dissertation, UCLA.

Graham, J. G. (1987) English language proficiency and the prediction of academic success. *TESOL Quarterly* 21, 505–21.

Klein-Braley, C. (1985) A cloze-up on the C-test: A study in the construct validation of authentic tests. *Language Testing* 2, 76–104.

Oltman, P. K. and Stricker, L. J. (1990) Developing homogeneous TOEFL scales by multidimensional scaling. *Language Testing* 7, 1–12.

Savignon, S. (1986) The meaning of communicative competence in relation to the TOEFL program. In C. W. Stansfield (ed.) *Toward Communicative Competence in Testing: Proceedings of the Second TOEFL Invitational Conference* (Research Rep. No. 21) (pp. 17–30). Princeton, NJ: Educational Testing Service.

4 An Investigation into the Validity of Written Indicators of Second Language Proficiency

ALISTER CUMMING and DEAN MELLOW

Seeking to provide construct validation for direct methods of assessing writing performance in a second language, particularly ratings of qualities of language use in students' written compositions, this study reviewed previous research then gathered empirical data to assess whether three morphological features of students' written texts (lexical articles, plural -s suffixes, and third person singular -s suffixes) or an index of lexical knowledge (type/token ratio of unique words to total words) might serve as valid and reliable indicators of second language proficiency. Analyses of compositions written in English by 24 adult Francophone and 42 adult Japanese learners of English found (1) accuracy of English article use, but not other variables, related significantly to analytic ratings of the quality of language use in these students' compositions; (2) none of the potential indicators relating significantly to the Francophone students' writing expertise in their mother tongue; (3) distinct differences across tasks for the Francophone students but not for the Japanese students; (4) the Francophone learners performing more accurately in the four aspects of language use than the Japanese learners; and (5) little consistent variation between accuracy in article use among either the French or Japanese learners at differing levels of English proficiency (intermediate and advanced). These findings provide limited evidence that accuracy of article use in English may be a stable indicator of second language proficiency (as concluded by Master, 1987), when compared to general assessments obtained through TOEFL scores or oral interviews, a finding that did not hold for the other aspects of English language use analyzed.

The present study sought to establish precise and valid indicators of second-language proficiency (SLP) for three purposes related to educational practice and research. First, theoretical and empirical validation is needed to support and refine the widespread uses of holistic, analytic or other impressionistic methods to assess students' written performance in second languages, for example, for such purposes as admissions to programs of higher education. Though endorsed from several perspectives (Jacobs *at al.*, 1981; Stansfield & Ross, 1988), holistic and analytic rating methods for assessing written compositions have only recently been subjected to intensive empirical scrutiny (Cumming, 1990a; Huot, 1990) and numerous scholars have begun to question their theoretical assumptions and practical realizations (Freedman, 1991; Purves, 1992; Raimes, 1990). For second language education, impressionistic rating schemes remain conceptually problematic in that students' writing expertise and language proficiency are assessed in conjunction (Cumming, 1989; 1990a). The present study sought specific indicators of the construct of SLP in the context of compositions written in a second language in order to supplement and verify impressionistic measures, while at the same time attempting to distinguish this construct from other cognitive capacities such as writing expertise that may also account for variation in students' performance in second language composing, for example, in relation to rhetorical organization, spelling or punctuation.

Second, the present research sought direct indicators of the acquisition of subsystems of language in order to develop research methods for training or longitudinal studies in second language writing. Theoretically, specific indicators of different subsystems of language are needed because such subsystems may develop differently and respond to instruction differently (Pienemann, Johnston & Brindley, 1988). To address this concern, instructional studies in second language acquisition are becoming more precise and constrained in terms of the pedagogically relevant factors they consider (Mellow, 1992). However, conventional methods such as tests of general ESL proficiency or holistic ratings of compositions do not provide sufficiently precise criteria of achievement for these purposes. Similarly, simple tallies of *total errors* in compositions are unsuitable because their frequency may not change with increased proficiency (Haswell, 1988).

Valid assessment procedures that measure specific aspects of language are required because without validation we do not know if there is logical evidence for content validity or if other factors might affect students' performance. For example, in composition tasks, learners may just avoid English structures they have not yet learned (Lennon, 1991). Furthermore, if a measure is valid as an indication of SLP, then we have reason to believe that the use of that language element might improve for learners of lower proficiency levels, and that the rate of acquisition might improve through instruction. If the element does not correlate positively with SLP, then this element may be more prone to *fossilize* during language acquisition, that is, to not develop further. In sum, our first purpose was to determine whether change in specific aspects of ESL learners' written language reflects a change in general underlying proficiency, particularly, whether any of several indicators adequately represent the construct of SLP. Bachman (1990a: 245) calls this approach *content coverage*. The second goal of our study was simply to better understand the typical development of these specific indicators.

The third purpose of the study was to determine the validity of *written* indicators of SLP because, due to task variability, it is not clear that assessing language use in a composition is a valid measure of acquisition of specific language forms (see Ringbom, 1987). For example, when composition measures are compared to other measures of instructional effects, inconsistent findings have been reported. For instance, Harley (1989) investigated the effect of instruction in two verb forms on Anglophones' development in French as a second language and found significant, short-term differences in regards to a cloze test and an oral interview but not on a composition test. A second training study, van Baalen (1983), also found different results for three grammatical elements on a composition (story-recall) test than on another test, a sentence completion task (a version of the Bilingual Syntax Measure). A third study, Ross & Berwick (1991), found differences in the use of derivational affixes in an expository essay and in a metalinguistic judgment task (a word well-formedness recognition task). In sum, no consistent results have emerged from studies which compared written composition results to other types of assessment to monitor the results of instruction in specific grammatical elements.

A previous analysis of some of the data analyzed here also did not indicate that assessing language use in a composition is a valid measure of SLP. Cumming's (1989) analysis of adult ESL compositions assessed the relationship of second language writing performance to ESL proficiency, writing expertise, and task variation. The earlier study analyzed three aspects of writing performance: qualities of compositions, attention devoted to aspects of writing, and problem solving behaviours used to control writing processes. Three qualities of the compositions were rated by two researchers who used procedures adapted from Jacobs *et al.* (1981): discourse organization, content, and language use. Overall, Cumming (1989) found that writing expertise and second language proficiency both accounted for large and distinct proportions of variance in the qualities of the compositions. With respect to language use alone, however, the students with advanced ESL proficiency performed better than those of intermediate proficiency but not to a degree that was statistically significant. Consequently, those results did not provide construct-related evidence for the validity of the analytic ratings as a measure of second language proficiency. In terms of task effects, for language use alone, there was not a clear difference according to task, although there was a tendency, especially at the advanced level, for students to perform better on the more cognitively demanding tasks of writing an argument or summary. The conflicting evidence regarding the use of composition measures to assess instructional effects, when combined with the results of Cumming's (1989) findings, suggests that careful investigation is required to discern whether composition measures are valid indicators of language proficiency or achievement.

Approach to Validation

Our approach used logical and empirical evidence to identify reliable and valid indicators of the construct of SLP (see Bachman, 1990a: 41–4, 236–71; Standards for Educational Research, 1985: 9). In the first of two phases of this research we sought logical (or content-related) evidence of reliability and validity, using insights from theories and previous research to (a) define and specify the target ability or ability domain, and (b) operationalize those abilities by choosing specific tasks or behaviours that are observable and representative of the set of behaviours associated with the construct. As discussed in detail below, the systematic, content-related judgments for the choice of indicators investigated here were based upon linguistic and psycholinguistic theories as well as expert judgments.

Some approaches to the construct validation of SLP have based content-related evidence on a general, component framework of language ability that divides SLP into competencies such as grammatical, discourse, sociolinguistic and strategic competence (e.g. Bachman 1990a: 42, 256–7; Harley et al. 1990: 9–13). However, the choice of such general competencies has been criticized in terms of their content validity; for example, Bachman (1990b: 29–31) and Schachter (1990: 39–47) suggest that Harley et al.'s (1990) approach to this problem did not sufficiently define and distinguish these components. In response to this concern for content-related evidence, our present approach considered extensive logical evidence to carefully define components of second language *performance* that might also be valid indicators of second language *proficiency*. We concluded that rather than being composed of several general competencies (as proposed in Harley et al., 1990b), SLP is composed of a large number of specific subsystems that may develop differently (e.g. plural inflection, interdental fricatives, requests, discourse deixis). During development (and in target-like use), several of these specific subsystems may be particularly interdependent, for example, topicalization, shared information, and article use.

The present investigation also considered the effects of the written mode and variations in genre (i.e. task effects), given that our efforts to establish content validity could be affected by the methods of assessment we used (Bachman, 1990a: 244, 258; Tarone & Parrish, 1988). Furthermore, the likelihood of cross-linguistic influences in second language learning and performance suggest that no one measure may be a universally valid indicator of second language development (Odlin, 1989; Ringbom, 1987). Accordingly, the present study considered data from both French and Japanese speakers learning English as a second language. Although data from two first languages is not representative of the variety of developmental relations that are possible cross-linguistically, the data may nonetheless be suggestive of such differences.

After using logical evidence to identify four potential indicators of SLP, the second phase of our research used empirical evidence to further assess the validity of the specific indicators. We assessed two sets of written compositions for the four potential indicators of SLP then used correlational analyses to determine if the patterns of variation for the four language features in these compositions corresponded to patterns in test scores obtained independently for the students who wrote them. Similar to. a method proposed in Standards for Educational Research (1985: 10) and Bachman (1990a: 248, 258), and used in several related studies (e.g. Bardovi-Harlig & Bofman, 1989; Laufer, 1991), the present study (a) used various criteria to establish two population samples representing *intermediate* and *advanced* levels of ESL proficiency; then (b) used statistical procedures to determine if the differences in the groups, as manifestations of the construct of SLP, were reflected in differences on the measures. Although the validity of these criterion measures is not clearly established, our empirical evidence might still best be described as *criterion-related* because these measures are widely used and are thought to be relatively valid.

For the reasons described above, the present study considered four linguistic features and the extent to which differences in their accuracy in compositions related to such measures of second language proficiency as TOEFL scores, oral interviews, class-placements, and self-reports of writing skill. The compositions were written by adults learning English in intensive ESL programs at Canadian universities, 24 Canadian Francophone Quebecois(e) studying in Ontario and 42 Japanese studying in Vancouver. Because language performance, as a potentially unique construct, is closely related to other cognitive processes, such as writing expertise, and is also complicated by the context of use, such as differences in writing tasks or genres, we also considered these factors in accounting for the accuracy with which linguistic features were used.

Choice of Specific Language Elements

Many measurement instruments conceptualize language use in a very general manner. For example, the definition of language use in Cumming (1989) followed the broad, holistic conception of Jacobs *et al*.'s (1981) *ESL Composition Profile*, including vocabulary (range, choice, usage, word form mastery, register), language use (complex constructions, errors of agreement, tense, number, word order/function, articles, pronouns, prepositions) and mechanics (spelling, punctuation, capitalization, paragraphing). The present study considered a much smaller range of language features as identified in previous studies of second language acquisition, reconceptualizing *language use* in regard to four specific language features.

Texts written by adult ESL students were analyzed for the accuracy of three morphological features and one index of lexical knowledge. The three morphological features were:

- *lexical articles* 'the' and 'a' (henceforth ART) considered in combination and separately (see Bardovi-Harlig & Bofman, 1989; Crookes, 1989; Huebner, 1983a, 1983b; Klein & Perdue, 1988; Master, 1987; Oller & Redding, 1972; Peyton, 1990; Pfaff, 1987; Tarone & Parrish, 1988; Thomas, 1989);
- the *plural -s suffix* on regular nouns (henceforth PLS, see Bardovi-Harlig & Bofman, 1989; Crookes, 1989; Peyton, 1990; Pienemann, Johnston & Brindley, 1988); and
- the *third person singular -s suffix* on verbs (henceforth TPS, see van Baalen, 1983; Bardovi-Harlig & Bofman, 1989; Ellis, 1988; Peyton, 1990; Pienemann, Johnston & Brindley, 1988).

The measure of lexical richness was a type/token ratio of (a) the number of unique, different words over (b) the total number of words in each composition (henceforth TTR, see Broeder, Extra & van Hout, 1989; Crookes, 1989; Johnson, 1944; Laufer, 1991). As noted, these four measures have been identified and assessed by other second language researchers, although, of those studies noted above, only Bardovi-Harlig & Bofman (1989), Johnson (1944), Laufer (1991), and Peyton (1990) analyzed these linguistic forms in written texts.

The measures were chosen so that they would be reliable and would have content validity. We consider it axiomatic that validity cannot be established unless reliability is also established for specific contexts of language performance. Establishing the reliability of the TTR was not problematic since a computer software package, *Textpac*, was used to identify lexical items mechanically and to compute the ratio. To establish reliability of the

measurement of morphemes, we first considered the nature of the decisions that the coders of the compositions would be required to perform,
and then, after training the coders, ascertained the inter-coder reliability on
100% of the remaining corpus. In order to provide relatively simple and
unambiguous decisions for the coders, we chose single morphemes: inflectional affixes and articles. Our coders considered all uses of these morphemes, not just the obligatory contexts for those elements, and therefore a score of the percentage correct for each morpheme indicates the
target-like use of the forms (Master, 1987: 21, 101 following K. Stauble).
Decisions regarding the correct use of the inflectional affixes were relatively
straightforward, requiring the determination of the plurality of nouns,
the person and number of the subject of the verb, and whether the noun
or verb required the regular suffix or was an irregular form (e.g. 'two
sheep', 'She *is* my mother'). These coding judgments proved to be problematic
only in instances where the writer had not clearly specified a referent or
subject, making the appropriate grammatical categories difficult to determine.

Judgments for appropriate article use were much more complex because
of the variety of structural and semantic properties involved. Structurally,
the prenominal position may be occupied by one of two lexical articles ('the',
'a'), or the zero article (*0*; the absence of an article, e.g. '*0* music is playing'),
or another prenominal element such as a demonstrative and possessive pro-
noun (e.g. 'this', 'that', 'my') or a noun marked for the genitive (e.g. 'cat's').
Each of the three articles is appropriate in a variety of semantic contexts
which have been subcategorized in a variety of ways. For example, Master
(1987: 40) argues for the need to use 19 categories to analyze second language
article use, including categories such as: generic 'a', generic 'the', generic *0*,
subsequent mention 'the' (specific definite), shared knowledge 'the' (specific
definite), count singular 'a' (specific indefinite), and interrogative 'a'
(ambiguous generic). In addition, Master (1987: 42) saw fit to restrict his
investigation to common nouns and did not consider proper nouns. Indeed,
given the difficulty in determining these distinctions, Roger Brown's
(1973: 350) influential work on the acquisition of grammatical morphemes
remarked that distinguishing these semantic contexts 'proved to be not
possible'.

Given these concerns regarding the complexity of interpretation,
we were surprised to find that most previous studies examining article
use in a second language had not reported multiple coders, coder training, inter-coder reliability, or intra-coder reliability (e.g. Huebner,
1983a: 38–40, 1983b: 52–3; Klein & Purdue, 1988: 11–22; Master 1987:
29–42; Parrish, 1987: 363–5; Pfaff, 1987: 88–99; Tarone & Parrish, 1988:

28). Of eight second language acquisition studies of article development we reviewed, only Thomas (1989: 345) reported inter-coder reliability: an agreement of 97% on 50% of her corpus, and this included coding only for the identification of the items in the text, not for the probable choice of articles by native speakers. In contrast to these studies, our approach to ensure reliability was to have two coders evaluate the native-like choice for each context and to simplify the decision making required of the coders.

Our relatively simple distinctions for articles required the two coders to chose from only four categories: 'the'-correct, 'the'-incorrect, 'a'-correct, and 'a'-incorrect. To simplify judgments by not double-coding instances and by not requiring a determination of the obligatory context, instances in which 'a' was required but 'the' was incorrectly provided were coded as 'the'-incorrect. Similarly, instances in which 'the' was required but 'a' was incorrectly provided were coded as 'a'-incorrect. As a result, this analysis emphasizes accuracy of usage instead of accuracy of suppliance in obligatory contexts. Our decision to simplify rating procedures follows Master's (1987) overall finding that such simple tallies of article use proved to be the most reliable indicators of SLP in his data. Although primarily structural, these categories also serve semantic and pragmatic functions, with 'the' used mainly for definite nouns for which the writer and the reader know the specific referent and 'a' used mainly for indefinite nouns for which either or both the writer and the reader do not know the specific referent.

We did not include the zero article in the analysis for three reasons. First, in written compositions, unlike a cloze task or a metalinguistic judgment task, a coder may not be reliably able to distinguish between the speaker's intentional use of the zero article and the unintentional omission of a lexical article (see Master, 1987: 22–3; Parrish, 1987: 373–4). The zero article was also excluded so that our analysis was parallel to our treatment of the two inflectional affixes: for plural -s and third person singular -s, we did not code the zero use of the affixes, particularly, the use of an uninflected noun or verb root. In other words, we examined the acquisition of morphemes, not the acquisition of linguistic sub-systems such as number agreement, subject-verb agreement or noun phrase categorization (through the article system). A third reason for excluding the zero article is that it has an especially heterogeneous set of sub-uses: in addition to the multiple types of nouns to which 'the' and 'a' may refer (generic or specific), and the multiple types of nouns to which 'the' may refer (common or proper, singular or plural, count or mass), the zero article may also be used to refer to nouns that are either indefinite or definite (for proper nouns). As a result of this heterogeneity, the zero article is primarily a structural category, whereas 'the' and 'a' are also rough semantic categories, as noted above. These choices regarding the coding of articles appear to have been justified since the coders achieved 93% agreement on 100% of the 2,085 instances in which articles appeared or were required in the corpus.

The logical and empirical evidence described above was used to help establish the reliability of our measures. In addition, the measures were chosen so that they would have content validity. We noted above that logical (or content-related) evidence may include (a) systematic observations of the behaviours associated with the construct and (b) theoretically-informed judgments. Three observations in previous research motivated our choice of these indicators. First, Master (1987: 168), after an extensive examination of many sub-categories of article use in the speech of ESL learners, found that the accuracy of overall article use consistently increased with learners' proficiency level in English, irrespective of learners' first language. Master's (1987: 29–30) analysis is slightly different than ours in that he used a different criterion for interlanguage level, excluded proper nouns, considered the zero article, and determined the accuracy ratio only for obligatory contexts of use.) Second, other investigations of article development in ESL acquisition indicate that 'the' develops before 'a', and that '*the* flooding' (the overuse of 'the' in prenominal positions) is a common developmental pattern (Parrish, 1987: 374; Peyton, 1990: 78–80; Thomas, 1989: 341, 349; Yamada & Matsuura, 1982: 56). The third observation of regular development of the indicators we selected appears in the results of the so-called *morpheme studies* (Dulay, Burt & Krashen, 1982: 200–29; Hatch, 1983: 44–57; Krashen, 1982: 12–15; Larsen-Freeman & Long, 1991: 88–92).

Although the methods of these studies have received considerable criticism and their findings vary somewhat, there are nonetheless claims that the three morphological features we have chosen represent three different stages in second language morpheme acquisition: PLS > ART > TPS; see Krashen (1982: 13). If this order is correct, then at different levels of proficiency some of these features may not (in Krashen's terms) be *acquired*, some may be *acquired*, and some may be at a variable stage below *acquisition*. If these previous observations are correct, differences in the accuracy of use of these three morphemes, either individually or in relation to one another, may indicate levels of second language proficiency. In sum, these precedents from earlier research provide content-related evidence suggesting that these morphological indicators may be developmentally appropriate and likely to distinguish between learners at these levels in their acquisition of English.

In addition to previous observations of the behaviours associated with the construct of SLP, we considered a further type of logical (or content-related) evidence: linguistic and psycholinguistic theories were also used to establish the validity of these choices. The four indicators we selected were considered to be linguistically appropriate in that they required language proficiency rather than writing expertise, e.g. rhetorical organization, punctuation and spelling were not considered. Furthermore, these indicators are part of various different language subsystems (e.g. verbal and nominal inflections; vocabulary, including derivational and inflectional word formation). By considering a range of subsystems, we hoped to increase the possibility that a measure would be developmentally appropriate for the proficiency levels of language learners in the study.

Theories that explain the apparent stages of morpheme development might also provide logical evidence for our choice of indicators. We did not look to Krashen's Monitor Theory and its Natural Order Hypothesis (e.g. Krashen, 1982) for an explanation because his hypothesis is really only a statement of certain observed facts and does not provide any explanation, linguistic or psycholinguistic, for the grouping of the development of these otherwise disparate features into one sequence (see Larsen-Freeman & Long, 1991: 248). For a linguistic grouping of these *grammatical morphemes*, we looked to generative linguistics (e.g. Chomsky & Lasnik, to appear). According to this linguistic theory, these grammatical morphemes belong to the group of elements known as *functional items*, rather than to the group of *lexical items*. Recent analyses of functional items, such as Speas (1991: 185) and Ritter (1991), organize these items in a hierarchical order of phrase markers that closely parallels the order of acquisition found in first language and second language morpheme studies. Recent first language acquisition analyses within this generative framework provide maturational explanations of aspects of functional item development (e.g. Guilfoyle & Noonan, to appear; Radford, 1990).

Because maturational accounts are not tenable for those second language learners who are cognitively mature, however, other explanations are required. One alternative is that various formal and semantic properties of the functional categories make certain language elements more difficult to learn (Hatch 1983: 54–5; Radford 1990: 263–8; Slobin, 1982: 150–3). A second explanation is that the order of development occurs because certain elements or constructions can be learned only after other constructions have been learned, i.e. the later elements logically require or are dependent on the former elements (Borer & Wexler, 1987: 126; Radford 1990: 269–70). A third account is that development reflects the difficulties that learners have in acquiring various 'marked', 'peripheral', or 'uncommon' properties of language (Borer & Wexler, 1987: 125; Hyams, 1986: 170–1; Radford, 1990: 271–4). Evaluation of these various hypotheses is beyond the scope of the present chapter. Rather, our purpose here is merely to demonstrate that the indicators we have chosen are supported not only by systematic observations of language development, but that they are also supported by theories of language and language acquisition that suggest these elements are related to each other in certain respects and may develop in a certain relative sequence.

Hypotheses

In the section above, we discussed logical and empirical evidence pointing toward the reliability of the linguistic indicators chosen for this study. In addition, we presented content-related evidence which suggested that these language elements might validly indicate the construct of SLP. In the remainder of this paper, we will discuss the implications of one type of empirical evidence: criterion-related, correlational evidence. We used empirical evidence to assess five hypotheses:

(1) that the relatively less proficient ESL students will show incomplete acquisition of the morphological features and a significantly lesser range of lexical use, whereas the relatively more proficient learners will demonstrate greater accuracy for all of the morphological features and display a significantly greater range of lexical items;
(2) that writing expertise will not account for any variance in the scores of the grammatical or lexical indicators (Cumming, 1989) (A possible relation between lexical richness and writing expertise might be expected though because better writers may draw more fully on their vocabulary; however, we hypothesized that the findings of Cumming (1989) would be confirmed, revealing no significant relation between vocabulary use, which was one aspect of language use in the earlier study, and writing expertise.);
(3) that task variation will be significantly reflected in the results of the analyses;
(4) that the first language of the learners will influence the development of accuracy of article use, with speakers of languages that have an article system (i.e. French) demonstrating greater accuracy at all levels of proficiency than speakers whose first language does not have an article system (i.e. Japanese);
(5) that students will exhibit developmental stages within article use, using 'the' more accurately than 'a' at all levels of proficiency.

Procedures

The study used data from two groups of young adults in intensive ESL courses. The first group was composed of 24 adult Francophone students who had entered university study in Ontario, but were first completing pre-requisite ESL courses. The students had similar backgrounds in regard to their age and level of education, where they were born and educated, why they had come to Ontario from Quebec, and their intentions upon the completion of their studies. Two levels of second language proficiency were defined and determined by the students' characteristics with respect to three highly correlated factors: scores on a university interview test, class placements, and length of residence in Ontario (see Cumming, 1989 for details). Eleven of these students were classified as having intermediate ESL proficiency and 12 were classified as having advanced ESL proficiency. Five of these students were classified as professionally experienced writers in their mother tongue, eight were classified as average writers in their mother tongue, and 10 were classified as basic writers in their mother tongue, according to analytic ratings of their L1 compositions, self-ratings and self-reports.

The second group was composed of 42 Japanese students studying ESL full-time at a university in British Columbia; for these students, TOEFL scores were the only available proficiency measure. These scores were used to divide the group into two equal groups – the 21 higher proficiency students scores having a mean TOEFL score of 512.8 with a range of 473 to 577, the 21 lower proficiency students having a mean TOEFL score of 438.4 with a range of 407 to 470.

The Francophone compositions had originally been solicited for Cumming (1989) but were reanalyzed for the present study. Each of the Francophone students provided three samples of writing, one on each of three tasks: an informal letter describing the course they were currently taking in English, a summary of a 48-page popular science booklet about the functional anatomy of cats, and an expository argument defending a position on women's social roles. These written texts were working drafts which were not handed in for grades.

Each of the Japanese students provided one sample of writing for a placement test which the students knew would be evaluated by their English teachers as well as the present researchers. Students were asked to write an essay of approximately 300 words on one of the following four topics: (1) Should smoking be permitted in public places? Write an argument addressing this question; (2) Discuss the effects of your studies in Canada may have on your future; (3) Compare yourself to one of your parents; and (4) Describe someone who has had a great influence on your life. These tasks were subsequently divided into three categories: argument (1), cause and effect (2), and description/comparison (3, 4). Since the students often chose a parent as the person who had a great influence on their life, topics 3 and 4 appeared virtually indistinguishable.

To obtain a measure for each of the grammatical items in the analysis, an accuracy score, expressed as a percentage, was determined. Two researchers coded each text by identifying all of the contexts in which those particular morphemes were required or supplied. Each instance was then coded as correct or incorrect, with incorrect instances including inaccurate use or the omission of the item. The two researchers trained together on 12 compositions until agreement exceeded 85%. For the 3,547 instances of the three grammatical indicators, inter-coder reliability was 92%. To achieve an accuracy score, for each composition the percentage of correct instances for each measure was determined for results from each coder. The percentages from the two coders were then averaged to give a final accuracy score for each composition.

In order to calculate an accuracy score for a composition on a specific indicator, we determined that the composition had to include at least three environments for that item, either an obligatory context for the item, or the production of the item in an 'incorrect' context. Like Ellis (1990: 317), we chose three as the minimum number of occasions, and like Ellis, we agree that is rather meagre (see Larsen-Freeman & Long, 1991: 90), but if the number had been set higher, the sample size would have been reduced unacceptably and a number of the comparisons would have been impossible to make. For most compositions, the number of occasions of articles and plural -s significantly exceeded the three instance minimum, with only 3% of the compositions having fewer than five instances of articles, and only 9% of the compositions having fewer than five instances of plural -s. Even with the number set at three, the TPS results had much missing data.

To assess vocabulary richness, a simple type/token ratio was computed by the *Textpac* language analysis program (Mohler & Zuell, 1991): the number of different words divided by the total number of words. To do this, each composition was entered as a document on a personal computer, double-checked, spell-checked, and then modified for spacing, characters, and ASCII formatting. *Textpac* considered plural words (with -s) to be separate words. Since *Textpac* separated *'s* as a unique word, contractions were fully spelled out as separate words and possessive -s was noted in the data so that the ratio could be modified (the number of instances of -s subtracted from both the numerator and the denominator). Spelling errors were corrected when their sense was evident from the context because the use of words, rather than spelling, was under investigation.

Analyses

Results were first analyzed using descriptive statistics, then similarities and differences within and across groups and tasks were assessed by examining mean scores and standard deviations. These results are presented in Tables 4.1 and 4.2 below. Finding these results to be suggestive, analyses of variance were performed using SYSTAT. Two types of analyses of variance were conducted. For data from the Francophone students, analyses considered one dependent measure at a time in a 2 (ESL proficiency) x 3 (writing expertise in L1) x 3 (tasks) repeated measures design. For the data from the Japanese subjects, analyses considered one dependent measure at a time in a 2 (TOEFL score) x 3 (task) design. The data showed a high degree of variance within groups (see standard deviations in Table 4.1 below). Not unexpectedly, the less proficient, intermediate level subjects exhibited more variation in their language use than the more advanced subjects. In addition, missing data appear for certain analyses (e.g. TPS did not appear in many compositions). These conditions suggest that the present results should be interpreted with caution.

Results

Hypothesis 1: Relations of indicators to second language proficiency

To test hypothesis 1 for the French L1 students, we used ANOVAs to assess whether students' level of ESL proficiency accounted for differences in the variation of each dependent variable over the three writing tasks. Results for the French L1 students were significantly different across proficiency levels for accuracy of article use ($F(1,18) = 9.6, p < 0.006$), particularly indefinite articles ($F(1,14) = 6.7, p < 0.02$) but not definite articles ($F(1,16) = 3.7$, n.s.). No significant differences emerged between proficiency levels for plural -s ($F(1,14) = 0.9$, n.s.), third person -s (too much missing data – see Table 4.1), or the type/token ratio of lexical richness ($F(1,17) = 0.2$, n.s.)).

Table 4.1 Accuracy scores for French over three compositions

ESL proficiency	1 (intermediate)			2 (advanced)		
	N	M	SD	N	M	SD
Articles	33	74.8	20.8	39	86.8	9.1
'the'	32	76.9	16.9	38	85.8	14.3
'a'	29	77.3	19.9	37	89.8	10.5
Plural -s	31	65.1	25.5	37	78.5	15.8
Third person -s	20	37.1	33.3	19	66.5	28.1
Type/token	33	47.3	8.5	38	48.3	8.3

ANOVAs were similarly used to test hypothesis 1 for the Japanese L1 students. Results for the Japanese L1 students were statistically significant for accuracy of article use (F (1,36) = 4.6, $p < 0.04$), but in this case students' accuracy on definite articles proved to be significantly related to their TOEFL scores (F (1,28) = 8.1, $p < 0.008$) but not so for indefinite articles (F (1,30) = 0.09, n.s.). No significant results emerged for plural -s (F (1,34) = 1.4, n.s.), third person -s (too much missing data – see Table 4.2), or the type/token ratio of lexical richness (F (1,36) = 0.2, n.s.).

Table 4.2 Accuracy scores for Japanese over three compositions

ESL proficiency	1 (intermediate)			2 (advanced)		
	N	M	SD	N	M	SD
Articles	21	67.6	20.5	21	77.8	12.0
'the'	14	62.5	25.9	20	77.8	13.3
'a'	18	74.2	21.9	18	79.6	20.3
Plural -s	19	72.4	25.3	21	79.0	15.1
Third person -s	05	61.6	19.7	06	86.2	22.1
Type/token	21	48.9	5.0	21	51.2	6.9

Hypothesis 2. Relations of indicators to writing expertise

Hypothesis 2 could only be tested for the French L1 students because data were not available on the Japanese students' writing expertise in their mother tongue. ANOVA assessed whether the French L1 students' writing expertise in their mother tongue accounted for differences in the variation of each dependent variable over the three writing tasks. No significant results emerged for accuracy of article use (F (2,18) = 0.7, n.s.), including indefinite articles (F (2,14) = 0.3, n.s.) and definite articles (F (2,16) = 0.2, n.s.), plural -s F (2,14) = 0.6, n.s.), third person -s (too much missing data), or the type/token ratio of lexical richness (F (1,17) = 0.1, n.s.). However, an interaction effect did emerge between writing expertise and second language proficiency for article use (F (2,18) = 4.0, $p < 0.04$) though not for any of the other dependent variables.

Hypothesis 3. Task effects

To test hypothesis 3, ANOVA assessed whether the interaction of task (within subjects and each ESL level) accounted for differences in the varia- tion of each dependent variable. For the French L1 students, significant differences emerged across the three writing tasks for accuracy of definite article use ($F(2,15) = 14.0$, $p < 0.0001$) and the type/token ratio of lexical richness ($F(2,16) = 9.5$, $p < 0.002$). But results were not statistically different across the tasks for article use in general ($F(2,17) = 1.6$, n.s.), indefinite articles ($F(2,13) = 1.9$, n.s.), third person -s (too much missing data – see Table 4.1), or plural -s ($F(2,13) = 2.0$, n.s.). Follow-up univariate F-tests (i.e. non-repeated measures for specific tasks) showed significant inter-actions between task and ESL proficiency for articles in the summary writing task only ($F(1,18) = 7.8$, $p < 0.01$) and particularly indefinite articles in that task ($F(1,14) = 10.3$, $p < 0.006$). For the Japanese L1 students, no significant differences emerged for any of the dependent variables across the three tasks. However, repeated measures analyses were not feasible because indi-viduals in this group did not write more than one task.

Hypothesis 4. Variability between languages

Table 4.3 compares group means for the four indicators across the French and Japanese compositions. Overall, the French accuracy scores were higher than the Japanese scores only for articles, and the Japanese scores were slightly higher on each of the other indicators measured. Although these data do appear to confirm the hypothesis, this comparison may be misleading since the groups were not necessarily at equal proficiency levels, and there were differences in the specific writing tasks and conditions for composing.

Table 4.3 Accuracy scores for French L1 and Japanese L1 over three compositions

L1	French			Japanese		
	N	*M*	*SD*	*N*	*M*	*SD*
Articles	72	81.3	16.6	42	72.7	17.4
'the'	70	81.7	16.1	34	71.5	20.6
'a'	66	84.3	16.5	36	76.9	21.0
Plural -s	68	72.4	21.7	40	75.9	20.6
Third person -s	39	51.4	33.9	11	75.0	23.7
Type/token	71	47.8	8.4	42	50.0	6.0

Hypothesis 5. Developmental sequences of articles

Group means for the French L1 data showed relatively little variation between accuracy of 'the' and 'a' at the intermediate (*M* for 'the' = 76.9; *M* for 'a' = 77.3) and advanced levels of proficiency (*M* for 'the' = 85.8; *M* for 'a' = 89.8). The design of the study allowed distinctions to be made between uses of 'a' and 'the' in the Francophone compositions through repeated measures comparing the same item, articles, for the same student under different conditions (e.g. definiteness vs. indefiniteness). These comparisons, however, showed no significant differences: $F(1,13) = 0.1$, n.s. Descriptive data for the Japanese students, however, showed distinct differences, with 'a' being used more accurately than 'the' at the intermediate level (M for 'the' = 62.5; M for 'a' = 74.2) but with equivalent accuracy at the more advanced level (M for 'the' = 77.8; M for 'a' = 79.6). However, these distinctions could not be assessed for the Japanese compositions through repeated measures analyses because each student only wrote one composition. Overall, for Japanese and French learners at both proficiency levels, the results did not confirm the expected finding that the definite article might be provided more accurately than the indefinite article.

Discussion

The purpose of this investigation was to identify linguistic indicators in the context of adult students' written compositions that might be validly related to second language proficiency. Among the four indicators analyzed, accuracy of article use alone proved to provide scores which corresponded to the construct of second language proficiency operationalized here. This result is similar to the findings of Master (1987: 176) who likewise concluded that 'the total accuracy of articles with common noun phrases' is a stable indicator of language proficiency in English, though using different coding and calculation methods. Articles may emerge as a specific indicator corresponding closely to more global measures of language proficiency, such as TOEFL scores or oral interview ratings, because acquisition of articles involve a composite of highly complex linguistic factors as well as semantic and discourse-related factors such as definite vs. indefinite, generic vs. specific, common vs. proper nouns, and count vs. mass nouns.

Differences related to students' first languages appeared in the analyses. As Master (1987) among others has pointed out, French and Japanese differ quite significantly in terms of their article systems: Japanese has no corresponding system, whereas French has an extensive article system (with more frequent uses of 'the' than English) – a fact that probably explains the comparatively higher rates of accuracy for English article use among the Francophone students. In addition, analyses of differences between definite and indefinite article use showed some suggestive trends, particularly as the Japanese population showed mastery over 'a' before 'the'. But the design of the study did not permit this trend to be assessed thoroughly, nor did comparable trends appear in the Francophone data. Moreover, other studies of second language acquisition such as Huebner (1983a), Peyton (1990) or Thomas (1989) have found contradictory results (i.e. the accurate use of 'a' occurring later than 'the'). One possible explanation of the surprisingly accurate use of 'a' here may be our inclusion in the analysis of forms such as 'a lot' which might have been used as a formulaic chunk by the learners (Nattinger & DeCarrico, 1992). However, the present ESL learners did make a few errors with the phrase 'a lot'. In addition, these learners also may have conceived of such forms as 'the cat' as a phrasal unit, potentially countering the presence of chunked indefinite articles. Alternatively, this finding may be an artifact of our coding system or a product of *'the' flooding* by learners at this level of English proficiency (P. Master, personal communication; Thomas, 1989: 240–1).

For the present data, the grammatical morphemes 'plural -s' and 'third person -s' did not prove to be valid indicators of second language proficiency, although the frequency of 'third person -s' was often not robust enough in the data to permit comparisons. The accuracy scores also contradicted a previously reported observation, that plural -s is usually acquired before articles. In our data, plural -s accuracy was slightly higher than that of articles for the Japanese learners, but lower than article accuracy for the French learners. These findings suggest that first language influence may be more important than those factors which tend to produce *natural order* effects.

The type-token ratio of lexical richness also did not yield significant results, suggesting that learners of English may not necessarily display more extensive lexical choices in their writing as their proficiency improves. Although a similar finding is reported by Laufer (1991), this counter-intuitive result may have arisen, as Youmans (1991) points out, because lexical type-token ratios quickly reach ceiling effects and thus seldom tend to reveal between-group differences.

The construct of language proficiency operationalized here proved to be empirically distinct from writing expertise, at least for the Francophone students, adding further support to the findings of Cumming (1989, 1990a). While numerous other sources of variation potentially related to second language proficiency were not eliminated from our analyses, the data indicate that the construct that does account for variance in some of the scores (i.e. articles in various forms) is distinct from writing expertise, at least for these Francophone learners of English. As such, accuracy of article use in English might reasonably be considered as an indicator for studies assessing the effects of writing on second language learning, as suggested in Cumming (1990b) and by Swain's 'comprehensible output' hypothesis (1985).

As in previous studies, task effects appeared for definite article use as well as the type/token ratio of lexical richness. The very distinct effects of task on the accuracy of definite article use suggests that students' language proficiency is displayed variably in different composition genres or topics. The summary task, which accounted for much of this task variation, called for frequent uses of general phrases like 'the cat's body . . .' as well as anaphoric references and specific descriptions – eliciting article use with a variety of noun phrases which were not obligatory in the more personal letter or narrative tasks or argumentative tasks. Task differences, however, did not appear in the Japanese data, perhaps because the topics, genres and conditions of writing were all elicited under very similar 'test-like' circumstances.

Acknowledgements

Funding for this research was provided through grants to the first author from the BC Ministry of Advanced Education, Training and Technology and from the Social Sciences and Humanities Research Council of Canada's grant #410-91-0722. While conducting the research the second author was supported by Social Sciences and Humanities Research Council of Canada's doctoral fellowship #753-91-0290. We thank Dennie Rothschild and Leslie Ogston for their valuable assistance in coding and reliability checks, Carole Trepannier for helping to collect the Japanese data, and Peter Master for commenting on an earlier version of this paper.

References

Bachman, L. (1990a) *Fundamental Considerations in Language Testing.* Oxford: Oxford University Press.
— (1990b) Constructing measures and measuring constructs. In B. Harley, P. Allen, J. Cummins and M. Swain (eds) *The Development of Second Language Proficiency* (pp. 26–38). Cambridge: Cambridge University Press.
Bardovi-Harlig, K. and Bofman, T. (1989) Attainment of syntactic and morphological accuracy by advanced language learners. *Studies in Second Language Acquisition,* 11, 17–34.
Borer, H. and Wexler, K. (1987) The maturation of syntax. In T. Roeper and E. Williams (eds) *Parameter Setting* (pp. 123–72). Dordrecht: D. Reidel.
Broeder, P., Extra, G. and van Hout, R. (1989) Processes in the developing lexicon of adult immigrant learners. *AILA Review* 6, 86–109.
Brown, R. (1973) *A First Language: The Early Stages.* Cambridge, MA: Harvard University Press.
Chomsky, N. and Lasnik, H. (in press) Principles and parameters theory. To appear in J. Jacobs, A. von Stechow, W. Sternfeld and T. Vennemann (eds) *Syntax: An International Handbook of Contemporary Research.* Berlin: Walter de Gruyter.
Crookes, G. (1989) Planning and interlanguage variation. *Studies in Second Language Acquisition* 11, 367–83.
Cumming, A. (1989) Writing expertise and second language proficiency. *Language Learning* 39, 81–141.

— (1990a) Expertise in evaluating second language compositions. *Language Testing* 7, 31–51.

— (1990b) Metalinguistic and ideational thinking in second language composing. *Written Communication* 7, 482–511.

Dulay, H., Burt, M. and Krashen, S. (1982) *Language Two*. New York: Oxford University Press.

Ellis, R. (1988) The effects of linguistic environment on the second language: Acquisition of grammatical rules. *Applied Linguistics* 9, 257–74.

— (1990) Are classroom and naturalistic acquisition the same? A study of the classroom acquisition of German word order rules. *Studies in Second Language Acquisition* 11, 305–28.

Freedman, S. (1991) Evaluating writing: Linking large-scale testing and classroom assessment. Occasional paper no. 27. Berkeley, CA: Center for the Study of Writing.

Guilfoyle. E. and Noonan, M. (in press) Functional categories and language acquisition. To appear in *The Canadian Journal of Linguistics*.

Harley, B. (1989) Functional grammar in French immersion: A classroom experiment. *Applied Linguistics* 10, 331–59.

Harley, B., Cummins, J., Swain, M. and Allen, P. (1990) The nature of language proficiency. In B. Harley, P. Allen, J. Cummins and M. Swain (eds) *The Development of Second Language Proficiency* (pp. 7–25). Cambridge: Cambridge University Press.

Harley, B., Allen, P., Cummins, J. and Swain, M. (eds) (1990) *The Development of Second Language Proficiency*. Cambridge: Cambridge University Press.

Haswell, R. (1988) Error and change in college student writing. *Written Communication* 5, 479–99.

Hatch, E. (1983) *Psycholinguistics: A Second Language Perspective*. Rowley, MA: Newbury House.

Huebner, T. (1983a) Linguistic systems and linguistic change in an interlanguage. *Studies in Second Language Acquisition* 6, 33–53.

— (1983b) *A Longitudinal Analysis of the Acquisition of English*. Ann Arbor: Karoma Publishers.

Huot, B. (1990) The literature of direct writing assessment: Major concerns and prevailing trends. *Review of Educational Research* 60, 237–63.

Hyams, N. (1986) *Language Acquisition and the Theory of Parameters*. Dordrecht: D. Reidel.

Jacobs, H., Zinkgraf, S., Wormuth, D., Hartfiel, V. and Hughey, J. (1981) *Testing ESL Composition: A Practical Approach*. Rowley, MA: Newbury House.

Johnson, W. (1944) Studies in language behaviour: I. A program of research. *Psychological Monographs* 56, 1–15.

Klein, W. and Perdue, C. (eds) (1988) Utterance Structure. *Final Report, Vol VI of Second Language Acquisition by Adult Immigrants*. European Science Foundation.

Krashen, S. (1982) *Principles and Practice in Second Language Acquisition*. Oxford: Pergamon Press.

Larsen-Freeman, D. and Long, M. (1991) *An Introduction to Second Language Acquisition Research*. London: Longman.

Laufer, B. (1991) The development of L2 lexis in the expression of the advanced learner. *Modern Language Journal* 75, 440–8.

Lennon, P. (1991) Error: Some problems of definition, identification, and distinction. *Applied Linguistics* 12, 180–96.

Master, P. (1987) A cross-linguistic interlanguage analysis of the acquisition of the English article system. Unpublished doctoral dissertation, University of California, Los Angeles.

Mellow, D. (1992) The effects of instruction: A review of constrained studies. Paper presented at TESOL 1992, Vancouver, Canada.

Mohler, P. and Zuell, C. (1990) *Textpac PC*. Release 4.0. Mannheim, Germany: Zentrum fur Umfragen, Methoden und Analysen.

Nattinger, J. and DeCarrico, J. (1992) *Lexical Phrases and Language Teaching*. Oxford: Oxford University Press.

Odlin, T. (1989) *Language Transfer: Cross-linguistic Influence in Language Learning*. Cambridge: Cambridge University Press.

Oller, J. and Redding, E. (1972) Article usage and other language skills. *Language Learning* 21, 85–95.

Parrish, B. (1987) A new look at methodologies in the study of article acquisition for learners of ESL. *Language Learning* 37, 361–83.

Peyton, J. (1990) Dialogue journal writing and the acquisition of English grammatical morphology. In J. Peyton (ed.) *Students and Teachers Writing Together: Perspectives on Journal Writing* (pp. 65–98). Alexandria, VI: TESOL.

Pienemann, M., Johnston, M. and Brindley, G. (1988) Constructing an acquisition-based procedure for second language assessment. *Studies in Second Language Acquisition* 10, 217–44.

Purves, A. (1992) Reflections on research and assessment in written composition. *Research in the Teaching of English* 26, 108–22.

Radford, A. (1990) *Syntactic Theory and the Acquisition of English Syntax*. Oxford: Basil Blackwell.

Raimes, A. (1990) The TOEFL test of written English: Causes for concern. *TESOL Quarterly* 24, 427–42.

Ringbom, H. (1987) *The Role of the First Language in Foreign Language Learning*. Clevedon: Multilingual Matters.

Ritter, E. (1991) Evidence for number as a nominal head. Paper presented at GLOW, 26 March 1991, University of Leiden.

Ross, S. and Berwick, R. (1991) The acquisition of English affixes through general and specific instructional strategies. *JALT Journal* 13, 131–42.

Schachter, J. (1990) Communicative competence revisited. In B. Harley, P. Allen, J. Cummins and M. Swain (eds) *The Development of Second Language Proficiency* (pp. 39–49). Cambridge: Cambridge University Press.

Slobin, D. (1982) Universal and particular in the acquisition of language. In E. Wanner and L. Gleitman, L. (eds) *Language Acquisition: The State of the Art* (pp. 128–72). Cambridge: Cambridge University Press.

Speas, M. (1991) Functional heads and the mirror principle. *Lingua* 84, 181–214.

Standards for Educational and Psychological Testing (1985). Washington, DC: The American Psychological Association.

Stansfield, C. and Ross, J. (1988) A long-term research agenda for the Test of Written English. *Language Testing* 5, 160–86.

Swain, M. (1985) Communicative competence: Some roles of comprehensible input and comprehensible output in its development. In S. Gass and S. Madden (eds) *Input and Second Language Acquisition* (pp. 235–53). Rowley, MA: Newbury House.

Tarone, E. and Parrish, B. (1988) Task-related variation in interlanguage: The case of articles. *Language Learning* 38, 21–44.

Thomas, M. (1989) The acquisition of English articles by first- and second-language learners. *Applied Psycholinguistics* 10, 335–55.

van Baalen, T. (1983) Giving learners rules: A study into the effect of grammatical instruction with varying degrees of explicitness. *Interlanguage Studies Bulletin* 7, 71–100.

Yamada, J. and Matsuura, N. (1982) The use of the English article among Japanese students. *RELC Journal* 13, 50–63.

Youmans, G. (1991) A new tool for discourse analysis: The vocabulary-management profile. *Language* 67, 763–89.

5 Multiple-choice Summary: A Measure of Text Comprehension

ARI HUHTA and ELINA RANDELL

This concurrent validation study aimed at finding out whether multiple-choice (MC) summary tasks would provide a practical alternative to more laborious techniques (e.g. summaries and open-ended questions) that purport to measure the comprehension of the main content in a foreign language text. To assess this prospect, we administered a battery of English reading comprehension tests (conventional multiple-choice and open-ended questions, a summarizing task, and an MC summary) to 295 students at the University of Jyväskylä, assessing their reading ability and determining the face validity of the tests. The best MC-summary format correlated with the other reading tests and with self-assessment questions, suggesting that it measures, at least partly, the same skills. The highest correlation was with the summarizing task, which was also the only significant predictor of the MC-summary score. The face validity of the new test equalled that of the other tests. However, the MC-summary format tried out here is still too unreliable for most testing purposes, though it may prove useful in teaching and practising reading comprehension.

English reading comprehension placement tests are a standard procedure at the beginning of a semester at many Finnish universities. The tests are used for deciding which students are exempted from specific-purpose reading courses in English and those which have to attend such a course. Teachers feel that the conventional multiple-choice (MC) tests commonly used for this purpose are not necessarily adequate: They would prefer using tests that appear to tap better the students' abilities to understand the main content of a text, which is the actual task the students are faced with during their academic careers. Because of the large number of students taking the pre-semester placement tests, and the pressure of time, teachers feel obliged to use test methods that are quick and easy to mark, such as conventional MC tests. This context therefore presents a distinct need for an easily scorable test that provides teachers with comparable information to what they would receive from open-ended reading comprehension questions or summarizing tasks.

Teachers of English reading comprehension in Finland have gradually broadened the range of different tests they use for exempting or grading their students; consequently, they find it frustrating to be confined to multiple-choice tests in large-scale testing. The MC tests referred to here follow a conventional format: one test consists of a 500-word text and ten questions, each of which has four alternative answers. The tests were analysed in the early 1980s as six-test batteries (i.e. 60 items), and their reliability turned out to be high.

Multiple-choice tests have come under various kinds of attacks in the age of communicative language assessment. One common criticism – do MC items cover the main content of a reading text? – is particularly relevant to our situation. The most straightforward ways of testing students' comprehension of the main content in a reading passage would probably be to ask testees to write a summary in their mother tongue, or to answer open-ended questions on the main points of the text. Although multiple-choice questions can also cover main content, the multiple-choice format requires a sufficient number of items to be reliable. Each MC-test used at our Language Centres comprises a 500-word text with ten questions. Given the brevity of the text, it is unlikely that such short texts could contain ten ideas worth asking about, and therefore, some MC questions are bound to require testees to concentrate on information that is less important than the main content of a text.

The study reported in this chapter is the starting point in an inquiry aiming to determine whether certain easily scorable test types might be used for measuring students' understanding of the main points of reading passages, yielding the same information about students' language proficiency as a summary or open-ended questions. We chose one type of easily scorable test, the multiple-choice summary, and set out to study whether it could substitute for the more open-ended and laborious tests.

The multiple-choice summary is a test format where the testee has to choose among alternative summaries the one that best corresponds to the original text. The idea comes from Valencia and Pearson (1987) who reported that their students practised reading comprehension by choosing among a number of summaries written by fellow students the one that they thought was the best. They did not, however, use the term 'multiple-choice summary'.

To study whether the MC-summary tests the comprehension of main ideas we set up a concurrent validation study where we compared this technique with a battery of other reading tests. Not wanting to rely only on information from other tests, however, we gathered additional evidence about the students' ability to comprehend the main points of reading passages in English. Accordingly, we included two self-assessment questions about the testees' reading skills in the English language as our external criteria; it has been shown (see, e.g. Oskarsson, 1984) that learners' self-assessment of language skills is often quite accurate. We also wanted to find out the most reliable and valid MC-summary format, particularly, in terms of the appropriate number of distractors. Therefore, we experimented with different versions of the new test.

Methods

Participants

295 students (humanities and social sciences majors) took part in the study. The group comprised men and women between the ages of 18–22 years, all of whom were freshmen at the University of Jyväskylä and were chosen on the basis of enrollment on the placement test in the fall of 1991. The students had not received any formal teaching about reading or writing for academic purposes in English. However, almost all had studied English at school for ten years. They had also studied Swedish (in addition to Finnish, Swedish is an official language of Finland) and one or two foreign languages for a shorter time.

Materials

The students took a five-part English reading comprehension examination which, in addition to the research purposes, served as their placement test:

> Parts 1 and 2: *two traditional standardized 10-item multiple-choice tests* (40 minutes).
> Part 3: *a test consisting of three open-ended questions* covering the main content of a text.
> Part 4: *a summary in L1*.
> Part 5: *a multiple-choice summary* (35 minutes).

The examination took place at the Language Center, which coordinates testing and teaching languages for specific purposes (LSP) in the university. The testees were given instructions on how to write a good summary in an attempt to even out differences between testees familiar with and those unfamiliar with the summarization task. The time allotted for Parts 3 and 4 was one hour and 15 minutes. The texts for Parts 3 and 4 were analysed by the two researchers who also constructed the criteria (e.g. a list of ideas that should be present in the summary) for marking the summaries and the open-ended questions.

There were four versions of Part 5 of the test (two different texts and two different methods: 3-choice and 5-choice), which were distributed to the testees so that each testee got only one version and the four groups were approximately equal. The four versions were:

(1) Text 1 (Impartiality is Not Enough) + 3 alternative summaries, one of which is the right one;
(2) Text 1 + 5 alternative summaries;
(3) Text 2 (Science, Technocracy and the Politico-Economic Power) + 3 alternatives;
(4) Text 2 + 5 alternatives (see Appendix 2).

A different text was used in each of the five parts of the examination. The texts were all about 500 words long and were chosen from examinations previously used for testing reading comprehension. An important selection criterion was that the texts could be used for both humanities and social sciences majors with regard to their content and vocabulary. In addition, the texts were selected to contain clear structure, definitions, illustrations, a logical argument and some indication of factual information versus the writers' own points of view or comments.

Because the MC summary is a new idea in language testing, and we had a fairly large number of testees, we considered it appropriate to try out different versions of the new task. We chose two different texts because a specific text often has a marked effect on how testees perform on a reading comprehension task. The texts were chosen carefully so that their discourse structures would not be identical. In the case of 'Science', this text appeared to be easier from the testees' point of view because of the clear structure together with the focusing question at the beginning of the text should help readers to concentrate on the main points. In contrast, 'Impartiality', despite its discourse markers and repetition, seemed to offer testees a slightly more difficult task in finding the most important points.

Also, we did not know what would be an optimal number of distractors. Conventional MC tests usually have four choices for each question, but because the choices in a MC summary are different in nature (e.g. they are much longer), the practice followed by conventional MC tests may not be the best one to apply in our case. We chose to use three and five alternative summaries in our tasks; we suspected that three choices might be too few in terms of reliability, but on the other hand, even that number gives the students quite a lot of text to read and analyse. We thought that five alternatives would quite likely be the maximum the students could cope with.

In addition to selecting the best summary, the students were required to justify their choices by writing the reasons for their choice. We hoped that this approach would improve the reliability of the MC summary. The multiple-choice summary was not taken into account when giving placement grades.

The students also filled in a questionnaire covering their language background and opinions on the test types and texts used. They were also asked to assess themselves on various aspects of their reading skills, which we hoped to use to validate the new MC-summary test: The students were asked which aspects of reading they found *difficult* when reading in English. A study by Bachman & Palmer (1989) suggested that this question type is more valid than the usual 'can do' questions, because learners may be more aware of areas where they have difficulties than of areas they find easy.

Designing Distractors for the Multiple-choice Summary

Several studies (e.g. Brown & Day, 1983; Winograd, 1984; Taylor, 1984, 1986; Johns, 1988; Pitkänen-Huhta, 1989) have concluded that poor summarizers typically concentrate on the beginning of a text and leave out important points if they occur near the end of the text; in general, they may completely omit some of the main or central ideas. Poor summarizers also add ideas that do not occur in the text. Further, they may not understand, or they cannot express, how the different parts of a text relate to each other. Moreover, poor summarizers include examples and irrelevant details in their summaries, at the expense of the main ideas.

On the basis of these observations the following distractor types were designed for the MC summaries:

(1) one distractor concentrated on the beginning of the text at the expense of the other parts;
(2) one distractor chose a subtheme as the main theme;
(3) one distractor contained information not found in the text;
(4) one distractor was incoherent: its sentences did not form a logical whole, although some of the main points of the original text were included.

A pilot test was run on the MC-summary section with a very small group of non-native testees before the actual placement test. These testees were asked questions about the plausibility of the distractors, and the distractors for the real test versions were selected accordingly. The two 3-choice MC-summary versions used distractor types 1 and 4, in addition to the correct alternative. The two 5-choice versions differed slightly from each other: The one based on the 'Impartiality' text used all the four distractor types, whereas the other version based on the 'Science' text did not contain a type 3 distractor, but rather used two type 2 distractors (see Appendix 2).

The fact that there are certain systematic differences between good and poor summarizers offers a substantive, theoretical basis for creating a systematic framework for designing distractors for MC summary tests. We are not aware of a comparable method of classifying and selecting distractors for conventional multiple-choice tests.

Procedures

Students were handed the examination papers and given general instructions about the purpose and the criteria of the test. They were then asked to read the specific instructions in their mother tongue for the test. After a short question period, when students were given a chance to check whether they had understood the instructions, they were all given permission to start with the first part of the test. All the parts were timed, and the testees were asked to wait for a signal to proceed to the next part.

Findings

Table 5.1 describes the means and standard deviations of the test scores, as well as the scales used for marking the tests. Note that the raw test scores were transformed into percentages to make comparisons of the test results possible. The means and standard deviations in Table 5.1 refer to these transformed scores, i.e. percentages.

Table 5.1 General descriptive test statistics

Test type	Assessment scale	Transformed scores (%)	
		Mean	SD
Conventional MC tests:			
Test 1	0–10 points	71	17
Test 2	0–10	64	19
Test 1 & 2	0–20	68	15
Open-ended questions	0–15	59	18
Summary	0–15	66	26
MC summary versions:			
(1) Text 1, 3-choice	0/1	21	—
(2) Text 1, 5-choice	0/1	25	—
(3) Text 2, 3-choice	0/1	85	—
(4) Text 2, 5-choice	0/1	80	—

The mean scores in Table 5.1 suggest that the MC summary versions, which were based on Text 2 ('Science'), were the easiest tests, whereas the most difficult tasks were the other two MC summaries based on Text 1 ('Impartiality'). The other reading tests differed very little in terms of their difficulty. The reason for the difficulty of the two MC summaries was probably that the versions based on Text 1 were not satisfactory as tests: only 21 or 25% of the students made the right choice. One of the distractors was apparently too similar to the right choice, because many of those who did very well on the other reading tests chose it.

The problems we had with the MC summaries based on Text 1 illustrate the fact that the selection of a text has an obvious effect on how easily a summary can be constructed. If the text has an opening paragraph that in fact summarizes the text, as was the case in Text 1, it appears to be relatively easy to select the right summary. It would probably also be quite easy to write a good summary of such a text. Testers who would like to use a MC summary as a test have two alternatives: Avoid using texts with this type of opening paragraphs or avoid using a distractor type that is based only on the beginning of the text.

It turned out that the MC summary tasks did not take as much time to complete as we had expected. Although the text and the three or five alternative summaries presented the students with a considerable amount of reading, the 35 minutes allowed to complete the task was more than enough, most of the students handing in their papers after 15 or 20 minutes. This suggests that five alternative summaries may not be the maximum or optimal number of tasks to include, at least when the alternatives are in the mother tongue and the testees at intermediate or advanced levels of proficiency in the second language. A test battery could contain more MC summaries, which would increase its reliability.

Reliability

The reliability of the two conventional multiple-choice tests was relatively low because both had only ten items: Cronbach's alpha was 0.38 for both, and 0.50 when the two were combined into a single 20-item test. An inter-rater reliability of the summary task and the test with open-ended questions was calculated by taking a random sample of 50 testees whose papers were then marked by one of the researchers (Elina Randell) along mutually agreed guidelines (the other writer marked all the papers). The inter-rater correlation for the summary and the open-ended questions was 0.89 and 0.94 respectively.

The reliability of the multiple-choice summary format tried out in this study is obviously problematic because each of the four versions consisted of only one item. To ensure that the testees did not merely guess they had to give justifications in writing for their choices by answering the question, 'Why do you think it [i.e. the alternative chosen] is a good summary?'. Unfortunately, this method did not yield the information we hoped for. Many answers were impossible to interpret, especially very general ones, such as 'It was the best summary' or 'It gave the best/a comprehensive picture of the text'. It is impossible to say whether these students had a valid reason for making the correct choice or whether they had just guessed. The students were advised to use the characteristics of a good summary provided in the summarizing task as their reasons for their choices. It turned out, however, that many students did not, or could not, make use of the list. Evidently this kind of activity requires some training.

Face validity of the tests

The face validity of the tests was assessed by asking students to evaluate each test by answering the question, 'How well do you think this test measured your English reading comprehension?' rating their responses on a 1 to 5 scale. The question was aimed at finding out the test takers' opinion on the task type used (e.g. multiple-choice), but their views on the texts may have affected their answers.

Differences in face validity between the tests were not very great, as Table 5.2 shows. Interestingly, the students did not consider the conventional MC test better than the other test types, although it was by far the most familiar one. In fact, the two open-ended test formats, the summarizing task and the open-ended questions, were regarded as slightly better tests than the others (we have not analysed these results statistically, however). The students seemed to indicate that they found something odd with the MC summary versions 1 and 2 (based on the 'Impartiality' text) because they received the lowest ratings. It was encouraging to notice, however, that those MC-summary versions (3 and 4) which did not have poor distractors were considered to be as good reading tests as the other tests. Many of the face validity ratings for all the tests were, however, at the middle point of the scale, which may indicate that many testees did actually not form an opinion on the validity of the tests.

The face validity of two tests apparently bore some relation to the test scores: The face validity estimates of the first conventional MC test and the summarizing task had a low correlation with the test score ($r = 0.18$, $p = 0.003$ and $r = 0.25$, $p = 0.000$, respectively).

Table 5.2 Face validity of the tests

Test type	Mean face validity (on 1 to 5 scale)	SD	N
Conventional MC tests:			
Test 1	3.3	0.80	262
Test 2	3.3	0.83	251
Open-ended questions	3.5	0.81	254
Summary	3.5	0.92	243
MC summaries:			
Version 1	3.0	1.10	45
Version 2	3.2	0.92	50
Version 3	3.4	0.80	50
Version 4	3.3	0.93	49

The students were also asked how familiar they were with the various test formats. The conventional multiple-choice format was by far the most familiar ($M = 4.8$ on a 1 to 5 scale), followed by the open-ended questions and the summarizing task ($M = 3.2$ and 2.0), and the new test, the MC summary ($M = 1.4$). This trend corresponds well to what we know about the test types used at schools in Finland. Students' familiarity with test types did not seem to affect the students' performance in the tests, however. The conventional MC tests were the only exception, where familiarity with the testing technique was associated with higher scores ($r = 0.20, p = 0.005, N = 159$).

Concurrent validity

Concurrent validation of the new test method was carried out by using various statistical analyses to compare the new test to the other tests and self-assessment questions, which served as external criteria. We present results here concerning the best version ('Science' 5-choice) of the four MC summaries that we tried out. The analyses of the remaining three versions are not included for reasons which will be explained below.

First, we computed Pearson correlation coefficients between the multiple-choice summary and the criterion tests and questions. Because the MC summary score is a dichotomous variable (right/wrong) and the others are continuous variables, the Pearson coefficients are in fact point-biserial correlation coefficients.

The 5-choice version based on the 'Science' text (see Appendix 1) turned out to be the best of the four MC summaries, at least judging by the fact that it correlated with the criterion tests. The two versions based on Text 1 ('Impartiality') did not correlate with the criteria because they were failures as tests: One of the distractors did not differ well enough from the right choice, as described above. This problem was not a complete surprise because the pilot testing of the MC summary had been on a very small scale. The 3-choice version of the 'Science' text did not correlate well with the criteria either; probably it was easy to choose (or merely guess) the right alternative in the 3-choice format. This tendency may have produced too little variance in the scores (85% made the correct choice in the 3-choice version), which could explain the low correlation in this case.

Table 5.3 Point-biserial correlations with the external criteria (the best MC-summary version)

	Summary	Open-ended questions	Conventional MC tests Test 1	Test 2	Both MC tests
MC Summary	0.35 $p = 0.001$	0.22 $p = 0.029$	0.20 $p = 0.047$	0.02 $p = 0.428$	0.15 $p = 0.102$
		Self-assessment question 1		Self-assessment question 2	
MC Summary		0.24 $p = 0.022$		0.20 $p = 0.045$	
N = 73					

Self-assessment question 1: can/cannot find main points in a text.
Self-assessment question 2: can/cannot figure out the message of a text as a whole.
Conventional MC tests: only questions aimed at the main content are included here.

Table 5.3 describes the point-biserial coefficients between the best MC summary (the 5-choice 'Science' version) and the criterion measures. The MC summary correlated best with the summarizing task (0.35), which is encouraging. The correlations with the other tests and self-assessment questions were in the range of 0.20 to 0.24. The only exception was the second conventional MC test which was uncorrelated with the new test, possibly because this test was the only one in which some of the test takers had problems with the time limit. In general, the relatively low reliabilities of the two conventional MC tests make it difficult to draw any firm conclusions about how well they could tap the ability to understand main ideas.

The intercorrelations (Pearson) of the criterion tests (summary, open-ended, and conventional MC questions) were rather low, ranging from 0.20 to 0.45 ($N = 293$). The low correlation between the multiple-choice and other tests may be explained by the low reliability of the MC tests: They had only 10 items each, or even less if the questions concerning details only are not considered. However, the low correlation between the summarizing task and the open-ended questions may suggest that they cover different aspects of reading; perhaps characteristics of the text also has some effect. This correlation was 0.38 ($p = 0.000$), or 0.42 after correction for attenuation.

The second approach we used to determine the validity of the new test was to combine all the tests and questions which we assumed to indicate an ability to understand the main points of a text. The idea was that a combination of measures of an ability would quite probably be more valid than any single measure. In this way the two groups – those who could choose the right MC summary and those who could not – were compared. Again, we only present the findings on the best MC summary ('Science' 5-choice).

On average, those who could select the right summary among the five alternatives were 12% better on the criterion tests than those who could not (67% vs. 55%, $t = 3.09$, $p = 0.003$, $N = 73$). The difference was even greater in the self-assessment (76% vs. 56%, $t = 3.79$, $p = 0.000$, $N = 65$). The t-tests indicate that both differences were statistically significant. All the tests and self-assessment questions were also analysed by MANOVA, and the analysis seemed to verify the t-test results ($F = 2.26$, $p = 0.048$, $N = 65$). These findings suggest that the multiple-choice summary taps the same construct as the external criteria, at least to some extent.

Finally, a logistic regression analysis was computed to study which tests and questions best predicted whether or not the testee could choose the right summary in the 5-choice (Science) version. The forward stepping method was used; it turned out that only the conventional summarizing task was a statistically significant predictor of failure or success in the multiple-choice summary ($p = 0.006$).

Table 5.4 shows that the prediction was quite accurate for those who chose the right MC-summary alternative but not for those who failed to do so. This inaccuracy of the prediction may have been the result of the fact that the test was rather easy for the testees so that the number of those who failed in the MC summary was very low.

Table 5.4 Number of correctly vs. incorrectly predicted MC-summarizers (5-choice 'Science' version)

	Predicted		
	Wrong	*Right*	*Percent correct*
Observed			
Wrong	3	12	20.0%
Right	2	56	96.6%
			Overall: 80.8%

Discussion

A tentative conclusion based on the findings of this validation study is that, to a certain extent, the multiple-choice summary measures skills similar to the more open-ended test methods (e.g. as indicated by a 0.35 point-biserial correlation with the summarizing task). The MC summary appears to be sensitive to the structure of the text used in the task, for example, certain types of distractors could not be used with certain text structures. Our results also indicate that five alternative summaries per text worked better than three. However, the format used in this study is not cost-effective: to achieve satisfactory reliability so many MC summaries need be used that the test as a whole would become impractical. The new method would probably be more useful as a teaching tool in reading comprehension courses. It could be used to retrieve the main content from a text and to illustrate and practise the writing of summaries, or to raise the students' awareness of different kinds of text organization.

From the point of view of testing, a fundamental problem appears to be how to make the MC summary more reliable and practical. A central problem here is how to determine whether testees merely make the right guess or whether they have a valid reason for choosing a particular alternative. One way of improving the test would be to increase the number of distractors. Constructing them for a MC-summary task appeared to be relatively simple because each alternative is in fact a text which can be varied in many ways to produce different distractors. In particular, the possibility of including information outside the text (see distractor type 3 above) makes the design of distractors relatively easy. The findings of this study indicate, however, that some distractors are probably quite implausible for students at intermediate and advanced levels of language proficiency (see, e.g. distractor 1 in Appendix 1). Reasons for this cannot be inferred from this limited study;

introspective data from test takers would probably supply useful information on this matter.

Another way of improving the reliability and practicality of the MC summary would be to improve the way the testees have to justify their choices. An open-ended question such as, 'Why do you think the summary you chose is a good one?' appeared to yield information that is not sufficiently specific to determine whether the student had guessed or not. If testees are forced to analyse the text in more detail when giving reasons for their choices, we could perhaps control for guessing more effectively. This could be done by presenting the testees with a series of statements which they have to mark as 'true' or 'false' after choosing one of the alternatives. These might include statements such as 'The summary covers the whole text', or if we want to make the task more guided, 'The summary covers the whole text, not just the beginning'. Testees should then choose the right reasons as well as the right alternative to be awarded full points.

Still another way of improving the MC summary might be to break the task into several smaller tasks, for example, by presenting a number of 'mini-summaries' after each paragraph. A 'mini-summary' would probably have to be at least two or three sentences long; otherwise this method would not differ from many conventional multiple-choice tests.

These different versions of the MC summary might solve some problems related to the format we experimented with in our study, but they may create other kinds of difficulties. For example, is it valid to make the testees analyse the text structure? How essential is this ability for advanced reading comprehension?

The findings of this pilot study clearly indicate that the multiple-choice summary, like any other test type, needs to be assessed extensively before it can be assumed to be a valid way to construct reading comprehension tests. Without pilot-testing the designer cannot be certain that all the distractors are satisfactory.

Other kinds of tests besides the multiple-choice summary may also offer ways to improve the practicality of testing students' comprehension of the main content in reading passages. Such possibilities might, for example, involve underlining the main points in a text; this approach is intuitively appealing because it is a behavior that many students do spontaneously when reading. In fact, at least one international English language test currently uses a task where the candidate has to underline sections in a text as a response to questions (the Certificate in Communicative Skills in English designed by the University of Cambridge and the Royal Society of Arts). However, we are not aware of any research on that particular test type.

Additional test methods could include filling in gaps in a summary of text (i.e. the testee is given a text and a summary of the text with some key words missing from the latter), filling in a chart representing the text structure, choosing among a list of statements ('propositions') the ones that represent the main ideas of a text, or perhaps ordering these propositions in a hierarchical order representing the text structure.

The next phase of our research will try out some of the methods mentioned above as well as an improved version of the multiple-choice summary. The search for more practical ways of assessing the understanding of main content in reading is not easy, but we hope in the end it will yield new methods for large-scale testing.

References

Bachman, L. F. and Palmer, A. S. (1989) The construct validation of self-ratings of communicative language ability. *Language Testing* 6, 14–29.

Brown, A. L. and Day, J. D. (1983) Macrorules for summarizing texts: The development of expertise. *Journal of Verbal Learning and Verbal Behaviour* 22, 1–14.

Johns, A. M. (1988) Reading for summarizing: An approach to text orientation and processing. *Reading in a Foreign Language* 4, 79–90.

Oskarsson, M. (1984) *Self-assessment of Foreign Language Skills: A Survey of Research and development work*. Strasbourg: Council of Europe.

Pitkänen-Huhta, A. (1989) *Summary Writing – Differences Between Good and Poor Summarizers*. Unpublished MA thesis, Department of English, University of Jyväskylä, Finland.

Taylor, K. K. (1984) Teaching summarization skills. *Journal of Reading* 27, 389–93.

— (1986) Summary writing by young children. *Reading Research Quarterly* 21, 193–208.

Valencia, S. and Pearson, P. D. (1987) Reading assessment: Time for a change. *The Reading Teacher* 40, 726–32.

Winograd, P. N. (1984) Strategic difficulties in summarizing texts. *Reading Research Quarterly* 19, 404–25.

Appendix 1: Text of the best multiple-choice summary (5-choice, 'Science' text)

Science, technocracy and the politico-economic power

Who counterbalances the establishment? There have been few historical examples of powerful groups that have not abused their power when other groups have been unable to offset their influence. Is there any group today which can or should counterbalance the power of 'the establishment', in our case the politicians and managers? Theoretically, such a group could exist. In the past, the universities, institutes of advanced studies and academies played a role of this sort. As they were then to a considerable extent independent of the State, it was normal for research workers to criticize and advise on complicated questions; and an academy's opinion was often of decisive importance. The extensive freedom of the universities was encouraged because their independent criticism was considered healthy for society.

In some European countries – I take Sweden as an example because I know it better than other countries – the situation has changed drastically over the past few decades. One of the reasons is that universities and academies have lost their independence. The universities used to constitute independent 'academic republics' within society; they now have been transformed into highly bureaucratic government departments and their working methods and development are decided arbitrarily by the State authorities, often without anything more than purely formal consultation.

Furthermore, the academies lost their backbone because their former independent financial status gave way to almost total reliance on State grants. They are now afraid to express any opinion that might annoy the authorities responsible for such allocations and their views therefore have scarcely any influence – except in unimportant matters.

None the less, research workers at the universities and institutes of advanced study have one considerable advantage over their colleagues in private companies or government departments; their contracts do not forbid them to express their views. Many occupy permanent posts from which they cannot be dismissed. They are therefore able to criticize freely, and this fact should limit the omnipotence of the politicians and managers. Quite often it actually does so. Research workers at universities and institutes have warned the public about pollution, dangerous substances in food and medicine, misleading and slanted use of statistics, etc. Thus, the kind of opposition required does exist.

On the other hand, the public is not generally aware of the effective methods employed by the authorities to silence such criticism when it becomes really uncomfortable. Research workers in universities today are virtually dependent on research grants: to determine the complicated processes which play an increasing part in modern society and in man's interaction with nature, it is often necessary to carry out a series of special projects requiring expensive instruments and a staff of skilled workers. This means that freedom of research can be effectively stifled through the machinery of grants.

Appendix 2. Alternative summaries and distractors

The task: the alternative summaries (translation from Finnish):

Name: .... Soc. sec. number: ....

Faculty: ....

First, read through the text 'Science, Technocracy and the Politico-Economic Power' and try to find the main point in it. Then look at the alternative summaries of the text below and choose the one that best describes the main content of the text. *Give reasons for your choice.* (The characteristics of a good summary presented at the beginning of test 4 (i.e. the summarizing task) may be of help to you.)

---

(1) History shows that those in power have usually abused their position unless they have had a counterforce. Universities were an important counterforce for those in power in the past, and they even had influence on important matters, which was considered beneficial to society. Nowadays, some European universities have grown to resemble state departments, for instance, in that they get their funding from the state.

(This is a type 1 distractor, which concentrates on the beginning of the text. None of the students in this 5-choice version chose it.)

(2) Universities have been a counterforce to the abuse of power by those who have been in power. State funding has meant that some European universities have lost their influence and independence and no longer dare criticize the establishment. On the other hand, those researchers who have tenure dare express criticism, and can sometimes have real influence on matters. However, researchers who are too critical can be silenced by denying them the funding they need for expensive research projects.

(This is the right alternative. It was chosen by 80% of the 73 students who had been given this MC-summary version.)

(3) The status of universities has changed in many European countries during the last few decades. In the past, universities were entirely independent communities and acquired their funding from other sources than the state. Now they resemble state departments in many respects: both get their funds from the state. Dependence has gone so far that the funds for even many research projects have to be applied from the state because modern research work is often very expensive.

(This is a type 2 distractor, which concentrates on a subtheme, not on the main theme of the passage. It was chosen by 7% of the students.)

(4) Many of those who have had power have abused it. Universities used to be independent in the past and act as a counterforce to those in power. This was considered beneficial for the society. Nowadays universities get their funding from the state. In some European countries, university staff dare not criticize those who have the political and economic power. Researchers' views have had an influence on decision making even in some important matters such as pollution.

(This is a type 4 distractor, which is clearly more incoherent/incohesive than the other alternatives. This was chosen by 9% of the students.)

(5) University researchers are in a different position from those who work in state departments and private enterprises. Researchers who are employed by the state or private companies are dependent on their employer, who pays their salaries, and therefore, they generally dare not criticise their employers. Although researchers at universities are also employed by the state they cannot be fired because of their opinions, since they usually have tenures. Thus, they have been able to exert influence on such important matters as pollution and food additives.

(This is a type 2 distractor, which concentrates on a subtheme. This was chosen by 4% of the students.)

The best summary is number: ....

Why do you think it is a good summary?

6 Using the Information Curve to Assess Language CAT Efficiency

MICHEL LAURIER

This study created two versions of a placement test in French, a Computerized Adaptive Test (CAT) and a Paper-Pencil Test (PPT), using an Interactional Ability approach and Item-Response Theory. To validate the test, we compared information curves between the two versions of the test. Because item difficulty on the test corresponds to students' abilities, the CAT version provided, in most cases, as much information as the PPT version while requiring fewer items. To demonstrate this difference, we calculated an efficiency index.

Recent research on validity (Messick, 1989; Moss, 1992; Shepard, 1993) promotes a unified view of construct validity as a multi-faceted process that aims at demonstrating the relevance of inferences and the appropriacy of decisions based on test results. However, according to Cook and Campbell (1979), threats to construct validity fall into two major categories: 'construct underrepresentation' or 'surplus construct irrelevancy'. The former concerns tests that lead to improper inferences because they fail to incorporate important dimensions of the construct. The latter refers to the test variance component that may be irrelevant to the construct. Messick (1989: 34) distinguishes two major types of such irrelevancy. 'Construct irrelevant difficulty' occurs whenever the task is too difficult for some individuals or the whole group. Conversely, 'construct irrelevant easiness' is found whenever the task is too simple. In both cases, undue abilities and tests strategies are likely to affect the test results.

Because they are intended for a broad range of ability levels, placement tests are particularly liable to 'surplus construct irrelevancy'. The use of adaptive procedures may increase test validity because they tailor the test according to the student's actual level of performance. During the course of the test, the difficulty of the task, at any given point, depends on the previous responses of the testee. As noted by Dunkel (1991: 205), placement

111

testing is one of the most promising use of computers among the numerous applications that have been made in language learning and testing. Following Larson & Madsen (1985) and Tung (1986), our research project[1] on adaptive language testing led us to design an experimental placement test in two different versions: a paper-pencil version (PPT) and a computerized adaptive version (CAT). This chapter compares the efficiency of these two versions then presents a simple efficiency index based on the amount of information that can be obtained from a test over a certain number of items. Within the framework of Item Response Theory (IRT), information is defined as a function that is related to students' ability. The interpretation of the information function is usually regarded as a reliability issue. However, in the context of most recent approaches to validity (Messick, 1989), studies on test efficiency form part of the long-term process of construct validation.

Characteristics of a Placement Test

The term *placement test* refers to the use of a test rather than its nature. Placement tests may serve one of three purposes distinguished by Clark (1972). When testers are primarily concerned with how well students will learn if they are placed in a given group, this purpose is *prognostic*. However, in most language programs, students' aptitude for learning is usually not considered as a primary criterion for placement. In most situations, the placement of students are determined in respect to a particular sequence of language course objectives; a placement test could then be designed in relation to purposes of *achievement*. However, the problem often arises that students have varied backgrounds so that it is difficult to relate different testing approaches and content to a specific curriculum, as well as to varied student populations who may experience that curriculum in different ways. Therefore, many placement tests are designed as *proficiency tests* that are validated in regards to a theoretical model of language competence.

Bachman (1990) claims that there are two approaches to the problem of authenticity in language proficiency tests. On one hand, a test may try to replicate a real-life situation. As there is no strict division between the ability and the behaviour that is elicited, the validity of the tests that are developed under this approach depends on the realism of the test situation and the magnitude of the inferential leap that must be made to the non-test situation. Because a computerized test cannot replicate a real-life situation, this approach does not work – unless one wants to test the ability to use foreign language software. On the other hand, according to Bachman, authenticity of language proficiency tests could be defined in terms of the kind of interaction that occurs between the test taker and the test tasks. Bachman (1990: 317) writes that this 'approach uses a theoretical framework of factors affecting test performance to construct tests that include features of language use that are relevant to both the interpretations and *uses to be made of tests scores*'.

Incorporating the features that are relevant to the uses of test scores means that we look at the type of decision that will be made on the basis of the test results. From Messick's (1989: 63) point of view, 'the evidential basis of test use is also construct validity but with the important proviso that the general evidence supportive of score meaning be enhanced by specific evidence for the relevance of the scores to the applied purpose and for the utility of the scores in the applied setting'. Therefore the comparisons between PPT and CAT must look at the way the testing mode may affect the placement decision. A placement decision has three main characteristics. *First*, it is validated against the performance the student will show in the language class. This means that the test must allow predictive inferences. *Secondly*, since wrong placement decisions are seldom beyond remedy, the error component of the test may be fairly large. *Thirdly*, the decision is unidimensional as it aims at locating the student on a single continuum – from a beginner's level to a very advanced level. We assume that this continuum represents the general construct of proficiency in the language.

In view of these decisions, we thought that a computerized administration may facilitate the placement process. We also thought that IRT, the psychometric theory that is currently popular in CAT development, was compatible with our purposes. However, we needed to compromise on the type of tasks for the test because we had to meet strong IRT assumptions (unidimensionality and item independence) and because we wished to avoid high technology (mass storage or interactive multimedia, for example) that was unavailable for the institutions involved. Also, we wanted the PPT and CAT versions to be comparable. We finally decided on multiple-choice questions that were displayed on a monochrome text screen. As a result, in our test the written mode was dominant, productive skills were almost absent, and highly integrative tasks were excluded.

Description of the Instrument

Despite these constraints, we believe that the test measures relevant features that are integral to general proficiency in French. The dimensionality studies (Blais & Laurier, 1993) and the correlational analyses (Laurier, 1993) that we have conducted so far did not reveal any 'construct underrepresentation'. However, since construct validation is an on-going process, these results will have to be supplemented with studies on more extensive data.

The test has three parts. The first part is based on what Jafarpur (1987) calls the 'short-context technique'. The students are asked to read a short paragraph in French before they answer a question to verify their general comprehension of the content.

Part I: Example

Avis au consommateur: Les magazins Zears ne s'engagent à remplacer cet appareil que s'il est défectueux. On doit alors le rapporter, accompagné de la preuve d'achat et de l'emballage d'origine, dans les 90 jours qui suivent la date d'achat. Aucun remboursement ne sera effectué.

A– Si l'appareil ne marche pas, on vous remettra votre argent.
B– La garantie de Zears est de seulement 90 jours.
C– Les magazins Zears remplaceront l'appareil, sans condition.
D– On ne doit pas avoir utilisé l'appareil pour l'échanger.

The second part focuses on sociolinguistic competence. The students read a description of the situation in their first language and choose the corresponding sentence. Howard (1980) and Raffaldini (1988) claim that students' abilities to produce appropriate statements can be measured with this type of item.

Part II: Example

Your boss will retire next year. You do not consider him as a friend but you talk with him often. At five, he leaves the office and usually drives downtown. Today, you have to go downtown. How would you start asking your boss for a ride?

A– Vas-tu au centre-ville, aujourd'hui?
B– Je veux aller au centre-ville aujourd'hui.
C– Passez-vous par le centre-ville aujourd'hui?
D– Emmenez-moi au centre-ville.

The format of the third part (Fill-in-the-gap) has been used in language tests for many years (see Lado, 1961) and is a useful technique to measure lexical or grammatical knowledge. If we accept Alderson's (1983) conclusions on Cloze tests – that the text span the student actually uses is relatively restricted – this type of item could even be an alternative to Cloze tests as a measure of general proficiency (see Oller, 1979).

Part III: Example

Je n'aurai probablement pas le temps d'arrêter au garage aujourd'hui. Je vais essayer .... y aller demain.

A– de
B– pour
C– d'
D– à

Procedures

An experimental PPT version, which included 50 items in each part, was administered to more than 700 examinees. Because the items were multiple choice, they may have encouraged a certain amount of guessing. Furthermore, because we could not assume the items were equally discriminating, the Rasch model was not appropriate for analyses. Therefore, we calibrated the items with a 3-parameter model: discrimination, difficulty and pseudo-guessing.

Three calibrated item banks were set up and used for the PPT and the CAT versions. We created two PPT forms and two CAT forms. The PPT forms were parallel: they have the same variance, the same mean and their information curve is similar. These forms use 60 different items – 20 in each part.

The CAT forms drew items from the whole banks but used different selection algorithms. The STRAT form was based on a *stradaptive* selection strategy similar to the one applied by Weiss (1982) in his comparison study between CAT and PPT with simulated data. Sets of relevant items were assigned to different strata that cover the whole ability range. The MATCH form tried to find the item with the *m* value that was the closest to the ability level. This value was calculated with Lord's formula (Lord, 1970) which estimates the ability level where a given item is the most informative.

In both CAT forms, prior information on a student's background or results on the previous parts were used to determine a starting ability level. Then the appropriate ability level was calculated using a maximum likelihood (ML) procedure; whenever ML failed, the program compared the simple level mean of wrong and right items. The program switched to the next part or stopped when the pre-set information threshold was reached or when 12 items had been administered.

The PPT score represented the number of correct answers. This is the way this type of test is usually marked. The PPT raw score or the CAT ability estimate was later converted on a proficiency-level scale which included the seven main levels plus six borderline levels (e.g. *Absolute Beginner +*):

Absolute Beginner	*Low Intermediate*	*Advanced*
False Beginner	*Mid-Intermediate*	*Very Advanced*
	High Intermediate	

Estimation of reliability

The ability continuum was divided so that the number of students placed at each level would be theoretically the same. For research purposes, we kept

50 answer sheets from the calibration sample (obtained with the 150 item paper-and-pencil experimental test) and made sure that we had approximately the same number of examinees at each level. We marked them considering only the items that were used in the PPT versions, that is, first using the answer key for *Form A* and then using the answer key for *Form B*. Using the actual answers of the experimental test as input, we also simulated, on the computer, adaptive administrations of the tests with STRAT and MATCH algorithms.

As shown on Table 6.1, we found that the students' levels were under-estimated with the CAT forms. The means and standard deviations were calculated after assigning a numerical value to each level, from 1 to 13. The discrepancy between PPT and CAT results can be explained in that a method effect might have arisen in the marking procedure (ML vs number correct) rather than because of a difference in the presentation mode (computer vs. questionnaire).

Table 6.1 PPT vs. CAT results

Version	M	SD
PPT Form A	7.08	4.194
PPT Form B	7.34	4.429
CAT STRAT	6.50	4.032
CAT MATCH	6.68	4.058

A correlation matrix (see Table 6.2) shows that the marking procedure may explain some differences in the students' results. However, the coefficients which involved the MATCH algorithm were consistently lower. This trend was not a surprise because the stradaptive strategy tended to select the best items whereas the matching of *m* values with students' abilities retrieved items that may have discriminated poorly. The MATCH algorithm would probably be a helpful solution to test-retest problems if the bank were larger and every one of the items had high discrimination values (*a* parameter). However, with small item banks like the ones we were using, the stradaptive algorithm was clearly superior. Therefore, we decided to concentrate on the STRAT form.

The correlation between the two parallel PPT forms ($r_{AB} = 0.969$) can be interpreted as a reliability coefficient once the scores have been con-verted to the 13-level scale. Classical theory reliability indices can also be used to estimate the error component on the PPT form subtests. Given the length of the sub-tests (20 items), KR-20s, calculated with the whole data for

Table 6.2 Correlations

	PPT-A	*PPT-B*	*STRAT*	*MATCH*
PPT Form A	1.000			
PPT Form B	0.969	1.000		
CAT STRAT	0.948	0.945	1.000	
CAT MATCH	0.907	0.915	0.932	1.000

both forms, are fairly high. They range from slightly below 0.8 for *Part II*, up to over 0.9 for *Part I*.

Green *et al.* (1984) showed that classical theory indices are not adequate for CAT because they concern all the subjects, whatever their ability, on the whole test. They proposed instead two reliability indices (marginal and conditional) that may not be totally accurate. However, within IRT framework, Thissen (1991) suggested that the information function can be used to estimate the error component. Birnbaum (1968) derived a formula to compute the item information as function of the ability.

$$I(\Theta, U_i) = \frac{P'^2}{P_i\, Q_i}$$

U_i is 1 if the answer on a given item is right, 0 if it is wrong. P_i for Θ (the ability level) is obtained with the standard logistic model formula that applies once the parameters are known. Q_i equals $P_i - 1$ and P'^2 is the first derivative of P_i. The information function is additive, which means that it grows arithmetically as the number of items increases. The sum of the information on each item is the test information $I(\Theta)$ for a given ability level. The standard error of measurement for this ability level is an inverse function of the test information, which means that as the information increases, the error is reduced:

$$SE(\Theta) = \frac{1}{\sqrt{I(\Theta)}}$$

A plot of the test information function helps to visualize the efficiency of the test at different levels. The peak of the information curve corresponds to the ability level where the test provides its maximum information.

Results

We analyzed the amount of information obtained at the end of each sub-test during the 50 CAT simulations. For each proficiency level, we averaged the number of items that were administered and the adaptive test information indices in order to draw a typical information curve.

Conventional test information indices, $I(\Theta)$, for PPT *Form A* and *Form B* were calculated using the entire data set. We plotted the information curves for these two 20 item conventional forms. Figure 6.1 shows the information curves for *Part I* (short-context technique) of *Form A* and *Form B*. The horizontal line represents the ability range whereas the vertical axe shows the amount of information that is obtained at a given ability level. Both versions provide more information at the intermediate levels ($-0.05 > \Theta > 0.5$). It should be noted that, in accordance with Samejima's (1977) definition of 'weak parallelism', we tried to get similar information curves for the three sub-tests of the PPT forms. As far as *Part I* is concerned, although *Form A* brings slightly more information than *Form B* at the *High Intermediate* and *Advanced* levels ($0.05 > \Theta > 1.0$), this criterion was generally met. 'Weak parallelism' was also found on the other sub-tests so that comparisons could be made on raw scores of any of the two PPT forms.

Figure 6.2 was created by superimposing CAT information curves obtained from the simulations. For the purposes of illustration, we will consider only the CAT curves for students who were placed at three different levels: *False Beginner*, *Mid-Intermediate* and *Advanced*. The thick segments on the ability line delimit these three levels. Curve shapes for other levels can be easily inferred. It can be observed that, at the *Mid-Intermediate* level, the CAT version provides less information than the two PPT forms. This tendency is due to the CAT procedure, whose information threshold interrupted the sub-test at a fixed level, around 9. This amount of information was obtained quickly, in most cases with only 7 items.

At the *False Beginner* level ($-0.88 > \Theta > -0.6$), the average number of items that was necessary to reach the information threshold was 11. In some cases, the maximum number of items, 12, was used. The peak of the curve is outside the ability area, which can be explained in two ways. *First*, this relation depended on the kind of decision that was made and the range of options available at a specific ability level. If the ability level was very low, the student could only be placed at the lowest level. If the ability level was higher, then the student could have been placed as *Low Intermediate*, *Mid-Intermediate*, or other levels up to *Very Advanced*. Had we plotted the information curve for the *Beginner*'s level, the peak of the curve would have been even higher and further from Θ. *Second*, the item bank was small and the *Intermediate* items were usually more efficient. Therefore, as the ability level departed from the mean $\Theta = 0$), some irrelevant information was collected. The same type of skewness can be observed at the *Advanced* level, and even more obviously at the *Very Advanced* level. At the *Advanced* level, PPT was slightly more informative but CAT generally required only nine items.

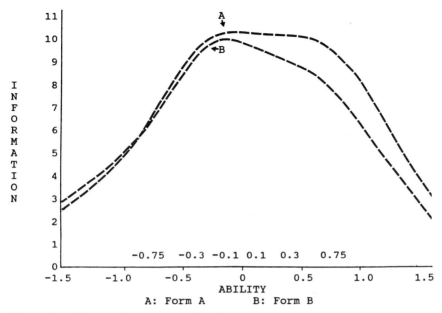

Figure 6.1 Information curves, *Part I*

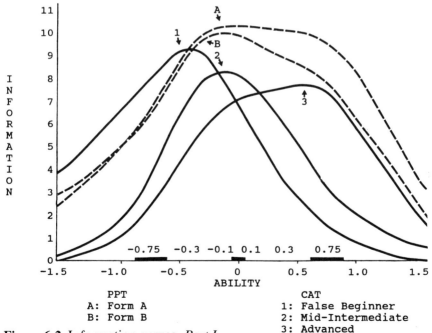

Figure 6.2 Information curves, *Part I*

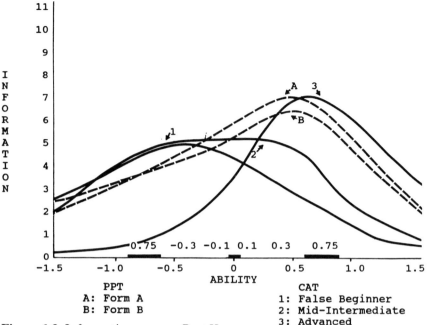

Figure 6.3 Information curves, *Part II*

The information curves are considerably flatter on *Part II* of the test and reflect the problems that arose in our development and calibration process. Many items had to be rejected because they showed poor *a* values (discrimination) or because they were misfitting, that is, they failed to meet the unidimensionality assumption. Although they may be considered as good indicators of communicative competence, judgments about the appropriateness of different statements with regard to a given situation are often unreliable. In addition, multidimensionality problems may affect the goodness of fit of the IRT model. As a result, we had to include in the bank some items that, from a psychometric point of view, were marginally acceptable. The PPT forms were parallel but, with as many items as *Part I* (20 items each), *Part II* is less informative. The maximum information was obtained at the *High Intermediate* level ($0.4 < \Theta < 0.6$).

The three information curves for CAT show that the same amount of information was obtained at each ability level. Because CAT selected the best items, an average number of 11 items was sufficient for the three levels. However, this pattern indicates that for some students, the maximum number of items was administered. Interestingly, on almost half of the cases, the ML procedure did not converge, so the program used the alternate procedure to estimate students' levels.

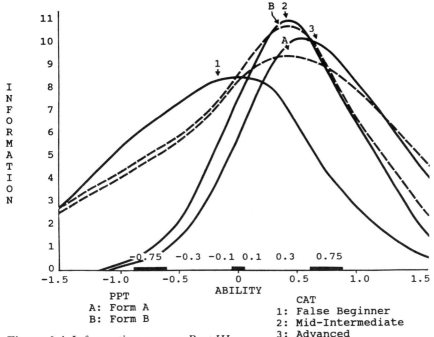

Figure 6.4 Information curves, *Part III*

The PPT information curves for *Part III* (Fill-in-the-gap) also have their highest point at the *High Intermediate* level. However, because of high discrimination item parameters, the curves are much steeper. At the highest point, *Form A* provided less information than *Form B*, but the two forms could still be considered as parallel. On this sub-test, the adaptive testing strategy was clearly superior than the linear conventional strategy. Overall, the CAT version provided at least as much information as PPT at the three levels. However, at these levels PTT required twice as many items. The skewness of the curve that we already explained for *Part I*, at the *False Beginner* and *Advanced* levels can again be observed.

Discussion

The information curves tell us how reliable a test is when different items were administered. The present comparison between the PPT version and the CAT version of our placement test showed that CAT was as reliable as PPT and was generally 50% shorter. CAT seems particularly effective at the extreme ends of the ability range. Because of the additive property of the information curve, a general efficiency index can be easily calculated using the following formula which gives a general ratio between the information and the number of items.

$$E = \frac{\bar{I}(\Theta)}{\bar{N}(\Theta)}$$

$\bar{I}(\Theta)$ represents the mean of the mean information that is obtained at each level and $\bar{N}(\Theta)$ the mean of the mean number of items that were administered at each level. As shown in Table 6.3, this ratio indicates that CAT is much more efficient than PPT (*Form A*). In fact, we can say that, on our placement test, CAT is generally twice as efficient as PPT.

Table 6.3 Efficiency indices

	Part I	*Part II*	*Part III*
CAT (STRAT)	0.81	0.44	0.78
PTT (*Form A*)	0.38	0.23	0.32

The relevance of an index based on the information function is an issue related to reliability. The index tells what measurement accuracy should be expected depending on the duration of the test. However, we all know that reducing the error component is a major step towards a more valid measure. In addition, one aspect of validity concerns the appropriateness of the test tasks. The CAT procedure selects tasks that are neither too easy nor too difficult, thereby reducing 'construct irrelevant difficulty' or 'construct irrelevant easiness'. This property of adaptive procedures improve the test validity. However, one could question the appropriacy of psychometric indices, such as the 'b parameter', to assess the difficulty of a task. In fact, we observed that the testees' perception of difficulty may differ from those indices.

Moreover, the validity problem is related to the type of task we usually find on adaptive language tests. Canale (1985) warned that the heavy dependence of CAT on the IRT model may 'require us to trivialize our theories' about language competence. For this reason, other psychometric approaches should be explored to allow more integrative tasks. Canale also pointed out that the use of the computer has great potential, provided we take full advantage of it. That is the reason why, in the further development of this test, we intend to make the computer environment less obtrusive and to create test items that will take advantage of newly affordable multimedia technology.

Note

1. This project is funded by the *Social Sciences and Humanities Research Council of Canada* (#410-92-1400).

References

Alderson, C. (1983) The Cloze procedure and proficiency in English as a foreign language. In J. Oller (ed.) *Issues in Language Testing Research* (pp. 205–17). Rowley, MA: Newbury House.

Bachman, L. (1990) *Fundamental Considerations in Language Testing*. Oxford: Oxford University Press.

Birnbaum, A. (1968) Some latent-trait models and their use in inferring an examinee's ability. In F. M. Lord and M. R. Novick (eds) *Statistical Theories of Mental Test Scores* (pp. 392–479). Reading, MA: Addison-Wesley.

Blais, J. and Laurier, M. (1993) The dimensionality of a placement test components. Paper presented at the 1993 Language Testing Research Colloquium, Cambridge/Arnhem.

Canale, M. (1985) The promise and threat of computerized adaptive assessment of reading comprehension. In C. Stansfield (ed.) *Technology and Language Testing* (pp. 29–47). Washington, DC: TESOL.

Cook, T. and Campbell, D. (1979) *Quasi-experimentation: Design and Analysis Issues for Field Testing*. Chicago: Rand-McNally.

Dunkel, P. (ed.) (1991) *Computer-assisted Language Learning and Testing: Research Issues and Practice*. New York: Newbury House.

Green, B. *et al.* (1984) Technical guidelines for assessing computerized adaptive tests. *Journal of Educational Measurement* 21, 347–60.

Howard, F. (1980) Testing communicative proficiency in French as a second language. *Canadian Modern Language Review* 36, 272–83.

Jafarpur, A. (1987) The short-context technique: An alternative for testing reading comprehension. *Language Testing* 2, 195–220.

Lado, R. (1961) *Language Testing: The Construction and Use of Foreign Language Tests*. London: Longman.

Larson, J. and Madsen, H. (1985) Computerized adaptive language testing: Moving beyond computer-assisted testing. *CALICO Journal* 2, 32–6.

Laurier, M. (1993) *L'informatisation d'un test de classement en langue seconde*. Québec: CIRAL, Université Laval.

Lord, F. (1970) Some test theory for tailored testing. In W. H. Holtzman (ed.) *Computer-assisted Instruction, Testing and Guidance* (pp. 139–83). New York: Harper & Row.

Messick, S. (1989) Validity. In R. L. Linn (ed.) *Educational Measurement* 3rd ed. (pp. 13–104). New York: Macmillan/American Council on Education.

Moss, P. (1992) Shifting conceptions of validity in educational measurement: Implications for performance assessment. *Review of Educational Research* 229–58.

Oller, J. (1979) *Language Tests at School*. London: Longman.

Rafaldini, T. (1988) The use of situation tests as measures of communicative ability. *Studies in Second Language Acquisition* 10, 197–215.

Samejima, F. (1978) Information function in tailored testing. *Applied Psychological Measurement* 1, 233–47.

Shepard, L. (1993) Evaluating test validity. In L. Darling-Hammond (ed.) *Review of Research in Education 19* (pp. 405–50). Washington: AERA.

Thissen, D. (1990) Reliability and measurement precision. In H. Wainer *et al.* (eds) *Computerized Adaptive Testing: A Primer* (pp. 161–86). Hillsdale, NJ: Lawrence Erlbaum.

Tung, P. (1986) Computerized adaptive testing: Implications for language test developers. In C. W. Stansfield (ed.) *Technology and Language Testing* (pp. 9–11). Washington, DC: TESOL.

Weiss, D. (1982) Improving measurement quality and efficiency with adaptive testing. *Applied Psychological Measurement* 6, 473–92.

7 Comparing the Scaling of Speaking Tasks by Language Teachers and by the ACTFL Guidelines

CHARLES W. STANSFIELD and DORRY MANN KENYON

Do classroom language teachers perceive the *level of ability* required to perform speaking tasks of differing levels of complexity in a manner compatible with the level of ability required for those tasks as posited by the ACTFL Speaking Proficiency Guidelines (ACTFL, 1986)? An affirmative answer would provide evidence for the validity of the Guidelines. This paper presents the results of the Rasch scaling of 38 speaking tasks (in terms of the level of ability required to perform each one) from data collected via a survey of 700 randomly selected French, Spanish and bilingual education public school teachers in the state of Texas. It compares the outcome of that scaling with the level of ability to perform those tasks as posited by the ACTFL Guidelines. It also examines differences in the scaling of the tasks by the language teachers and the bilingual education teachers.

Background to the Guidelines

The Proficiency Guidelines of the American Council on the Teaching of Foreign Languages (ACTFL):

> represent a hierarchy of global characterizations of integrated performance in speaking, listening, reading and writing. Each description is a representative, not an exhaustive, sample of a particular range of ability, and each level subsumes all previous levels, moving from simple to complex in an 'all-before-and-more' fashion. (ACTFL, 1986)

The ACTFL Guidelines have been widely used in the field of foreign language education in the United States since their original publication in 1982. The Guidelines, by providing an *a priori* description of developing foreign language competence, have served as the basis for the widely-used, face-to-face tailored assessment of foreign language speaking ability known as the Oral Proficiency Interview (OPI). The Guidelines also form the basis for a series of tape-mediated speaking tests known as Simulated Oral Proficiency Interviews (SOPIs) developed by the Center for Applied Linguistics (Stansfield, 1989). In this performance-based assessment of speaking ability, the Guidelines guide both the development of the speaking tasks (i.e. the items) that appear on the test and the scoring of examinee performance.

The Guidelines describe foreign language proficiency at four main levels: Novice, Intermediate, Advanced and Superior. They also describe sublevels within the first three main levels. Inherent in each description are the types of speaking tasks speakers at each level of ability can accomplish. Thus, an Intermediate Low level speaker can 'perform such tasks as introducing self, ordering a meal, asking directions and making purchases' (ACTFL, 1986). Superior level speakers can, for example, 'discuss special fields of competence and interest with ease' (ACTFL, 1986).

Despite the wide dissemination and application of the Guidelines and their demonstrated practical utility, their validity as a description of developing competence in a second language has been widely contested. Many have directly challenged their validity (e.g. Bachman & Savignon, 1986; Lantolf & Frawley, 1985), while others have cited the lack of research to validate the scale levels (Clark & Lett, 1988; Shohamy, 1990).

This paper attempts to address one part of the validity issue through a study that compares judgements made by 'naive' judges about the level of ability required to perform speaking tasks with the level posited by the ACTFL Guidelines themselves. To the degree that these agree, it may be said the ACTFL Guidelines present a scale of developing competence in a foreign language.

The Use of the Many-Faceted Rasch Model as a Method of Scaling

Although there are various approaches to and methods of scaling (e.g. Torgerson, 1958), the method used here is a multi-faceted Rasch approach. Rasch methodology has provided practitioners with useful tools in the analysis of scales (e.g. Wright & Masters, 1982). The study reported in this paper provides an illustration of the information that may be gained from applying one of the newest Rasch computer programs, FACETS (Linacre & Wright, 1990) in a scalar analysis. Although most programs for Rasch and other item analysis only handle two facets (examinees and items), the FACETS program can handle multiple facets and provides calibrations on the logit scale for each element in each facet. Since the ACTFL scale assumes an underlying unidimensional trait of developing second language proficiency, it appears appropriate to consider using a Rasch model.

It is important to clarify that the motivation of the Rasch model is the construction of a measure, not the description of data. Accordingly, although the original data was not produced in an effort to build a measure, the analyses and interpretations in this paper will be in terms of measurement construction. The interpretation of support for the validity of the ACTFL Guidelines will be presented in the context of (1) whether the analysis shows evidence for the existence of an underlying scale that conforms to the Guidelines, and (2) whether further measurement construction, as indicated by information provided by the Rasch analysis, indicates development in a direction moving closer to the ACTFL scale or not.

Background to the Study

In 1990, the Center for Applied Linguistics (CAL), under contract with the Texas Education Agency (TEA), developed the Texas Oral Proficiency Test (TOPT), a simulated oral proficiency interview (SOPI) for use in the certification of Texas French, Spanish and bilingual education teachers (Stansfield & Kenyon, 1991). The TEA began using the TOPT for teacher certification purposes in November, 1991. The test consists of 15 speaking tasks. The development of these tasks was guided by the descriptions contained in the ACTFL Guidelines. In addition, the scoring of the test is also based entirely on the ACTFL scale.

The data for the study reported here was collected during a job-relevancy study conducted before the actual writing of test items began.

The Scaling of Speaking Tasks

In the TOPT, examinees are asked to perform 15 speaking tasks ranging from 'giving directions' to 'supporting an opinion'. Each of these tasks is *a priori* designated at one of the main proficiency levels on the ACTFL scale. (Novice level tasks are not included on the TOPT since it is assumed that teacher certification candidates would all be above that level.) Each item on the TOPT is designed to elicit performance at the ACTFL level associated with the item's speaking task. As an example, Appendix 1 presents an outline of the 15 speaking tasks on the Spanish TOPT and their levels on the ACTFL scale.

In the first phase of the test development project, a job relevancy survey was conducted to determine the relevancy to teaching of 38 individual speaking tasks. The survey presented teachers with a brief description of each speaking task and asked them to rate each on a five-point scale in response to the following question: *Is the **level of ability** required to perform this task needed by bilingual education* (Spanish language/French language, changed as appropriate) *teachers in Texas public schools?* A booklet sent with the survey contained the label for each task, followed by a more complete description of it (Appendix 2). Teachers indicated their response on a machine-readable answer sheet. A rating of 5 indicated 'Definitely Yes', 4 meant 'Probably Yes', 3 meant 'Maybe', 2 meant 'Probably No', and 1 meant 'Definitely No'.

700 teachers from throughout the state of Texas were chosen in a geographically stratified random sampling design to receive the survey: 400 bilingual education teachers, 200 Spanish language teachers and 100 French language teachers. Four hundred and two (402) teachers returned the survey for a response rate of 57%. Table 7.1 presents a summary of the demographic information of those returning the survey. It reveals an adequate response rate (57%) which was consistent across all three groups of teachers. In terms of the experience of the teachers and their sex, little difference appears across the three groups. In terms of educational level taught, Table 7.1 reflects the fact that bilingual education is offered only in K through 5th grade in Texas. In terms of ethnicity of respondents, there is great, though expected, variation among the groups. TEA staff and members of the test advisory boards felt that, based on the demographic data, the survey results may be seen as an accurate reflection of each group. For the purposes of the test development project, all speaking tasks that received a mean rating above 3.50 were considered acceptable to be used on the TOPT.

Study 1: Scaling by all teachers

In the first part of the current study, the complete data matrix of ratings from all teachers was analyzed. This study viewed the data set as containing three facets. The primary facet of interest was the speaking task, of which there were 38 elements. The second facet was the teachers. The third was the group to which each teacher belonged.

Table 7.2 presents the *a priori* classification of the 38 speaking tasks into the three highest main levels on the ACTFL scale. Within each level, tasks are listed in alphabetical order. These classifications were made by the test developers and were based on, as primary references, the ACTFL Guidelines

(ACTFL, 1986) and the FILR Skill Level Descriptions (Liskin-Gasparro, 1987). As a secondary reference, Omaggio's influential text, *Teaching language in context* (Omaggio, 1986), was also used to classify the tasks.

Table 7.1 TOPT job-relevancy survey sample: Summary of demographic information

Total number of surveys sent:		700		
Bilingual Education (BE) Teachers		400		
Spanish Language (SP) Teachers		200		
French Language (FR) Teachers		100		
Total number of valid returned surveys:			402	(57%)
	n	*% Ret'd*	*% of Responses of total group*	
Bilingual education	229	57%	57%	
Spanish	113	57%	28%	
French	60	60%	15%	
Level taught:	*BE*	*SP*	*FR*	
Elementary	96%	14%	0%	
Jun. High/Middle School	1%	21%	14%	
High School	1%	65%	86%	
Other	2%	0%	0%	
Experience:	*BE*	*SP*	*FR*	
1–5 years	41%	37%	34%	
6–10 years	28%	24%	25%	
11–15 years	20%	17%	20%	
16+ years	11%	22%	21%	
Sex:	*BE*	*SP*	*FR*	
Male	10%	18%	12%	
Female	90%	82%	88%	
Ethnicity:	*BE*	*SP*	*FR*	
Hispanic	87%	43%	9%	
White	11%	52%	89%	
Black	1%	3%	2%	
Other	1%	2%	0%	

Table 7.2 *A priori* scaling of the 38 speaking tasks used in the TOPT job-relevancy survey

Intermediate tasks
Describe a Place
Describe Health Problems
Describe Your Daily Routine
Give a Brief Personal History
Give Directions
Introduce Yourself
Make Arrangements for Future Activities
Make Purchases
Order a Meal
Talk About Family Members
Talk About Personal Activities
Talk About Your Future Plans

Advanced tasks
Compare and Contrast Two Objects or Places
Correct an Unexpected Situation
Describe a Sequence of Events in the Past
Describe Expected Future Events
Describe Habitual Actions in the Past
Describe Typical Routines
Explain a Familiar Simple Process
Express Personal Apologies
Give a Brief Organized Factual Summary
Give Advice
Give Instructions
Hypothesize About a Personal Situation
Lodge a Complaint
State Advantages and Disadvantages

Superior tasks
Change Someone's Behavior through Persuasion
Describe a Complex Object in Detail
Discuss a Professional Topic
Evaluate Issues Surrounding a Conflict
Explain a Complex Process in Detail
Explain a Complex Process of a Personal Nature
Give a Professional Talk
Hypothesize About an Impersonal Topic
Hypothesize About Probable Outcomes
Propose & Defend a Course of Action with Persuasion
State Personal Point of View (Controversial Subject)
Support Opinions

Table 7.3 Scaling of the 38 speaking tasks for all teachers by the FACETS program

Logit	Task		Error
13.00	(S)	Describe a Complex Object in Detail	0.21
12.76	(S)	Give a Professional Talk***	0.21
12.48	(S)	Explain a Complex Process in Detail	0.21
12.41	(S)	Explain a Complex Process of a Personal Nature	0.21
11.99	(S)	Discuss a Professional Topic	0.21
11.96	(S)	Evaluate Issues Surrounding a Conflict	0.21
11.40	(S)	Hypothesize About Probable Outcomes	0.21
10.95	(S)	Hypothesize About an Impersonal Topic	0.21
10.88	(A)	Correct an Unexpected Situation	0.21
10.61	(A)	Hypothesize About a Personal Situation	0.21
10.50	(S)	State Personal Point of View (Controversial Subject)	0.21
10.36	(A)	Lodge a Complaint	0.21
10.12	(S)	Propose & Defend a Course of Action with Persuasion	0.21
9.98	(S)	Support Opinions	0.21
9.88	(I)	Talk About Your Future Plans	0.21
9.81	(S)	Change Someone's Behavior through Persuasion	0.21
9.43	(I)	Describe Health Problems	0.21
9.18	(A)	Describe Habitual Actions in the Past	0.21
9.15	(A)	State Advantages and Disadvantages	0.21
8.66	(A)	Give Advice	0.24
8.60	(I)	Make Arrangements for Future Activities	0.24
8.32	(A)	Give a Brief Organized Factual Summary	0.24
8.18	(I)	Make Purchases***	0.24
7.97	(I)	Give a Brief Personal History	0.24
7.87	(I)	Talk About Personal Activities	0.24
7.83	(I)	Order a Meal***	0.24
7.69	(A)	Compare and Contrast Two Objects or Places	0.24
6.72	(A)	Describe Expected Future Events	0.28
6.55	(I)	Talk About Family Members***	0.28
6.34	(A)	Express Personal Apologies***	0.28
5.82	(I)	Describe a Place	0.28
5.51	(I)	Describe Your Daily Routine	0.31
5.09	(A)	Explain a Familiar Simple Process	0.31
4.78	(A)	Describe a Sequence of Events in the Past	0.31
4.33	(I)	Give Directions	0.35
4.26	(A)	Describe Typical Routines	0.35
2.21	(A)	Give Instructions	0.45
1.00	(I)	Introduce Yourself***	0.52

*** = Positive outfit (standardized mean square) > 2

Table 7.3 presents the results of the scaling of the 38 speaking tasks by the FACETS program. There was relatively little error in the logit measure for each in comparison to the width of the entire scale. The Rasch equivalent to the KR20 reliability of determining the measure of the tasks was 0.99. In the context of the survey, an 'easier' task would receive a higher average rating, indicating more teachers felt that a Texas classroom teacher should have the ability to perform this task. In Table 7.3, however, the original logit scale was transformed so that the 'easiest' speaking task had a rating of 1.00 and the 'most difficult' had a rating of 13.00.

We next compare the scaling of the 38 speaking tasks based on the FACETS analysis with the level of ability required to complete each one as posited by the ACTFL Guidelines and designated by their *a priori* classifications. Had the two scalings completely matched, then in Table 7.3 the 12 tasks identified *a priori* as Intermediate would have been the bottom 12 tasks, the 14 tasks identified *a priori* as Advanced would have been the middle 14 tasks, and the 12 tasks identified *a priori* as Superior would have been the top 12 tasks. This ideal outcome is presented in Table 7.4.

Table 7.4 Comparing the *a priori* classifications with the actual scaling: the ideal outcome

A priori expected ordering	Actual scaling		
	I	A	S
I (12)	12	0	0
A (14)	0	14	0
S (12)	0	0	12
Correct Order	12 (100%)	14 (100%)	12 (100%)

Table 7.5 presents the comparison based on the actual scaling results. This comparison is presented as a 'best case' scenario. In other words, tasks that are statistically equivalent (i.e. become reordered when one unit of measurement error from each logit value is taken into account) and cross an ACTFL level boundary have been grouped according to their *a priori* designations. This affected only two pairs of tasks. 'Lodge a Complaint', designated *a priori* as an Advanced task but located as the lowest calibrated task among the top 12 is considered belonging to the Advanced level group, while 'Propose and Defend a Course of Action with Persuasion', designated *a priori* as a Superior task but located as the highest calibrated task among the middle 14 is considered belonging to the Superior level group. Similarly, 'Order a Meal' is considered to have been scaled as an Intermediate task, while 'Compare and Contrast Two Objects or Places' is seen as scaled in the Advanced level.

Table 7.5 Comparing the *a priori* classifications with the actual scaling by all
teachers 'Best case scenario'

A priori expected ordering	Actual scaling		
	I	A	S
I (12)	6	6	0
A (14)	6	6	2
S (12)	0	2	10
Correct Order	6 (50%)	6 (43%)	10 (83%)

Tables 7.3 and 7.5 indicate that Superior tasks, in general, were similarly
scaled by both the Texas teachers and the ACTFL Guidelines. However,
Intermediate and Advanced level tasks seem to be totally intertwined.

One of the advantages of the Rasch model is its ability to examine fit
and to incorporate information to continually assess and improve the quality
of a measure. In an analysis of the fit of the speaking tasks, the standardized
mean square outfit statistic, a common criterion, was used. For the purposes
of this study, all tasks with a standardized outfit statistic above 2 were considered misfitting. Tasks with an outfit below -2 are considered overly
consistent or overfitting (not contributing unique information to the
measurement), and were not a concern of this study, as the purpose of the
original project was not to construct a measure. Misfitting tasks have been
marked with three asterisks (***) in Table 7.3. Six tasks (16%) were misfitting
by this criterion. From most misfitting to least these were: 'Make Purchases',
'Order a Meal', 'Introduce Yourself', 'Give a Professional Talk', 'Describe
Expected Future Events' and 'Talk about Family Members'. Given the
criterion, the tasks have generally scaled well, though there is not overwhelm-
ing evidence for the hypothesis that a unidimensional construct underlies
these data. Generally, less than 10% of the items should be misfitting before
adequate fit is claimed.

One of the facets in this analysis was group membership. Table 7.6
shows the results for this facet. The calibration logit indicates that the least
and the most severe groups differed by less than 0.06 logit. This difference
is not much greater than the model error (0.03) for the most lenient group,
the French teachers. Thus, group membership of the teachers did not contribute much to the overall severity of the scaling of the tasks. In terms of fit,
however, the French group showed itself to be extraordinarily consistent,

while the bilingual education group had a high incidence, on a group level, of misfit (inconsistent ratings). This indicates that the members of these two groups may well have viewed the underlying construct quite differently.

Table 7.6 Results of analysis of the groups facet

Groups	Logit	Model error	Outfit statistic
French	−0.68	0.03	−7
Spanish	−0.73	0.02	0
Bilingual	−0.74	0.01	9

The last facet was the teacher. Applying widely-used criteria of fit to the teachers indicated some misfit. In terms of the outfit mean squared statistic, of the 380 teachers without perfect ratings, for the standardized outfit statistic only 29 teachers (7.6%) had a statistic above two. Of these, 23 (79%) were bilingual education teachers and six (21%) were Spanish language teachers. None of the French teachers were inconsistent with the entire group.

In summary, Study 1 suggests that classroom teachers recognize those speaking tasks which require the greatest amount of ability to perform (the 12 Superior level tasks) in a manner generally consistent with the ACTFL Guidelines. However, they do not tend to rank the ability required to perform the remaining 26 Advanced and Intermediate speaking tasks in a manner consistent with the ACTFL Guidelines.

The analysis of fit also suggests that the groups of teachers may have been operating with different understandings of the construct. Thus, in Study 2, we analyze and compare the results of scaling the speaking tasks by the French and Spanish language teachers alone and by the bilingual education teachers alone.

Study 2

Table 7.7 duplicates Table 7.3, except that it presents the results of the scaling of all 38 speaking tasks by the French and Spanish teachers only. The Rasch equivalent to the KR20 reliability of the tasks measure was 0.99.

Table 7.8 duplicates Table 7.5 in presenting the comparison of the ranking of all 38 speaking tasks as scaled by the French and Spanish language teachers with their ranking based on their *a priori* designations.

Table 7.7 Scaling of the 38 speaking tasks for French and Spanish teachers only

Logit	Task		Error
13.00	(S)	Describe a Complex Object in Detail	0.18
12.98	(S)	Give a Professional Talk	0.18
12.80	(S)	Explain a Complex Process in Detail	0.18
12.34	(S)	Explain a Complex Process of a Personal Nature	0.18
12.28	(S)	Discuss a Professional Topic	0.18
12.24	(S)	Evaluate Issues Surrounding a Conflict	0.18
12.12	(S)	Hypothesize About Probable Outcomes	0.18
11.24	(S)	Hypothesize About an Impersonal Topic	0.18
11.06	(S)	Change Someone's Behavior through Persuasion	0.18
10.90	(S)	Propose & Defend a Course of Action with Persuasion	0.18
10.88	(A)	Correct an Unexpected Situation	0.18
10.76	(S)	State Personal Point of View (Controversial Subject)	0.18
10.76	(A)	Hypothesize About a Personal Situation	0.18
10.56	(S)	Support Opinions	0.20
10.10	(A)	Lodge a Complaint	0.20
9.88	(A)	State Advantages and Disadvantages	0.20
9.82	(A)	Give Advice	0.20
9.31	(I)	Describe Health Problems	0.20
8.87	(I)	Talk About Your Future Plans	0.22
8.51	(A)	Give a Brief Organized Factual Summary	0.22
8.43	(I)	Make Arrangements for Future Activities	0.22
7.83	(A)	Describe Habitual Actions in the Past	0.24
7.79	(A)	Compare and Contrast Two Objects or Places	0.24
7.41	(A)	Describe Expected Future Events	0.26
7.13	(I)	Give a Brief Personal History	0.26
6.81	(A)	Express Personal Apologies	0.28
6.43	(I)	Talk About Personal Activities	0.30
6.19	(I)	Describe a Place	0.30
6.13	(A)	Explain a Familiar Simple Process	0.30
5.95	(I)	Make Purchases***	0.32
5.79	(A)	Describe a Sequence of Events in the Past	0.32
5.23	(I)	Give Directions	0.36
5.23	(I)	Order a Meal***	0.36
5.17	(A)	Describe Typical Routines	0.36
5.17	(A)	Give Instructions	0.36
4.95	(I)	Describe Your Daily Routine	0.38
4.43	(I)	Talk About Family Members	0.42
1.00	(I)	Introduce Yourself***	0.84

*** = Positive outfit (standardized mean square) > 2

Table 7.8 Comparing the *a priori* classifications with the actual scaling by French and Spanish language teachers 'Best case scenario'

A priori expected ordering	Actual scaling		
	I	A	S
I (12)	8	4	0
A (14)	4	10	0
S (12)	0	0	12
Correct Order	8 (67%)	10 (71%)	12 (100%)

Again, Table 7.8 presents a 'best case' scenario. The grouping takes measurement error into consideration. In this scaling, only one pair was affected. 'Correct an Unexpected Situation', designated an Advanced task but scaled among the top 12 tasks is considered to have been scaled as an Advanced task, while 'Support Opinions', designated a Superior task but scaled among the middle 14 tasks, is viewed as having been scaled a Superior task.

Tables 7.7 and 7.8 indicate that when analyzed separately, the scaling of the speaking tasks by the language teachers alone much more closely approximates the scaling according to the ACTFL scale than the scaling based on the data from all teachers together.

As for fit, only three of the six tasks that were misfitting in the first study remained so for these teachers: 'Introduce Yourself', 'Order a Meal', and 'Make Purchases'. 'Talk about Family Members', 'Give a Professional Talk' and 'Describe Expected Future Events' were no longer misfitting. This outcome lends support to the hypothesis that for these teachers, a unidimensional construct underlies these data.

Table 7.9 shows the results of the calibration and fit analysis for group membership. The calibration logit indicates that although there was a minor differences between the two groups in terms of their overall severity, with the Spanish teachers generally awarding higher ratings (i.e. the tasks were less difficult) than the French teachers. However, in terms of fit, we again see that these two groups appear to be operating differently in their understanding of the underlying construct. As a group, the French teachers are very consistent in their approach, while the Spanish teachers are more prone to awarding outlying ratings.

Table 7.9 Results of analysis of the groups facet French vs. Spanish teachers

Groups	Calib. logit	Model error	Outfit statistic	
Spanish	−0.60	0.02	9	(Lower ratings)
French	−0.75	0.03	−5	(Higher ratings)

On the level of the individual teacher, 12 teachers (7%) were misfitting. All of these, however, were Spanish language teachers. Again, none of the individual French teachers were misfitting.

Let us now examine the results of the scaling of the speaking tasks by the bilingual education teachers alone. Table 7.10 parallels Table 7.7, presenting the results of the scaling of the 38 speaking tasks by the bilingual education teachers only. The reliability of the tasks measure was 0.98.

Table 7.11 parallels Table 7.8 in presenting the comparison of the ranking of the 38 speaking tasks as scaled by the French and Spanish language teachers with their ranking based on their *a priori* designations.

Again, Table 7.11 presents a 'best case' scenario in that the scaling takes measurement error into consideration. Thus, 'Make Purchases', an Intermediate task, was exchanged with 'State Personal Point of View (Controversial Subject)', a Superior task.

Tables 7.10 and 7.11 indicate that when analyzed separately, the scaling of the speaking tasks by the bilingual education teachers diverges much more from the scaling according to the ACTFL scale than for either the group of teachers as a whole, or, in particular, for the French and Spanish teachers.

As for fit, the tasks scaled better for the bilingual education group by themselves than for the entire group. Only four (11%) were misfitting, all of which were also identified in Study 1, and three which were likewise misfitting for the language teachers. However, two of the six from Study 1 were no longer misfitting: 'Express Personal Apologies', and 'Talk About Family Members'.

As for the teacher facet, only eight teachers (3%) had a standardized outfit statistic above two. The low amount of misfit for tasks and teachers indicate the validity of the scaling of the speaking tasks by this group. As a group, these teachers were very consistent in how they felt about the level of ability required to perform these speaking tasks.

Table 7.10 Scaling of the 38 speaking tasks for bilingual education teachers only

Logit	Task		Error
13.00	(S)	Describe a Complex Object in Detail	0.31
12.65	(S)	Explain a Complex Process of a Personal Nature	0.31
12.46	(S)	Give a Professional Talk***	0.31
12.07	(S)	Explain a Complex Process in Detail	0.31
11.83	(I)	Talk About Your Future Plans	0.31
11.76	(S)	Discuss a Professional Topic	0.31
11.72	(S)	Evaluate Issues Surrounding a Conflict	0.31
11.56	(A)	Describe Habitual Actions in the Past	0.31
11.41	(A)	Correct an Unexpected Situation	0.31
11.33	(A)	Lodge a Complaint	0.31
11.10	(I)	Make Purchases***	0.31
11.02	(S)	Hypothesize About an Impersonal Topic	0.31
10.94	(A)	Hypothesize About a Personal Situation	0.31
10.90	(I)	Order a Meal***	0.31
10.75	(S)	State Personal Point of View (Controversial Subject)	0.31
10.59	(S)	Hypothesize About Probable Outcomes	0.31
10.44	(I)	Describe Health Problems	0.31
10.36	(I)	Talk About Personal Activities	0.35
10.01	(I)	Give a Brief Personal History	0.35
9.85	(S)	Support Opinions	0.35
9.85	(I)	Make Arrangements for Future Activities	0.35
9.66	(S)	Propose & Defend a Course of Action with Persuasion	0.35
9.27	(I)	Talk About Family Members	0.35
9.19	(A)	Give a Brief Organized Factual Summary	0.35
9.04	(A)	State Advantages and Disadvantages	0.35
8.84	(A)	Compare and Contrast Two Objects or Places	0.35
8.46	(S)	Change Someone's Behavior through Persuasion	0.39
7.91	(A)	Give Advice	0.39
7.41	(A)	Describe Expected Future Events	0.39
7.41	(I)	Describe Your Daily Routine	0.39
7.33	(A)	Express Personal Apologies	0.39
7.06	(I)	Describe a Place	0.43
5.78	(A)	Explain a Familiar Simple Process	0.47
5.50	(A)	Describe a Sequence of Events in the Past	0.47
5.31	(I)	Give Directions	0.47
5.23	(A)	Describe Typical Routines	0.47
2.59	(I)	Introduce Yourself***	0.62
1.00	(A)	Give Instructions	0.74

*** = Positive outfit (standardized mean square) > 2

Table 7.11 Comparing the *a priori* classifications with the actual scaling by bilingual education teachers 'Best case scenario'

A priori expected ordering	Actual scaling		
	I	A	S
I (12)	4	7	1
A (14)	7	4	3
S (12)	1	3	8
Correct Order	4 (33%)	4 (29%)	8 (66%)

Discussion of the Studies

As pointed out earlier, this discussion is in the context of test construction rather than data analysis. However, we do want to examine whether the ordering of the tasks by the randomly sampled Texas classroom teachers across three disciplines reflects the ordering based on the ACTFL scale. The FACETS program has provided much information that is useful to understanding what happened in this survey.

First, the teachers discriminated between the 38 speaking tasks. This is seen in the logit calibrations presented in Tables 7.3, 7.7 and 7.10. The low level of misfit among all three analyses for the teachers as individuals indicate that they were able to rather consistently apply an understanding of the task they were asked to do and award a rating to each speaking task.

Second, the three groups of teachers appeared to apply different standards. In Study 1, on the group level, the bilingual education teachers showed an extraordinary amount of misfit. These teachers comprised 79% of the misfitting teachers (although they only comprised 57% of the survey population). The distinction between the language teachers and the bilingual education teachers was more clearly shown in Study 2. There, each subgroup had a better fit (only three or four misfitting speaking tasks and a small percentage of individual misfitting teachers) than for the combined group. The fit statistics for the French and Spanish groups suggest that even these two groups may be analyzed separately.

Three, although consistent as single groups, the two subgroups differed radically in their scaling of the 38 speaking tasks. The language teachers scaled the tasks in a way that, when compared with the group as a whole, more closely approaches the scaling according to the ACTFL Guidelines.

The bilingual education teachers diverged quite greatly from the Guidelines. While all the tasks viewed as Superior according to the Guidelines were also scaled as Superior by the language teachers, only eight of these 12 tasks were scaled as Superior by the bilingual ed. teachers. In fact, one Superior task, 'Change Someone's Behavior through Persuasion', was scaled among the bottom 12 tasks for the bilingual ed. teachers, while the Intermediate task, 'Talk About Your Future Plans', was scaled among the top 12 tasks.

Why may have this happened? We would like to suggest that three factors may have been involved. First, the language teachers through their training may have been more metalinguistically alert to the issues involved in the question of the amount of ability required to perform these speaking tasks. The tasks themselves may have been ones they have had experience with in their classroom teaching. The training of the bilingual education teachers more likely focused on content and pedagogy than on the development of linguistic awareness. One indication of this is that the language teachers scaled 'Introduce Yourself' as the easiest task, whereas the bilingual ed. teachers scaled 'Give Instructions' as the easiest. Perhaps the bilingual ed. teachers felt 'Give Instructions' was the task they most often perform in the classroom, and thus gave it a rating of '5' on the survey more often than they awarded a '5' to 'Introduce Yourself', a task requiring minimal ability in a foreign language.

Second, the number of native speakers of the language was probably far fewer for the language teachers (particularly the French teachers) than for the bilingual ed. teachers, 87% of whom indicated they were hispanic. This may have been a contributing factor.

Third, some of the language teachers, through their training and experience, may have had experience with the ACTFL Guidelines and the associated proficiency concepts. Although no mention is made of the Guidelines in the survey, and the task asked of the recipients was not directly to scale the tasks as has been done in these studies, there may have been some influence. The ACTFL Guidelines are most likely virtually unknown to the bilingual education teachers.

Considering the above speculations, even the scaling by the language teachers was not as close as may have been expected. To what extent may the wording on the survey instrument have influenced this outcome? Rasch analysis, as a measurement model, provides much feedback regarding the instrument. Let us examine what we learn about the survey instrument from the Rasch analysis.

First, three speaking tasks were consistently misfitting across both the language and the bilingual education teachers: 'Make Purchases', 'Order a Meal' and 'Introduce Yourself'. These are presented in Table 7.12 as taken from the original survey. All were *a priori* designated as at the Intermediate level. Upon closer examination, two of them ('Make Purchases' and 'Order a Meal') seem very different from the other 36 tasks (see Appendix 2). These two tasks seem very concrete and less dependent on linguistic skills. One may be able to fulfil these tasks in another country through signs and gestures without any proficiency in a foreign language at all. On the other hand, each could potentially involve complications requiring much linguistic skill. Perhaps teachers as a group had trouble picturing just how much ability would be involved in performing these tasks. This could account for the lack of consistency among the teachers in assigning a rating to these tasks.

'Introduce Yourself' was located as item number 1 on the survey and very few teachers awarded it less than a '5'. An item consistently receiving an extreme score by the vast majority of raters is highly susceptible to statistically being indicated as misfitting if a few raters award it another rating. This is most likely what happened here.

Table 7.12 Speaking tasks that were misfitting in all groups as presented in the survey

Task no.	Task
1.	*Introduce Yourself* Be able to give your name and basic personal information such as would be given at a first meeting.
6.	*Make Purchases* Be able to request items, discuss prices, and handle currency in a situation involving a purchase.
14.	*Order a Meal* Be able to ask questions about menu items, order food, and ask for and settle a bill.

However, even with discounting the misfitting tasks, there is still an intermingling of the Intermediate and Advanced level tasks in the scaling, even for the language teachers. If the ACTFL scaling were valid, why might this have happened? First, in the set of speaking tasks as presented to the teachers, the discourse type required (sentences, paragraphs, extended discourse), one of the important characteristics that distinguishes the Intermediate, Advanced and Superior levels of the ACTFL scale, appears to have been inadequately incorporated into the task descriptions, if at all. Briefly, the Guidelines posit that Intermediate level speakers use 'sentence-level' discourse. Intermediate level tasks can be accomplished with such discourse. Advanced level speakers use 'paragraph-level' discourse to narrate and describe. To carry out tasks at the Advanced level, more organized speech is required. Tasks at the Superior level require an extended level of discourse, in which thoughts are elaborated into 'paragraphs' and these are solidly connected to get meaning across.

The expected discourse type required to perform the task was clearly lacking in the description of most of the speaking tasks that were designated *a priori* as Intermediate but scaled by the language teachers as requiring much ability to perform. For example, 'Describe Health Problems' was designated *a priori* as Intermediate. As an Intermediate level task, however, the expectation is that one can say, at the sentence level, 'I have a pain in my stomach', but not necessarily go into great detail. In completing this survey, the language teachers may well have pictured to themselves much more complicated discourse. Similarly, the survey did not make clear that the expectation for fulfilling other high-ranking Intermediate level tasks, such as 'Talk About Your Future Plans', 'Make Arrangements for Future Activities' and 'Give a Brief Personal History' was simple sentence-level discourse.

In contrast, the description of the Superior level tasks on the survey tended to convey the idea of complexity by using words and phrases such as 'abstract', 'complex', 'controversial', 'explain in detail' and 'discuss at length'. Perhaps such descriptions more adequately gave, to the language teachers at least, a sense of the complexity of the discourse required to perform the Superior level tasks.

There is evidence that a second trend, frequency of use in class, was also operating among this set of language teachers. This trend may have worked to place certain Advanced speaking tasks lower on the scale than expected. Three of the four easiest ranked Advanced tasks ('Give Instructions', 'Describe Typical Routines' and 'Explain a Familiar Simple Process') are tasks that may actually occur in the classroom on a frequent basis. Thus, when the teachers were asked whether a teacher in Texas needed the ability to perform this task, they may have ranked these as '5' (Definitely Yes). In terms of linguistic ability, these tasks cannot satisfactorily be completed using sentence level discourse, since in most cases an organized, elaborated response would definitely be required. As mentioned previously, there is evidence that this trend may have been even stronger among the bilingual education teachers.

The FACETS analysis revealed a wealth of information helpful in understanding what may have been going on in this survey. The randomly-surveyed teachers did generally perceive a single trait as underlying the tasks, although this was more true in the subgroups than as a whole. Where the task description matched the intent of the Guidelines, results for the language teachers were as expected, though results for the bilingual education teachers were more confusing. In our opinion, this study does provide some evidence to support the validity of the Guidelines as a scale of speaking ability. Were such a survey to be undertaken again, a greater effort should be made to better match the task descriptions to the levels of the Guidelines and to include sample speaking tasks with appropriate responses for the meta-linguistically naive. If such a survey were taken, we believe that the teachers would even more closely scale the speaking tasks in accordance with the Guidelines.

References

American Council on the Teaching of Foreign Languages (1986) *ACTFL Proficiency Guidelines*. Hastings-on-Hudson, NY: ACTFL.

Bachman, L. F. and Savignon, S. J. (1986) The evaluation of communicative language proficiency: A critique of the ACTFL oral interview. *The Modern Language Journal* 70, 380–90.

Clark, J. L. D. and Lett, J. (1988) A research agenda. In P. Lowe, Jr and C. W. Stansfield (eds) *Second Language Proficiency Assessment: Current Issues*. Englewood Cliffs, NJ: Prentice Hall Regents.

Lantolf, J. P. and Frawley, W. (1985) Oral proficiency testing: a critical analysis. *The Modern Language Journal* 69, 337–45.

Linacre, J. M. and Wright, B. D. (1990) *FACETS: Rasch-model Computer Program* Version 2.4. Chicago: MESA Press.

Liskin-Gasparro, J. (1987) *Testing and Teaching for Oral Proficiency*. Boston: Heinle & Heinle Publishers.

Omaggio, A. C. (1986) *Teaching Language in Context*. Boston: Heinle & Heinle.

Shohamy, E. (1990) Language testing priorities: A different perspective. *Foreign Language Annals* 23, 385–94.

Stansfield, C. W. (1989) Simulated oral proficiency interviews. *ERIC Digest*. Washington, DC: Center for Applied Linguistics.

Stansfield, C. W. and Kenyon, D. M. (1991) *Development of the Texas Oral Proficiency Test (TOPT): Final Report*. Washington, DC: Center for Applied Linguistics. (ERIC Document Reproduction Service, ED 332 522.)

Torgerson, W. S. (1958). *Theory and Methods of Scaling*. New York: John Wiley & Sons.

Wright, B. D. and Masters, G. N. (1982) *Rating Scale Analysis: Rasch Measurement*. Chicago: MESA Press.

Appendix 1: Structure of the TOPT – Spanish

Task	Item	Level	Speaking Task
	Warm-up	I	Answer personal questions
1	Picture 1	I	Give Directions
2	Picture 2	I	Describe a place/activities
3	Picture 3	A	Narrate in present time
4	Picture 4	A	Narrate in past time
5	Picture 5	A	Narrate in future time
6	Topic 1	A	Give instructions
7	Topic 2	A	State advantages/disadvantages
8	Topic 3	A	Give a brief factual summary
9	Topic 4	S	Support an opinion
10	Topic 5	S	Hypothesize on an impersonal topic
11	Situation 1	A	Speak with tact
12	Situation 2	S	Speak to persuade someone
13	Situation 3	S	Propose and defend a course of action
14	Situation 4	S	Give a professional talk
15	Situation 5	A	Give advice
	Wind down	I	

Key

A = Advanced
I = Intermediate
S = Superior

Appendix 2: Texas Oral Proficiency Test (TOPT). Bilingual education teachers

JOB-RELATEDNESS SURVEY

RETURN BY MAY 4, 1990

INTRODUCTION

The Texas Education Agency is developing a test of oral proficiency in Spanish which will be required of individuals seeking a certificate or an endorsement for bilingual education. The Texas Oral Proficiency Test in Spanish (TOPT-Spanish) will be a tape-mediated test. From a master tape and via a test booklet, examinees will be presented with approximately twenty speaking tasks. These tasks will allow them to demonstrate their ability to speak Spanish. Successful performance of these tasks requires various levels of Spanish speaking ability; some are fairly easy to perform, while others are considerably more challenging. The examinees' responses will be recorded on examinee response tapes. After examinees complete the test, their performance, as recorded on the tapes, will be scored by trained raters.

This survey presents you with 38 speaking tasks, such as may appear on the TOPT-Spanish. For each task, you are to indicate whether, in your professional opinion, bilingual education teachers need to have the **ABILITY** to carry out this task in order to perform successfully in bilingual education classrooms in the state of Texas. Note that the question is not whether bilingual education teachers need to carry out the task in the classroom, but whether bilingual education teachers need the **level of ability** necessary to carry out the task.

You are one of a sample of Texas bilingual education teachers selected to receive this survey. The results will assist the TEA in determining the level of speaking skills in Spanish needed by bilingual education teachers in Texas. Your responses are important and your assistance to the TEA is appreciated.

DIRECTIONS

Your survey packet contains: this survey booklet, a blue and white machine-readable survey response sheet, and a stamped, pre-addressed return envelope. Note that data for this survey are being collected with machine-readable response sheets. Please **do not fold** the survey response sheets.

There are five steps to completing this survey. Follow all directions carefully and use a **No. 2 pencil**. It is estimated that this survey will require **15 to 20 minutes** to complete.

STEP 1   ID NUMBER

Please write your social security number in the boxes in the area entitled ID NUMBER on the top left-hand corner of the machine-readable survey response sheet. Then fill in the circle corresponding to the number in each box. NOTE: Your social security number will only be used for data processing purposes and will not be used to identify any individual respondent to this survey.

EXAMPLE

This is what your response sheet would look like if your social security number were 123-45-6789:

STEP 2   DEMOGRAPHIC INFORMATION

For demographic purposes, please answer each lettered question presented on the next page in the box labeled DEMOGRAPHIC INFORMATION. Write your answer in the area entitled SPECIAL CODES on the top left-hand corner of the response sheet. For each lettered question (A through G), write the number of your answer in the block on the answer sheet. Then fill in the circle corresponding to the number of your answer.

EXAMPLE

This is what your response sheet would look like if you were an elementary school teacher (Question A) with a certificate in bilingual education (Question B) and between 3 and 5 years of experience (Question C), etc.:

DEMOGRAPHIC INFORMATION

A. What is your current level of assignment?

(0) Elementary   (2) High School
(1) Junior High or Middle School   (3) Other

B. Do you hold a certificate or endorsement in bilingual education?

(0) Yes
(1) No

C. How many years of bilingual education teaching experience do you have?

(0) 1-2 years   (3) 11-15 years
(1) 3-5 years   (4) 16-19 years
(2) 6-10 years   (5) 20 or more years

D. What levels of bilingual classes have you taught during the past three years? (select only one)

(0) Early Childhood
(1) Grades 1-3
(2) Grades 4-6

E. What is the highest degree that you hold?

(0) No degree   (2) Master's
(1) Bachelor's   (3) Doctorate

F. What is your ethnic group?

(0) Hispanic   (2) White
(1) Black   (3) Other

G. What is your sex?

(0) Male   (1) Female

STEP 3   RESPONSES TO SPEAKING TASKS

Listed on the survey response sheet is a series of speaking tasks requiring various degrees of language ability to perform. For each task, indicate whether, in your professional opinion, bilingual education teachers need to have the **language ability** necessary to carry out the task in order to perform successfully in a bilingual classroom. In other words, for each task, ask yourself:

Is the **level of ability**
required to perform this task
needed by bilingual education teachers
in Texas public schools?

Important: The question is NOT "Do bilingual teachers need to carry out this task in the classroom?" Rather, the question is "Do bilingual education teachers need to have the Spanish language **ability** to carry out this task?"

Fill in the letter that represents your response to this question in the appropriate column on the response sheet. The columns are as follows:

A	=	Definitely Yes
B	=	Probably Yes
C	=	Maybe
D	=	Probably No
E	=	Definitely No

Following the examples below are detailed descriptions of the speaking tasks. Be sure to read them before making your response.

EXAMPLES
  Here are two example tasks with responses completed for you:

Example A

Extend an Invitation

Be able to politely invite someone to your home for a party or other social function.

If, in your opinion, bilingual education teachers should __definitely__ have the __level of ability__ required to perform this speaking task (independent of whether they would need to do the task in the classroom), then you would darken circle "A" in the first column of the response sheet.

Example B

Negotiate Renting Temporary Living Quarters

Be able to negotiate a rental agreement with a landlord, ask questions about
what is included in the rent, and ask for clarification of the rental agreement.

If, in your opinion, bilingual education teachers should **probably** *have the* **level of ability**
*required to perform this speaking task (independent of whether they would need to do the
task in the classroom), then you would darken circle "B" in the second column of the
response sheet.*

*If you made the above two responses to the example tasks, your survey response sheet
would look like this:*

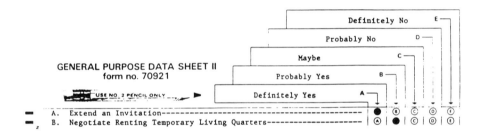

Now please make your response for each of the 38 speaking tasks listed on the
following pages on the appropriate line of the survey response sheet.
Remember to ask yourself, for each task:

> **Is the level of ability**
> required to perform this task
> needed by bilingual education teachers
> in Texas public schools?

SPEAKING TASKS

1. Introduce Yourself

    Be able to give your name and basic personal information such as would be given at a first meeting.

2. Explain a Familiar, Simple Process

    Be able to explain how to accomplish everyday processes such as writing a check, borrowing a book from the library, or taking attendance in the classroom.

3. Describe a Sequence of Events in the Past

    Be able to use and sequence language indicating past time in order to narrate an event or incident which occurred recently.

4. Propose and Defend a Course of Action with Persuasion

    In light of at least two possible choices of action, be able to propose and defend a course of action in such a way as to persuade others to accept your choice.

5. Describe Typical Routines

    Be able to use and sequence language indicating present or habitual time in order to narrate recurring events or routines, everyday activities, etc.

6. Make Purchases

    Be able to request items, discuss prices, and handle currency in a situation involving a purchase.

7. Talk About Personal Activities

    Be able to talk about your leisure activities, favorite pastimes, and preferred hobbies.

8. Hypothesize About an Impersonal Topic

    Be able to discuss various possibilities ("what if" situations) surrounding an abstract, impersonal topic.

[FOR SURVEY PURPOSES ONLY]

9.   Talk About Family Members

       Be able to give the names of the members of your family and simple descriptive
       information, such as their occupations and physical characteristics.

10.   Give a Brief, Organized Factual Summary

       Be able to summarize in an "oral report" fashion factual information about
       topics of a personal or professional nature.

11.   State Your Personal Point of View on a Controversial Subject

       Be able to state what you believe on a controversial subject and why you hold
       those beliefs.

12.   Describe Expected Future Events

       Be able to use and sequence language indicating future time in order to narrate
       expected occurrences of a personal nature, such as a planned trip or activity.

13.   Explain a Complex Process in Detail

       Be able to explain in detail a non-routine process of an impersonal nature, such
       as how to carry out a scientific investigation or how to write a term paper.

14.   Order a Meal

       Be able to ask questions about menu items, order food, and ask for and settle a
       bill.

15.ʹ   Express Personal Apologies

       Be able to apologize clearly and appropriately to an offended party.

16.   Give Advice

       Be able to give advice to someone faced with making a decision between two or
       more choices, giving supporting reasons for the advice given.

17.   Hypothesize About a Personal Situation

       Be able to say what you would do in a hypothetical situation.

                         [FOR SURVEY PURPOSES ONLY]

18.   Describe Your Daily Routine

       Be able to narrate your typical daily activities.

19.   Give Instructions

       Be able to give instructions and explain the steps involved in carrying out an
       activity.

20.   Give a Brief Personal History

       Be able to talk about your personal background.

21.   State Advantages and Disadvantages

       Be able to state the advantages and disadvantages of a situation (such as living
       in a big city), a decision (such as going to college), or an object that has
       affected society (such as the computer).

22.   Support Opinions

       Be able to state, support and defend a personally-held opinion or belief about
       an issue.

23.   Describe Health Problems

       Be able to describe health problems or conditions.

24.   Discuss a Professional Topic

       Be able to discuss at length and in detail a topic of professional interest.

25.   Describe a Complex Object in Detail

       Be able to describe a complex object such as a car or bicycle in detail and with
       precise vocabulary.

26.   Lodge a Complaint

       Be able to lodge a complaint, giving the reasons for and details behind the
       complaint.

                        [FOR SURVEY PURPOSES ONLY]

27. <u>Talk About Your Future Plans</u>

Be able to state and describe your personal or professional plans, goals and ambitions.

28. <u>Give a Professional Talk</u>

Be able to present a talk on a topic of professional interest.

29. <u>Make Arrangements for Future Activities</u>

Be able to inquire about and to make arrangements for future activities, and to set the date, time and place.

30. <u>Evaluate Issues Surrounding a Conflict</u>

Be able to present arguments on both sides of a familiar issue or topic and evaluate their relative merits.

31. <u>Give Directions</u>

Be able to give directions on how to get from one place to another.

32. <u>Describe a Place</u>

Be able to describe in detail a particular place, such as a school, a store, or a park.

33. <u>Explain a Complex Process of a Personal Nature</u>

Be able to describe and explain in detail a non-routine process such as how to get a job, or how to apply to college.

34. <u>Hypothesize About Probable Outcomes</u>

Be able to discuss what could happen if something unexpected occurs.

35. <u>Correct an Unexpected Situation</u>

Be able to handle an unexpected outcome, such as receiving faulty merchandise.

[FOR SURVEY PURPOSES ONLY]

36.   Change Someone's Behavior through Persuasion

Be able to persuade someone to do something he or she is not inclined to do, or to cease doing something which is annoying to you.

37.   Describe Habitual Actions in the Past

Be able to describe people, places or things in the past, such as the work schedule you used to have or leisure activities you used to do.

38.   Compare and Contrast Two Objects or Places

Be able to compare and contrast two objects, places, or customs.

STEP 4   ADDITIONAL COMMENTS

Please use the space provided in the three WRITE-IN AREAS on the back of the survey response sheet for any additional comments you wish to make regarding the oral language functions to be included on the TOPT-Spanish.

STEP 5   RETURNING THE SURVEY

Unfold the enclosed pre-addressed, stamped envelope. Insert the blue and white machine-readable survey response sheet into the envelope, being careful not to fold it. Return **the machine-readable survey response sheet only** as soon as possible, but postmarked no later than **MAY 4, 1990**, to:

> Mr. Dorry Kenyon
> Center for Applied Linguistics
> 1118 22nd Street, NW
> Washington, DC 20037

Thank you for your participation in this survey.

RETURN BY MAY 4, 1990

8 A Communicative Test in Analysis: Strategies in Reading Authentic Texts

INGRID F. WIJGH

The introduction of a communicative section in the Dutch final examinations in reading comprehension at the end of secondary education aimed to include a broad variety of text types as well as to elicit more varied reading behaviors, particularly to assess the quality of students' strategies for reading in foreign languages and to determine if they could adjust their reading strategies to their reading goals and to the text types in question. We set up a validation study to find out if 13 students' behaviors were adequate for these purposes, using thinking-aloud methods to trace these students' reading strategies, which produced protocol analyses of students' actual reading behavior that we compared to the idealized, intended behavior as formulated by the researchers.

Foreign language teaching and testing in Dutch secondary education have increasingly oriented themselves towards communicative language learning. This trend toward communicative language education is evident in the national criteria developed for foreign language learning in the first stage of secondary education as well as in the final examinations at the end of secondary education. The present chapter focuses on MAVO, Junior General Secondary Education, which is a four-year education cycle attended by about 35% of the total school population.

Since 1986, final examinations for reading comprehension in French, English and German have consisted of two sections; a traditional and a communicative one. In the traditional section, candidates answer about 40 multiple-choice questions on edited texts laid out uniformly. In addition, in the communicative section, candidates answer about 10 multiple-choice questions on a variety of short texts in their original lay-out.

All eyes in The Netherlands were focused on this latter section when it was introduced in 1986. Teachers, test constructors, as well as others related to schools watched this change in the existing examinations, a rare thing, and difficult to bring about. Generally speaking, the new items were welcomed by teachers and pupils with some enthusiasm; they were not short on face validity. Nor was this new section of the test condemned by psychometricians. The item difficulty of the communicative items did not differ much from that of the traditional ones, nor did the new items appear to affect the reliability of the examination.

Does this mean that the introduction of a communicative section in the final examination was an improvement that enabled students to show they were good readers? Even though final examinations have been product-oriented by tradition, this changing situation prompted test constructors to ask seriously what kinds of communicative reading processes they were actually testing. Under the influence of the communicative methodology they became more interested in reading goals and reading strategies. A shift was taking place from product to process orientations, from text comprehension to reading skills. The communicative part of the examination aimed at testing efficient uses of reading strategies in view of a given reading goal.

Psychometric data and positive reactions, however, did not provide sufficient information on the behavioral component of the new section of the reading test. For this reason, the present validation project was initiated, its main question being: Does the real-life behavior of the candidates correspond to the behavior aimed at by the test constructors? The validation study mainly concentrated on the construct of *reading skills*, meaning the psychological processes students use preceding their proper comprehension of a text. It was the test constructors' aim to elicit such reading processes as students' selection of relevant information, formulation of hypotheses about the content of a text, and use of world knowledge while reading. The validation study aimed to examine whether discrepancies existed between the behaviors demonstrated in the testing situation and this construct of reading skills.

Characteristics of the Communicative Test

The communicative philosophy of reading underpinning the test can be summarized in the question, In *what situations* do we read *which texts* for *which purposes*? Test constructors had characterized relevant *situations* in a general way as 'leisure time' and 'tourism'. The starting point for test development was an inventory of text types and tasks based on such objectives for reading as understanding the gist of a paragraph, identifying relevant information, comparing information, or drawing conclusions. Wherever possible, the *purposes* of the tasks on the tests were related to these text types.

The communicative section of the examination consisted of 10 short *texts* such as leaflets, brochures, photographs with subscripts, classified ads, or short news items. The multiple-choice questions accompanying the texts were presented in candidates' mother tongue (i.e. Dutch) so as not to cause problems in the understanding of the examination questions.

The texts had to meet the following criteria:

- they must correspond with the intellectual level of 16-year-old students;
- their subject matter must be of interest to that age group;
- their difficulty must be in accordance with the foreign-language proficiency of the students;
- they must be authentic and in the original lay-out, not edited nor specially written for educational purposes.

The principles for communicative language learning guiding test construction suggested that pupils should know how to handle different text types as well as to be effective and efficient readers, adjusting their strategies to their reading goals. So the test tasks and questions had to elicit specific behaviors related to a particular text type and reading goal. The present validation study aimed to find out if pupils really did this, specifically in terms of their reading strategies.

Research Questions

The validation study addressed the principal question: Does the reading behavior intended by test-constructors correspond to the real-life behavior of the students? This question was specified into four sub-questions:

- *How do students react when they meet with unknown words?* By definition, authentic texts contain more unknown words than edited texts traditionally used in the exams. Does this difference have a negative psychological effect? Are pupils confused by a greater number of unknown words than usual? Does this hinder them in the fulfilment of their task?
- *Do students select their strategies according to the task set?* Or do they use the same strategy, regardless of the specific task? In other words is their behavior task-based or learner-based?
- *Are students able to select the most efficient strategy for each task?* Or do they use trial-and-error methods? If so, does the factor of time influence their finding correct answers?
- *Do students make use of extra-linguistic information?* For example, in the form of illustrations, photographs, or text lay-out. Do they use their knowledge of the world in answering the questions?

Method

The study was carried out by two researchers, both of them experienced test constructors, who followed the research questions with the guiding aim of coming to know students' behavior on the reading tests in the most direct way possible. For this reason, think-aloud protocols formed the methodology for the study. We adopted research steps prescribed by Elshout, a Dutch cognitive psychologist (Breuker *et al.*, 1986), who based his techniques on Ericsson & Simon's (1984) methods for gathering and analyzing verbal reports. Although Dutch cognitive psychologists usually use think-aloud methods for concept-development and theory-building, the present circumstances called for validation of a test instrument, which required some adaptation of Elshout's original scheme. The study had no need to develop a new theory of reading; rather, the purpose of the study was confirmatory.

Protocol analyses present three well-known problems: (1) subjectivity, (2) introspection on the part of the test-taker and (3) interpretation on the part of the researcher in analyzing the protocols. The present study tried to avoid these pitfalls in the following ways. The two researchers doing the study analyzed the protocols independently of each other, comparing their interpretations afterwards. The same procedure was used when describing the ideal behavior for each task. There was scarcely any disagreement between the two descriptions or between the results of the protocol analyses, so it was decided that no special measures, such as reliability checks, were necessary.

A primary concern with think-aloud methods is, of course, that the test-takers actually think aloud. How does one get them to express their thoughts? Because the test takers were 16-year-olds, we feared they might describe their reading behaviors in simple terms like 'Well, I don't know' or 'Just like that'. However, Vrolijk's (1991) method of the Free Attitude Interview, developed to keep young people talking in an educational setting, offered some valuable suggestions, enabling us to stimulate the test-takers without actually influencing them. We did this by repeating student responses, by asking what they were doing, and by offering several choices.

A second concern is that, when thinking aloud, if students reflect extensively on their reading behavior this could modify the authenticity of their verbal reports. We considered it important to tap the strategies students were using to read (i.e. introspection) and not to prompt them to think too much about those strategies (i.e. retrospection). The test-takers were instructed in such a way as to keep them from introspection and to really think aloud.

To avoid interpretation problems in analyzing the protocols the two researchers first identified and coded the strategies used by the first two pupils participating in the study, then compared their results. The remainder of the protocols were analyzed independently with the list of coded strategies as a guideline. We took care to assure that this analysis could be verified by researchers who had not participated in the study, justifying and explaining each step of our analysis in a final report. In this way, we aimed to deal with the subjective aspects of our protocol analysis.

Procedure

We first selected 13 communicative items out of a reading test consisting of 32 items previously taken by about 300 students. This assured the availability of reliable psychometric data on the items and allowed us to use difficulty and discrimination indices to make the selection. The selection included a wide range of text types and of tasks.

Appendix 1 outlines the specific steps we took in the analysis of protocols. The first step consisted of consulting documents on reading related to communicative language learning and on ways of describing such test items. The two most important sources for communicative reading were the *Threshold level* (van Ek, 1980), its German version for secondary schools, the *Rahmenrichtlinien*, and Westhoff's dissertation on predictive reading (1981). For the description of the items, we used a model developed by CITO (The Dutch Institute for Educational Measurement). This model defined items using two parameters: content and behavior. Also, psychometric information on the task set by each item was collected. (See the item and step one in Appendix 5.)

Secondly, we distinguished the following aspects of the items: text type, linguistic content and type of behavior the question was referring to, reading objective, and knowledge and skills required to find the right answer. The exemplary behavior (i.e. most efficient behavior for a particular reading objective) was described in terms of sequenced strategies (see the description in step two of Appendix 5). The items proved to cluster into two groups: tasks consisting in finding and understanding factual, explicit information, and more complex tasks on combining information and drawing conclusions from comparisons.

Out third step involved collecting the protocols. Thirteen students at two different schools, in three parallel classes, did the test items. They had all been taught the same number of hours of French. Both researchers were guest teachers in the classes concerned for one period before the think-aloud session. Our lessons used the same type of materials as appeared in the test. In this way, the students became acquainted with the people conducting the research and its purposes.

The think-aloud sessions took half an hour on average for each student. We saw no needs for a retrospection phase because students demonstrated few problems in reporting their thinking processes while they took the tests. However, some pupils had to be encouraged to continue their thinking aloud. Pupils also appeared to want feedback, asking questions like, 'Am I doing alright?', 'That is correct, isn't it?'. Feedback was only given at the end of a task, so as not to disturb the thinking-aloud process. (For an example, see the last remark of the researcher in the typescript of one pupil's protocol, step four in Appendix 5.) The typescript in Appendix 5 shows the student hypothesizing (the expected behavior for the task) at the beginning of the task: 'so you could still think of a book.' In the next part she is looking for evidence for her hypothesis by going backwards and forwards in the text, by using her general knowledge and by looking for cues: 'I am still going to read backwards for a moment . . . I first thought of a book because you can send it back . . . I shall look for a picture or a book or so.'

Step four was our first analysis. Both researchers described two protocols in terms of the exemplary behavior – reading strategies and skills. Even though this description was done independently, the descriptions resembled each other very much. The description of the exemplary behavior for each item made beforehand turned out to function adequately as an instrument to analyze students' actual behavior. Of course the pupils did not always show the ideal behavior, aimed at by the test constructors. So new categories like *checking the answer* (e.g. when, after finding the right answer, students monitored if it was really the right one by going back to the text) and *repeating* (e.g. when pupils repeated the same reading strategy) were added to the list. To facilitate analysis the specific strategies and skills were coded. Appendix 2 provides an overview of all skills, processes and strategies used by the students. Appendix 5, step four, displays an example description of one student's behavior in terms of her reading strategies and skills.

Step five consisted in both researchers independently analysing all the protocols then comparing the two coded sets afterwards. Cases of disagreement, which were rare, were discussed then resolved as a single interpretation. We then compiled the frequencies of strategies expected and realised for each task on the test, as shown in Appendix 3. This made a content analysis of the items possible and provided information to answer our research questions. The analysis also turned out to provide valuable information on the quality of the test items. For an example, see step five in Appendix 4. Our final step was to evaluate our results. For each item, we compared data on students' actual behavior with our expected or idealized behavior for the item.

Findings

Appendix 3 reports the frequency of the strategies that students used for each item on the test, distinguishing between those strategies figuring in the descriptions of the ideal behavior and those strategies which did not but which students nontheless employed. The results do not provide a definite answer to our main research question, Do the tasks set elicit the behavior the test constructors aimed at? Generally speaking, the exemplary behavior was recognizable in the strategies the pupils used. But discrepancies did occur when pupils did not find the right answer immediately.

Two groups of items were distinguished in advance: those asking for factual information and those where pupils had to combine or compare information. In the category of combination-items, it was particularly clear that pupils did not choose the most efficient reading strategies (see Appendix 3, numbers 2, 4, 5, 6). They did not quickly orient themselves, nor did they skip irrelevant parts of the text. Students just began to read at the start of the text and continued until the end, whereas they were expected to jump around in the text to locate relevant information. This pattern was evident in their high frequency of global reading (GR), which is not in accordance with the exemplary behavior.

Unknown words

Our first sub-question – 'How do students react when they meet with unknown words?' – could not be answered with the data in Appendix 3. However, during the administration of the protocols the researchers noticed that students were not at all hindered by any unknown word. When translating passages, students just tended to ignore unknown words, a finding that may be reassuring to the test constructors.

Reading strategies

The second and third sub-questions were, 'Do students select their strategies according to the task set?' and 'Are students able to select the most efficient strategy for their task?'. Neither of these questions can be answered affirmatively. The students usually followed the same basic strategy, which was not always the most efficient one: They read the question (RQ) and armed with cues from the question, they read the text globally (GR), translating (TR) from time to time. If this method failed, they chose other, sometimes more time-consuming, strategies like eliminating alternatives (e.g. item 7 and 10 in Appendix 3).

From the fact that most of the pupils used the same basic strategy of reading the test question then reading the text globally, one may conclude that in general they did not chose reading strategies corresponding to the reading objective intended by the test question. This implies that, most of the time, these students did not adjust their strategies to the type of text they were reading nor to the purposes for which they were reading. Either the students cannot be considered as 'good, efficient readers' or the reading tasks did not elicit such behaviors. Although students found the correct answers to the test items in most cases, for some of them, this process took a considerable amount of time. Indeed, some pupils needed twice as much time as others, a finding pointing toward important differences among individual students in this factor, even though this test (like all others in the Dutch educational system) was not a speed test.

Extra-linguistic information

The fourth sub-question was, 'Do students make use of extra-linguistic information?' This question referred specifically to students' uses of their knowledge of the world (UGK) or other non-textual information (UI). Appendix 4 shows where those two strategies were used by the students and if they were expected to do so in that context (i.e. the ideal behavior). Using non-textual information and general knowledge is considered to be very important for finding one's way in a text. As Appendix 4 shows, for five out of 13 items students did use these strategies when they were not expected to do so. They were used as a second choice, when students did not find the right answer by just reading the text. In these instances, lay-out and illustrations were used as source of information. Some of the better pupils did this at the very beginning of the task, managing to compensate for their lack of vocabulary in this way.

For seven items the use of general knowledge or non-textual information was foreseen in the ideal behavior. Only in three cases did a reasonable number of students use this information. Curiously, students did not make explicit use of extra-linguistic information on items such as: Item 4, which included posters of movies to be selected; Item 8, which concerned the choice of a camp site, accompanied by a key to the symbols necessary to find the right answer; nor Item 11, which included a coupon. For Item 7, which contained a photograph with subscript, only five pupils started the task by looking at the picture, whereas the others just began to read the subscript. In sum, these students appeared very text-directed, making little use of information other than linguistic information.

Additional observations

In addition to information on the research questions, the protocols provided other interesting details on students' reading processes during the test.

Item 10 was a *brain-twister*. The item difficulty was only 0.57. The think-aloud session revealed that problems with this item were only caused by the fact that most pupils did not remember the French names of the days of the week. They had studied these names in their first year of French; by the time of their final examinations, half of the students had forgotten them.

We also observed, in reference to Appendix 3, that pupils only read alternatives when these consisted of a full sentence, that is, when they could perceive a meaningful content. When alternatives consisted of just names or numbers, students did not read them, although in some cases this strategy would have been useful to quickly eliminate passages of the text and to find the answer efficiently. This information appears in the distribution of the frequency of RQ (reading question) and of RQA (reading question and alternatives) between ideal and deviant behavior in Appendix 3.

Concluding Remarks

On the basis of this analysis we cannot conclude that the behavior aimed at by the test constructors was the same as students' actual behaviors in performing the test; nor would it be fair to say that the test constructors failed completely in their intentions. The truth lies somewhere in between. Answers were found to our original research question, but not definite ones. The students participating in our study may not have been very efficient or skilled readers in foreign languages. Many often used the same basic strategies, which were not always the most efficient ones. We should reiterate, however, that the pupils taking part in this study had no training in reading strategies. Only very recently has such training appeared in course books and in the national curriculum. Even the national curriculum is a brand-new phenomenon in The Netherlands. So, maybe within a few years, the effects of communicatively-oriented reading tests may help promote teaching and learning that creates students who are better readers than the group in the present study.

The study nonetheless yielded valuable findings. First, rather than just psychometric data on test-and-item analyses, we can provide feedback to constructors of reading tests that shows some of the thinking processes students actually use when performing reading tasks – indicating areas of discrepancy between what test constructors expect to elicit and what tests actually do elicit. Furthermore, the results of this research make clear that one cannot always speak of a single, most efficient behavior for answering questions on tests. Though not all roads lead to Rome, often more than one does. Protocol analysis made clear the variety of thinking processes that students may use in preparation to actually giving an answer to an examination question.

However, this variety should not constrain test constructors from being specific in the tasks they set. Nor do we think it should stop us all from thinking what it is that we demand from pupils and what those demands should be in a test situation.

Acknowledgment

I thank my CITO colleague, José Noyons, for his valuable remarks on this chapter.

References

Block, E. (1986) The comprehension strategies of second language learners. *TESOL Quarterly* 20, 463–94.

Breuker, J. A., Elshout, J. J., van Someren, M. W. and Wielinga, B. J. (1986) Hardopdenken en protocolanalyse [Thinking-aloud and protocol analysis]. *Tijdschrift voor onderwijsresearch* 11, 241–54.

Cohen, A. D. (1984) On taking language tests: What the students report. *Language Testing* 1, 70–81.

Ericsson, K. A. and Simon, H. A. (1984) *Protocol Analysis: Verbal Reports as Data*. Cambridge, MA: MIT Press.

Ippel, M. J. and Elshout, J. J. (eds) (1990) *Training van hogere-orde denkprocessen* [Training of higher-order thinking skills]. Amsterdam/Lisse: Swets & Zeitlinger.

van der Linden, E. (1986) L'analyse des protocoles: une méthode plus efficace pour l'analyse des erreurs [Protocol analysis: a more efficient method of error analysis]. *Rapports/het Franse boek* 1, 28–43.

Olshavsky, J. (1976/77) Reading as problem solving: an investigation of strategies. *Reading Research Quarterly* 12, 654–74.

Potter, F. (1982) The use of linguistic context. *British Journal of Educational Psychology* 52, 16–23.

Rahmenrichtlinien, Sekundarstufe I, Neue Sprachen (1980) [Framework for foreign language objectives for the first stage of secondary education]. Wiesbaden: Der Hessische Kultusminister.

van der Kamp, L. and van der Kamp, M. (eds) (1982) *Methodologie van onderwijsresearch* [Methodology of educational research]. Lisse: Swets & Zeitlinger.

van Ek, J. A. (1980) *Threshold Level English*. Oxford: Pergamon Press.

Vermunt, J. D. H. M., Lodewijks, J. G. L. C. and Simons, P. R. J. (1986) Hardopdenken als onderzoeksmethode naar regulatieprocessen bij tekstbestudering [Thinking-aloud as method of research on regulation processes in learning from text]. *Tijdschrift voor onderwijsresearch* 11, 187–202.

Vrolijk, A. (1991) *Gesprekstechniek* [Conversation Techniques]. Houten: Bohn, Stafleu, van Loghum.

Wearn, Y. (1980) Thinking aloud during reading. *Scandinavian Journal of Psychology* 21, 123–32.

Westhoff, G. J. (1981) *Voorspellend lezen* [Predictive Reading] Doctoral dissertation, Utrecht University, The Netherlands.

Appendix 1. Steps for protocol analysis

(1) *Getting information on the task.*

  – a   Communicative language teaching: implications for the reading skill and for the selection of texts. What is a good reader?

  – b   A descriptive model for reading tasks based on content and behavior.

  – c   Psychometric data on the items used in the study.

(2) *Designing the ideal production process for each task*, at two levels, a concrete level and a theoretical one.

  – a   Describe for each task the content and behavior, using the model mentioned under 1. Indicate the most efficient sequence.

  – b   Describe the sequence of strategies for a pupil's ideal behavior for each task (the concrete level).

  – c   Cluster tasks aiming at the same behavior.

(3) *Collecting of protocols.*

  – a   Start with an example as instruction.

  – b   Pupils do the tasks, while thinking aloud. The whole session is taped.

  – c   At the end of the session: listen to the tape with the student and ask for explanation, if necessary. Make notes.

  – d   When necessary, encourage pupils to talk and make use of advice from Free Attitude Interview.

(4) *Preliminary analysis* to check step 2.

  – a   Listen to some protocols, making them readable.

  – b   Compare protocols to the description of the ideal process (step 2). If necessary, adjust the description, but do not go beyond the theoretical framework (step 1) in doing so.

  – c   Make all protocols readable.

(5) *Protocol-analysis.*

  – a   Analyze all protocols according to the concrete and abstract description of the exemplary behavior.

(6) *Explain where the analysis succeeded and where it failed.*

  – a   Make clear in which cases pupils demonstrated the behavior aimed at and in which cases they did not.

  – b   Look for clusters of tasks.

Appendix 2. Codes used in the analysis of protocols

Strategy	Code
reading question	RQ
reading question and alternatives	RQA
memorizing cues	MC
translating	TR
global reading (focused on cues)	GR
eliminating passages	EP
eliminating alternatives	EA
analyzing structure	AS
using non textual information	UI
using general knowledge	UGK
combining relevant information	COM
repeating	R
understanding relevant part of text:	
– by translating	UT
– by context	UC
testing hypothesis of right answer	TH
checking answer	CHK
formulating of hypothesis	hypothesis

Appendix 3. Frequencies of (non)expected strategies

$N = 13$

Real behavior in in accordance with ideal		Deviant behavior	
item 1			
RQ	6	3	RQA
MC	1	2	GR (without RQ)
GR	10	2	TR (without RQ)
TR	1	11	UT/UC
COM	1	1	CHK
UGK	1	1	hypothesis

Appendix 3. Frequencies of (non)expected strategies *continued*

N = 13

Real behavior in in accordance with ideal		Deviant behavior	
item 2			
RQ	11	2	RQA
MC	10	6	GR
EP/EA	12	6	R
UT	10	1	guess
		1	CHK
item 3			
RQ	8	5	RQA
MC	—	6	TR
GR	11	4	UC
UT	12	3	MC
		1	guess
		1	UGK
		1	CHK
item 4			
RQ	13	7	GR
MC	3	1	TH
UI	7	1	AS
EP	9	7	CHK
(UGK)	2		
UT	12		
item 5			
RQ	13	9	GR
MC	1	8	EP/EA
UT/COM	12	1	UI
(UGK)	1	1	TH
		8	CHK
item 6			
RQ	11	2	RQA
MC	4	10	GR
EP/EA	8	2	TR
UT	12	2	UI
		2	TH
		4	CHK

Appendix 3. Frequencies of (non)expected strategies *continued*

N = 13

Real behavior in in accordance with ideal		Deviant behavior	
item 7			
RQ	8	5	RQA
MC	1	5	TR
UI	5	3	EA
GR	7	2	UGK
UT	13	1	TH
		2	CHK
item 8			
RQ	11	2	RQA
MC	4	11	EA/EP
AS	4	2	COM
GR	9	3	CHK
UI	10	1	TH
UC	11		
item 9			
RQ	6	7	RQA
MC	—	4	EA
GR	7	3	TH
COM	—	10	UT
or:			
RQ	—		
TR	7		
COM	—		
UGK	—		
item 10			
RQ	7	6	RQA
MC	8	4	COM
GR	10	3	AS
MC	3	1	TH
EP	6	3	EA
TR	2	1	hypothesis
UT	11	1	CHK

Appendix 3. Frequencies of (non)expected strategies *continued*

N = 13

Real behavior in
in accordance with ideal   *Deviant behavior*

Item 11			
RQ	7	6	RQA
AS	2	4	EA
GR	10	2	MC
UT/COM	11	2	TH
(UGK)	7	1	CHK

item 12			
RQ	11	2	RQA
MC	1	1	UGK
GR	8	4	TR
COM	11		
U(T)	13		

item 13			
RQ	7	6	RQA
MC	—	5	TR
GR	7	5	TH
TR	—	1	hypothesis
UC	—	4	EA
		1	UI
		5	CH

Appendix 4. Frequencies of use of general knowledge & non-textual information

Item number	Frequency of expected use	Frequency of non-expected use
1	UGK 1	—
3	—	UGK 1
4	UI 7 UGK 2	—
5	UGK 1	UI 1
7	UI 5	UGK 2
8	UI 10	—
9	UGK —	—
11	UGK 7	—
12	—	UGK 1
13	—	UI 1

Appendix 5. Example of research steps for one item

Item (number 11)
If you fill in this coupon, you'll receive
- (a) a book by Jules Verne
- (b) a picture of Jules Verne
- (c) a travel guide
- (d) pictures of a space voyage

STEP 1. Information on the task

Item difficulty	74*	4	12	9
Discrimination	29*	−6	−15	−13

STEP 2. Ideal production process

text type	coupon
characteristics	meaning of sentences, production task
question	(i.e. answer cannot be found in text literally, a conclusion must be drawn)
reading objective	understand what is being offered in the ad
knowledge, skills	− recognizing words that give clues about what is being offered: tome, série des *Voyages extraordinaires*, ouvrage, volumes;
	− making use of general knowledge: recognize Jules Verne as bookwriter.
exemplary behavior	− read line-printed circular;
	− conclude that it does not give relevant information;
	− read text globally, with cue in mind (what?);
	− find 'tome', 'série', 'ouvrage', 'volume';
	− conclude from vocabulary and/or general knowledge that it is about a book.

STEP 3. Collecting of protocols

STEP 4. First analysis
Typescript of Lysette's protocol

Lisette: If you fill in this coupon and send it in, you'll receive . . . book, photograph, travel guide or pictures, . . uh . . well I'll just read it . . uh . . I just do not really follow the beginning but I just continue. . . . . so, a 'voyages extraordinaires' . . . special voyages, the first series, so you could still also think of a book . . .

Ingrid: Yes

Lisette: A series of pictures and then, I am still going to read backwards for a moment, yes there I can find it, so I continue reading . . uh . . uh . .

Appendix 5. Example of research steps for one item *continued*

> what is that? . .' la première série numérotée', so this is again about
> that series . . . uh . . . then I shall look for a picture or a book or
> so. . . if it says anything about that, uh . . uh . ., what is this, 'je vous
> le retournerai' . . . you could send it back . . so . . eh . . it could be a
> 'voyages extraordinaires' . . there a little bit, I think . . . 'la
> première série', that's more like a series, I first thought of a book,
> because it says that you can send it back if desired, but because it
> really says 'séries' you also think a bit of photographs but you don't
> send or have a look at a picture or a series of Jules Verne. 'Envoyer'
> is to send . . . yeah, I don't know, . . . I should think . . well let's take
> the book anyway, because at the end they say . . . . return.

Ingrid: that seems the most likely then, in that case, yes, it is the right one,
          yes.

Description of protocol according to step 2.
– Reads question;
– Reads alternatives globally;
– chooses and retains key-words;
– reads text passage;
– does not understand;
– hypothesizes on the basis of key-words and information from
  alternatives;
– reads back and forwards to check hypothesis (book or picture);
– reads back and forwards, general knowledge 'return': book. Séries:
  pictures;
– cannot really make a choice.

STEP 5. Analysis
Students read the question, half of them also read alternatives. Two of them
analyze the structure of the text. While reading globally or translating, they
find the key-passage. There are some unknown words, so they try to figure
out their meaning on the basis of the context, the alternatives or their knowledge of the world.

Comments on item:
In fact it is just a vocabulary test. The meaning of the unknown words can be
deduced from context.

STEP 6. Evaluation
Real behavior more or less conform behavior aimed at.

9 What Makes an ESP Reading Test Appropriate for its Candidates?

CAROLINE CLAPHAM

Recent studies into the effect of academic discipline on performance in English for Specific Purposes (ESP) reading tests have come up with conflicting results: some have reported that students found tests to be easier if they were related to their own academic subject area, but some have found little conclusive evidence of this (see Clapham, 1991, 1993). It now seems that one of the reasons for these differences in the results may have been the choice of reading passages used in the studies: in spite of their apparent appropriateness for the students concerned, it might be that some of the texts were not sufficiently specific to the intended subject areas. This appeared to be the case with some of the passages investigated in a recent paper (Clapham, 1991).

In this study, 507 students each took two of the International English Language Testing System (IELTS) reading modules, one in their own subject area and one outside it. [IELTS has separate modules for students in three broad subject areas: Business Studies and the Social Sciences (BSS), the Life and Medical Sciences (LMS), and the Physical Sciences and Technology (PST). Each module contains three or four subtests which are based on reading passages from different disciplines within the module's overall subject area, and these are accompanied by different types of comprehension questions.] Repeated measures analysis of variance showed that over the tests as a whole students did significantly better at those in their own subject areas. However, when their performance was compared on individual subtests, this was not always the case. Although a highly significant subject effect was shown between performance on some of the pairs of subtests, there were others which showed no significant effect, and there was one instance where BSS and PST students not only did no better at the subtest in their own subject area, they did significantly worse. It looks, therefore, as if some of the subtests are not specific to a particular subject area, although they are intended to be so. ('Specific' means that the topic and the type of reading passage are appropriate to students in the relevant subject area, and, by extension, not appropriate to students in the other subject areas.) If there is a passage in a supposedly ESP test which turns out to be inappropriate for its own audience, or

171

indeed more appropriate for another audience, then it is not fulfilling its function. **The purpose of this study, therefore, is to analyse the content of the IELTS reading modules to see if some reasons can be given for the variation in specificity. The analysis will mainly concentrate on the reading passages, but will also briefly discuss the test items.**

The IELTS Reading Modules

Table 9.1 gives the names and sources of the passages used in the subtests, and lists the abbreviations by which they will henceforth be called.

Table 9.1 Reading passages in the three IELTS reading modules

---

Business Studies and Social Sciences (BSS)

(1) (Qual) 'Quality Circles' (from *Study Document 342*, Incomes Data Services Ltd, Great Portland Street, London)

(2) (Educ) 'The Purposes of Continuing Education' (adapted from *Adult Learning: Issues and Innovations*, edited by Robert M. Smith. ERIC Clearinghouse in Career Education, 1976)

(3) (High) 'Access to Higher Education' (from a Department of Education and Science White Paper on Higher Education, London 1988)

Life and Medical Sciences (LMS)

(1) (Teeth) 'The Mystery of Declining Tooth Decay' (from *Nature*, Vol. 322, 1986)

(2) (Child) 'Our Children's Teeth' (from *The British Medical Journal*, Vol. 298, February 1989)

(3) (Genes) 'Three Ways to Make a Transgenic Beast' (from the *New Scientist*, 7 July 1988)

(4) (Nitro) 'Nitrogen Fixation' (from 'Agricultural Microbiology', *Scientific American*, 1981)

Physical Science and Technology (PST)

(1) (Sun) 'Life Without a Sunscreen' (from the *New Scientist*, 10 December, 1988)

(2) (Fuel) 'Energy from Fuels' (from a textbook written for young non-scientists; source unknown)

(3) (Ship) 'The Recovery of the Mary Rose' (from *The Structural Engineer*, Vol. 62a, No. 2, 1984)

Table 9.2 Level of significance of subject area effect for pairs of subtests (Repeated measures analysis of variance)

2.1		*LMS module*				*PST module*		
		Tooth	Child	Genes	Nitro	Sun	Fuel	Ship
	Qual	NS	NS	0.000	0.000	0.000	0.01[1]	NS
BSS module	Educ	0.05	NS	0.000	0.000	0.000	0.05	NS
	High	NS	NS	0.000	0.000	0.050	NS	NS
		BSS & LMS students				BSS & PST students		

2.2		*PST module*			*BSS module*		
		Sun	Fuel	Ship	Qual	Educ	High
	Tooth	NS	0.05	0.05	NS	0.05	NS
LMS module	Child	NS	0.05	NS	NS	NS	NS
	Genes	NS	0.05	NS	0.000	0.000	0.000
	Nitro	0.01	0.001	0.001	0.000	0.000	0.000
		LMS & PST students			LMS & BSS students		

2.3		*LMS module*				*BSS module*		
		Tooth	Child	Genes	Nitro	Qual	Educ	High
	Sun	NS	NS	NS	0.01	0.000	0.000	0.05
PST module	Fuel	0.05	0.05	0.05	0.001	0.01[1]	0.05	NS
	Ship	0.05	NS	NS	0.001	NS	NS	NS
		PST & LMS students				PST & BSS students		

[1] The significance in this case was the other way round. That is students did significantly better at the subtest which was *not* in their own subject area.

Table 9.2 shows the difference in the effect of academic subject area for each pair of subtests. Table 9.2.1. shows the subject area effect when BSS and LMS students took both the BSS and LMS subtests, and when BSS and PST students took both the BSS and PST ones. Similarly, Tables 9.2.2 and 9.2.3 show the pairings with LMS students and PST students respectively. It will be seen from this chart how the subtests vary in their 'specificity', that is in the extent to which they appear to have significant subject area effects when paired with subtests from other modules. The LMS subtest Nitro, for example (Table 9.2.2), has significant subject area effects when paired with all the subtests from the other modules (0.01, 0.001 and 0.001 with the PST subsets Sun, Fuel and Ship respectively, and 0.000 with the three BSS subtests). On the other hand (LMS)Child has no significant subject effects with any of the BSS subtests and only with one PST subtest – Fuel. When BSS and PST students' scores are compared on (BSS)Qual and (PST)Sun (Table 9.2.1) there is a highly significant subject effect (sig. = 0.000), but when those same students' performances are compared on (BSS)Qual and (PST)Fuel it can be seen that the students did significantly better at the subtest which was *not* in their own subject area. Of course any interpretation of these results is confounded by the fact that there are always two subtests contributing to an effect, and one of these may be subject specific and the other not. However, some subtests have consistently higher significant effects than others. For example, (LMS)Nitro, as shown above, has significant effects with every one of the subtests, whereas (LMS)Child has almost none.

When a subtest has highly significant subject area effects when paired with all or almost all the other subtests it can be presumed that the subtest is highly specific to students in that subject area. Such subtests will therefore be labelled 'highly specific'. So (LMS)Genes and (LMS)Nitro are both highly specific subtests. Subtests such as (BSS)Qual and (PST)Sun, which have highly significant effects with some but not all the other subtests, will be called 'specific', and subtests which have few or no significant effects will be called 'general'. (LMS)Tooth, (LMS)Child, (PST)Fuel and (PST)Ship are all 'general' according to this definition.

The question now therefore is Why? What makes some tests more specific than others?

There must be many factors that go into the specificity of a text which cannot be investigated here. What I can do, though, is look at the most likely causes of this variation in specificity. Firstly I shall briefly look at the comments by students on the familiarity of the subject matter of the reading passages. Secondly, I shall look at the source of each reading passage (i.e. academic paper, popular article, textbook, etc.), to see whether there is a simple relationship between this and text specificity. Finally I shall approach the problem another way by using Bachman's Test Method Characteristics (TMC) Instrument (see Bachman, 1990) to analyse further aspects of the reading passages and their accompanying items.

Appropriacy of Subject Area

Students' familiarity with subject area

All students who took the tests were asked in a questionnaire how familiar they were with the general subject area of each of the reading passages. (The results of this are described in more detail in Clapham, 1991). Table 9.3 shows the percentage of students in the three academic subject areas who said that they were familiar with the subject areas.

Table 9.3 Percentage of students familiar with the general subject area of each subtest

Level of specificity			BSS students (N = 269)	LMS students (N = 61)	PST students (N = 68)
BSS	S	Qual	54%	28%	38%
	S	Educ	68%	40%	46%
	S	High	58%	33%	34%
LMS	G	Tooth[1]	32%	62%	27%
	G	Child[1]	32%	62%	27%
	HS	Genes	13%	69%	14%
	HS	Nitro	10%	69%	35%
PST	S	Sun	39%	81%	76%
	G	Fuel	60%	72%	92%
	G	Ship	4%	13%	16%

Key: HS = Highly Specific according to Table 9.2
S = Specific
G = General

[1] The answers relating to (LMS)Tooth and (LMS)Child are identical as they both cover the same subject area – tooth decay.

In the case of 'highly specific' subtests it will be seen that the students became progressively less familiar with the subject area as it became more removed from their own: for example for (LMS)Nitro, the figures were: LMS students 69%, PST students 35% and BSS students 10%. In subtests which appear 'general', such as (LMS)Tooth, and (LMS)Child, the trend is still there but less obvious: although 62% of LMS students were familiar with the subject area, 32% of BSS students also were. For the (PST)Fuel subtest, the figures were: PST students 92%, LMS students 72%, and BSS students 60%, so although a greater proportion of PST students were familiar with the subject area than BSS students, more than half the BSS students were also familiar with it. This may well account for some of the subtest's lack of specificity. On the whole, Table 9.3 reinforces the classification of the subtests into HS, S and G. The one exception is (PST)Ship, which was labelled 'General' and which might therefore have been expected to be familiar to many students in all three subject areas. This is undoubtedly not the case. Far from being general, it is familiar to almost no one. Indeed, only 16% of the PST students for whom the subtest was intended were familiar with the subject area. The passage covers an area of engineering which, it turns out, is not only unfamiliar to BSS and LMS students, but to most physical and technological scientists as well. In this case, therefore, it seems that the subtest is not 'general', but 'too specific' and for the rest of this paper it will be described in that way. This over specificity accounts very well for the fact that the subtest does not have significant subject area effects when paired with the other subtests. If a subtest is too specific, it is suitable for so few of the students in the designated subject area that such students are not likely to do significantly better than students in other subject areas.

Subject specialists' views

Since it seems that the test specifications were not sufficiently detailed to ensure that the reading passages would be appropriate for candidates in the relevant subject areas, a small number of university lecturers at Lancaster University were asked to read all ten passages and to say how appropriate the passages were for their students and how familiar these students would be with the subject matter. There is no space to report the results of this survey here, but on the whole the lecturers' comments agreed with the students' ratings.

Source of Reading Passages

As can be seen from Table 9.1, the passages come from varied sources. The BSS module contains the greatest variety of texts with one coming from a study document, one from a British government paper, and one from an adaptation of a paper on career education. The sources of the two science modules' texts are more uniform – with one exception the passages come from either academic journals – *Nature*, *The British Medical Journal* and *The Structural Engineer*, or popularisations of academic science reports – the *New Scientist* and the *Scientific American*. The one exception is the (PST)Fuel text which comes from a textbook written not for science students but for young *non-scientists*. This surprising fact may well account for the lack of specificity of this subtest as although the subject matter may be appropriate for PST students its intended audience is certainly not. The content of the passage is not sufficiently specialised for PST students, and it is therefore insufficiently academic. It seems likely that the more academic a piece of writing is the more highly specific will be its subject matter, as it will be aimed at a progressively more specialised audience. Articles in learned journals are considered to be more academic than ones in popularisations such as the *New Scientist* and the *Scientific American*, and these in turn are thought to be more academic than say articles in quality newspapers. However, it is not clear that there is any agreement about what the word 'academic' means. It is used frequently without explanation. Everyone would probably agree that a research article is academic. Writers such as Fahnestock (1986) and Myers (1991) have described the differences between research articles and popularisations, and imply that popularisations are less academic. Presumably the more academic an article is the more closely it is related to one discipline, so it might follow that texts from academic journals would be more subject specific than popularisations. Since all but one of the texts from the two IELTS science modules come from either academic journals or popularisations, we can see whether this is the case here. Table 9.4 shows the source of each of the LMS and PST reading passages.

Table 9.4 Specificity of passage by source and rhetorical function

Specificity	Passage	Source	Rhetorical function
G	Tooth	Academic Article	Introduction: reporting research
G	Child	Academic Article	Introduction: listing findings
HS	Genes	Popularisation	Description of processes
HS	Nitro	Popularisation	Description of process
S	Sun	Popularisation	Introduction: explanation
G	Fuel	Textbook for non-scientists	Exposition
TS	Ship	Academic Article	Description of plans and narration of outcomes

Key: HS = Highly Specific
　　　S = Specific
　　　G = General
　　　TS = Too Specific

Contrary to expectations, with the exception of (PST)Ship which has been shown to be 'too specific', neither of the passages from academic journals seems to be specific whereas all the three popularisations *are*. This may seem surprising. However, although the descriptions of research articles given by genre analysts such as Swales (1990) may show that research articles are highly specific to their field of study (see also Bazerman, 1988), academic articles as a whole take so many forms that it is difficult to generalise about them. Even in one discipline they may vary from general survey articles which the lay reader would understand, to ones which are so technical that even experts in the esoteric sub-discipline have difficulty understanding them. In addition, an article may contain sections which vary in their specificity and in their discourse types. The introduction, for example, may contain an easily accessible review of the literature, but this may be followed by a highly specialist description of an experiment or process. Authors such as Dudley-Evans & Henderson (1990) have described the different styles used in different parts of a single article. Although the two 'general' LMS passages come from learned journals they are both so general in approach that they present no problems to a BSS reader. The first passage, Tooth, introduces the concept of fluoridation in water supplies, and reports on some studies on the effect of fluoridation on tooth decay. Very few technical terms are used, and those that there are, are explained in the text. The second passage, Child, discusses tooth decay in children, and shows how this is related to social class. This passage is perhaps slightly more technical than the first in that it includes some statistics, but there are no concepts or terms which would be unfamiliar to a social scientist. The section of an academic article from which a passage is selected will, therefore, itself have an effect on the suitability and easiness of the passage.

Unlike the two LMS texts which come from academic articles, the two that come from popularisations are not introductions or surveys. They are either wholly or partially descriptions of processes, and this may partly account for their difficulty for non-LMS students. (LMS)Genes describes methods of transferring genes to mice, and (LMS)Nitro describes the process of nitrogen fixation. Both passages have unexplained technical vocabulary, and both demand an understanding of biological concepts. To a biologist such concepts are elementary, but to a non-scientist they are obscure. Myers (1991) has shown how the lexical cohesion which makes scientific research articles so difficult to read for non-scientists is replaced by more helpful, explanatory cohesive devices in popularisations, but in (LMS)Genes and (LMS)Nitro any such devices seem inadequate for the layman. The texts are not contextualised for non-life-science readers (see Bachman, 1990), and therefore BSS and PST students have difficulty with them.

In Table 9.4 above, the fourth column shows the rhetorical function of each passage and this does appear to have some relationship with the specificity or non-specificity of the passages. The passages from academic journals come from general introductions. The two 'highly specific' texts come from popular rather than academic journals, *but* they are descriptions of processes.

Recapitulation

I shall be returning to the above concept of contextualisation later, but first I shall give a brief summary of what has been learnt so far. From the students' questionnaires, I have shown that familiarity with subject area has an important effect on the specificity of reading passages. I have also shown that the fact that a passage is extracted from an academic article will not itself guarantee that the text is subject specific, and although it is dangerous to generalise from such a small number of texts, it looks as if the rhetorical function of an extract may be of more importance than the source.

In order to try and confirm the above findings, and to find other factors that may affect specificity, I shall now turn to the use of Bachman's Test Method Characteristics (TMC) Rating instrument. This instrument is designed to assess reading passages and items on a range of variables many of which are directly or indirectly relevant to my purposes.

The TMC and CLA Instruments

Bachman and his colleagues designed two rating scales, the TMC Scale and the Communicative Language Ability (CLA) Scale, for the Cambridge – TOEFL Comparability Study (Bachman, Davidson, Ryan & Choi, 1995). The scales were drawn up in order to find a quantifiable way of comparing the content of two test batteries; Bachman (1990) discusses the theoretical framework behind these scales. The CLA facets are rated on a five-point scale and relate to the level of ability required of the test takers in the areas of grammatical, textual, illocutionary, sociolinguistic and strategic competence. The TMC facets relate to test items and test passages, and concern the testing environment, test rubric, item type, and the nature of test input. Among the facets of test input are: complexity of language, rhetorical organisation, degree of contextualisation, test topic, cultural bias, and pragmatic characteristics. For each facet raters assess an item or a passage according to a scale which generally has three points. For example:

	Very simple		Very complex
Rhetorical Organisation	0	1	2

Some facets are rated according to the number of occurrences of a feature, for example:

	No Occurrences	One Occurrence	Two or more Occurrences
Cultural References	0	1	2

Since the first TMC trials, the scales have been steadily refined. They were used to investigate the relationship between item content and item difficulty

(Bachman, Davidson, Lynch & Ryan, 1989), and to compare the content of different versions of a test (Bachman, Davidson & Milanovic, 1991). The version of the instrument that I have adapted was prepared in March 1991.

The complete 1991 versions of Bachman's rating instruments consist of 63 TMC and 13 CLA facets. They are designed to apply to listening, speaking, reading and writing tests in a wide range of sociolinguistic settings. Not all these facets are applicable to the IELTS reading tests since these all have the same overall test design, and since they only test reading, and contain only academic or quasi academic passages. For my version of the scales, therefore, I was able to reduce the number of facets. However, in spite of this reduction, my first draft of the scales consisted of 35 TMC and 12 CLA facets to be assessed for 10 reading passages and 95 test items. This was too daunting for the volunteer raters and I had radically to reduce the scope of the exercise. Some facets were amalgamated – grammar, for example, was no longer assessed according to embeddings, sentence type and voice, but only under the one umbrella term, 'grammatical complexity' – and the CLA scale was dropped completely. The only addition I made to the existing facets was that 'Degree of Contextualisation – Topic Specificity' was expanded so that raters were asked to assign ratings for students in the three subject areas of BSS, LMS and PST separately. The final rating instrument consists of 17 facets, some of which relate to items, some to passages and some to both. It is heavily based on Bachman's (1991) instrument, but has been adjusted to cover perceived ambiguities in the original instrument. (An abbreviated copy of parts of the modified instrument is provided as an Appendix.) It should be pointed out that although these alterations appeared to clarify the raters' task, they may in some cases have obscured the purpose of the Bachman originals. To try to guard against this, raters were referred where possible to the relevant sections of Bachman's (1990) explanations of the facets concerned.

The raters

Three raters assessed the tests. All three were applied linguists, and experienced teachers of English for Academic Purposes. Two were British and one had a Canadian/British background, and all three were educated in the humanities. Their most recent EAP experience covered Indonesia, Thailand and the UK. None of them were familiar with the tests before they embarked on the rating procedure.

Training the raters

At an initial meeting to discuss the first draft of the modified TMC instrument, several problems arose because the group felt that the explanations of some of the facets were ambiguous. Possibly the most important problem, and certainly the most enduring, related to those facets where the assessment had to be made in relation to the expected test taker. For example, raters were asked to decide on the frequency of the vocabulary used in a test passage or item, using a three-point scale ranging from 0 if the vocabulary was frequent, to 2 if it was infrequent. The raters wanted to know for whom this vocabulary should be considered frequent or infrequent. Should it be for all members of the English speaking world, or all learners of English, or the specific test takers, i.e. in IELTS' case, prospective E2L university students? Eventually, with Bachman's approval, it was decided that the question should be related to IELTS candidates, but even then the raters wanted to know which IELTS candidate, since there was no such thing as a typical IELTS test taker. Bachman supplied some very detailed comments on this and other problems which arose (Bachman, personal communication), and the TMC Instrument was further modified.

Once the contents of the TMC scale was finally settled, I went through one passage and its items with each of the three raters seeing if we could agree on which level to assign to each facet, and the raters then carried out the rest of the rating by themselves. The rating itself took each rater approximately three hours.

None of the three raters were confident about their assessments. They felt that although some facets were unambiguous and straightforward to answer (such as 'Figurative Language' [see Appendix 1], where the rating would be the same for any group of test takers), they were still worried by others. They all said that they would not expect to give the same ratings another time as they felt their internal rules for assessing the facets kept changing. As a check on this, Rater 2 carried out the whole exercise again eight weeks later.

Agreement among raters

Although the raters assessed both items and passages, for the sake of clarity only the passages will be discussed here.

It was not possible to calculate a standard reliability index for the raters, as the number of rating categories was too small. It was only possible to check the agreement between raters. Table 9.5 gives the weighted Kappa statistic for each pair of judges, weighted to take account of the fact that if raters differed by two points when assessing a facet this was a more serious disagreement than if they had differed by one. The fourth row shows the agreement between Rater 2's first and second marking. (Note that a Kappa of 0.00 would show that any agreement could have been due to chance, and that 1.00 would show perfect agreement.)

Table 9.5 Weighted Kappa statistics

Raters	Weighted Kappa	95% confidence interval
1/2	0.36	0.21 to .51
1/3	0.48	0.34 to .61
2/3	0.45	0.31 to .58
1st/2nd rating	0.45	0.32 to .58

All four weighted kappas are significantly different from chance at the 0.05 level; they show a moderate agreement between the raters. No one rater stands out as having performed very differently from the other two, but Raters 1 and 2 showed the least agreement. The fact that the agreement between Rater 2's first and second marking is also only moderate shows that the raters were probably right to doubt their consistency.

A weighted RAP (Rater Agreement Proportion) statistic was calculated on each facet for each passage. The RAP statistic is used by Bachman *et al.* (1991) to measure the proportion of rater agreement on each facet/item. In their research, for example, where there were five raters, the RAP was 1.0 (5/5) if all five raters agreed, and 0.8 if four did. If two agreed it was 0.2 and no agreement was 0.0. To find out the agreement over facets or items, the mean RAP was calculated for each variable. This statistic is easy to conceptualise but it has one disadvantage: it does not take account of extreme judgements. So, for example, if three raters gave a 2, and two raters gave a 0, the RAP index would be the same as if three had given a 2 and two a 1. For the present study, the scale has been adjusted to account for extreme ratings. If all three raters agree, the RAP figure is 1, and if two agree with a difference of 1 between the ratings, then the RAP is 0.67 (2/3). If, however, two agree, but the third is *two* points away from the others, then the RAP is 0.33. If no-one agrees the RAP is 0.0. This therefore could be called a weighted RAP (WRAP). Table 9.6 gives the mean WRAPs for all the facets. (A more detailed table giving the mean WRAPs for all the passages is provided in Table 9.7.)

It will be seen from these figures that, in spite of the raters' doubts, there was quite high agreement for some of the facets. The raters mostly agreed about 'Grammar' and 'Cohesion', although in both cases Bachman's detailed facets had been conflated into single variables. 'Frequency of Vocabulary', too, which had caused such anxiety, had a mean WRAP of 0.80 and so did 'Rhetorical Organisation' which two of the raters had felt was impossible to rate in the manner outlined in the TMC instrument. There was, however, little agreement on some of the other facets. Since it is possible to get a mean WRAP

Table 9.6 Mean WRAP figures for each facet[1]

Facet	Mean WRAP	Facet	Mean WRAP
Vocabulary		*Organisational*	
Infrequent	0.80	*characteristics*	
Specialised	0.77	Grammar	0.87
Ambiguous	0.80	Cohesion	0.90
		Rhetorical organisation	0.80
Degree of		N. of types of rhet. org.	0.70
contextulisation			
Cultural content	0.73	*Sociolinguistic*	
Topic Specificity		*characteristics*	
BSS	0.70	Cultural references	0.68
LMS	0.66	Figurative language	0.80
PST	0.66		
Topic			
Culture specific	0.77		
Academic specific	0.57		
Specialised topic	0.67	Overall mean WRAP	0.74

[1] All the mean WRAPs are very slightly inflated since one passage (PST)Sun was used for training purposes.

of 0.48 by chance alone, it seems that where facets have a mean WRAP of less than about 0.7 there is too little agreement for us to believe that the raters were using the same criteria for their judgements. What is interesting is that the facets which led to such disagreement are, with one exception, those most obviously related to the problem of text specificity, namely 'Contextualisation – Topic Specificity', 'Specialised Topic' and 'Academic Specificity'. The only exception is 'Cultural References' (mean WRAP = 0.68) where raters had to rate passages according to the number of cultural references in the text. This appeared to be a fairly mechanical task which should have led to high agreement. It may be that the raters interpreted this facet in different ways, or it may be that they have varying perceptions of what cultural references are. The facet which led to the greatest disagreement among raters was 'Topic: Academic Specific'. Raters were asked to state how specifically academic each reading passages was, regardless of the test taker. It is possible that since all the IELTS passages are supposedly suitable for academic study, there was not enough range in the passages for the raters to have a feel for what a 0, a 1 or a 2 would mean. On the other hand it may be that some passages are very difficult to rate in this way. As was discussed earlier, there may be no clear concept of what 'academic' means. There was total disagreement over the academic specificity of two of the passages – (LMS)Tooth and (LMS)Child: in each case one rater gave a 0, one a 1, and one a 2. These were two of the passages that I had labelled 'general', and although they both came from academic journals (see Table 9.4) the subject matter was not only familiar to readers in many disciplines, but it was presented in a non-specialised way. The other passage where 'Academic Specificity' produced little agreement among the raters was (PST)Ship, which I have labelled 'too specific'. Its WRAP was 0.33. What the TMC instrument may be confirming is what I suspected earlier, namely that there is as yet no consensus on what makes an 'academic' text.

The other facets with low mean WRAPS were the three 'Contextualisation – Topic Specificity' ones. Here the raters had to rate the passages according to the viewpoint of BSS, LMS, and PST students. This may seem to have been a strange thing to ask them to do, but that is what item writers are doing when they select a text for an ESP test. Since all three raters had social science backgrounds it might be expected that they would agree most on the BSS facet, and indeed they did, but the mean WRAP was still low, only 0.70. It may not only be the difficulty of judging the contextualisation from different viewpoints which is the problem here. All three raters found it difficult to grasp the concept behind this facet. They said that they never managed to internalise it, and kept having to re-read the instructions. What can be deduced from the above, I think, is that for some facets the low agreement is due to inadequate explanation, and in some it is because the concepts are not yet sufficiently defined. In the case of the 'Contextualisation – Topic Specificity' facets, the raters may not have the appropriate background knowledge to be able to agree on an answer, but they are also not happy with the concept.

Use of the TMC Instrument

Test items

Although I am not going to discuss the results of TMC assessment of the test items here, it is worth saying that there did not seem to be any great differences in the rubric, item types, frequency of vocabulary, and grammatical complexity of the items across the three reading modules. On the whole the raters considered that although some of the item types were unusual, the items were clearly explained, and were generally presented in simple language. The tentative conclusion from the analysis of the items is that item content does not appear to have affected the specificity of the subtests.

Linguistic complexity

We now need to see whether any of the facets can throw light on the specificity of the reading passages, and it is certainly possible to show the ones which do not. Table 9.7 gives a complete picture of the ratings on all facets for all passages. The three raters' assessments have been totalled, so that, for example, if each gave a 1, the total is 3. So for the (LMS)Child passage, the raters' combined rating for 'Infrequent Vocabulary' (separately 2, 2, and 1) is 5. In this table the facets are grouped under three headings: Linguistic Complexity, Subject Specificity, and Culture. Looking at the facets across the three subject areas of BSS, LMS and PST it can be seen that those grouped under Linguistic Complexity do not seem to differentiate across the modules. For 'Ambiguity', for example, all the passages are considered to be relatively unambiguous, and have total scores of 3 or less. Some of the facets seem to work in pairs, witness 'Grammar' and 'Cohesion', which appear to be almost identical, and are very steady across all 10 passages. With the exception of (BSS)Qual, which has a lower rating for 'Cohesion', the passages have all been rated as having very complex Grammar and Cohesive Devices. This consistency may show that it is difficult to distinguish between such academically sophisticated texts, or it may be that my reduction of Bachman's more detailed facets has obscured interesting differences. On the other hand, since the 'Cohesion' facet comes directly after 'Grammar' it may be that 'Cohesion' is suffering from a halo effect. It is possible that the raters were rating both facets according to some general recognition of linguistic complexity. 'Rhetorical Organisation' and 'Rhetorical Complexity' too have almost identical ratings, and so do 'Specific Vocabulary' and 'Specialised Topic'. This latter pair is particularly interesting as the facets appear in different parts of the TMC instrument, and might not therefore be expected to suffer from a halo effect. It seems that the raters are using the same criteria to assess these facets, although for 'Specialised Vocabulary' they are supposed to hold IELTS test takers in mind, and for 'Specialised Topic' they are not.

Culture

Here differences can be seen between the three subject areas. The most outstanding feature is that the PST passages appear to be the least culturally specific. Two out of the three texts are considered to contain no Culture Specific content (Sun and Fuel) and the amount of unexplained information for which prior cultural knowledge is required (Contextualisation – Cultural Content) is low for all three passages. In the BSS and the LMS modules, however, the figures are much higher. (BSS)Qual and (BSS)Higher have high ratings on at least two of these variables, and so does (LMS)Child. In the case of Higher and Child at least these are easily explained. Higher is part of a British government report on projections for higher education in Britain. Since the text is aimed at a readership which is familiar with the British educational system it uses terms such as 'polytechnic' and 'Highers' without any explanation. Similarly, the (LMS)Child passage compares tooth decay in different areas of Britain. This time it is not the vocabulary that might give problems to candidates without prior knowledge of Britain, but knowledge of the relative wealth of different areas in Britain. Without this knowledge it is difficult to make sense of various of the references. Whether these differences relate to the specificity of the texts is not clear, but it would be worth investigating further.

Table 9.7 TMC ratings on all facets for all passages

	BSS			LMS				PST			
	S	S	S	G	G	HS	HS	S	G	TS	Mean
	Qual	Educ	High	Tooth	Child	Genes	Nitro	Sun	Fuel	Ship	WRAP
Linguistic complexity											
Infr. vocab.	5	5	6	4	5	6	4	6	4	6	0.80
Fig. lang.	6	6	5	3	3	6	2	0	2	6	0.68
Ambiguity	0	1	3	0	0	1	0	3	0	2	0.80
Grammar	5	5	6	6	6	6	6	6	5	5	0.87
Cohesion	3	5	6	6	6	6	6	6	5	5	0.90
Rhet. org.	3	3	5	3	3	3	2	3	3	2	0.80
N rhet. org.	6	3	5	3	3	3	2	4	4	3	0.70
Subject Specificity Context:											
ASS	3	2	5	3	2	5	6	5	2	4	0.70
LMS	4	2	6	1	2	2	2	3	2	4	0.66
PST	4	2	6	3	2	4	4	2	1	2	0.66
Ac. specific	2	2	6	3	3	4	6	4	4	2	0.57
Special. top.	5	2	6	3	3	6	6	4	3	6	0.67
Special. voc.	5	4	6	4	4	6	6	6	3	6	0.77
Culture											
Cult. ref.	5	0	4	3	3	1	1	0	0	2	0.68
Cult. cont.	3	1	5	1	5	1	1	3	2	1	0.73
Cult. specif.	4	2	6	2	5	1	1	0	0	2	0.77
Mean WRAP	0.81	0.63	0.79	0.79	0.60	0.81	0.75	0.92	0.60	0.74	

Subject specificity

Since all the subject specificity facets had low agreement among raters it is not possible to make any deductions from the total ratings. However, it is possible to look at them in more detail, and to see if we can account for the lack of agreement. Table 9.8 shows the totals for the facets relating to subject specificity for the three passages which had been labelled 'general'. The WRAP statistic for each facet is shown in brackets. Table 9.9 shows the same facets for the 'highly specific' subtests.

Table 9.8 Totals and WRAP statistics for the three 'General' passages

	(LMS)Tooth	*(LMS)Child*	*(PST)Fuel*
Contextualisation			
BSS	3 (1.0)	2 (0.67)	2 (0.67)
LMS	1 (0.67)	2 (0.67)	2 (0.67)
PST	3 (1.0)	2 (0.67)	1 (0.67)
Academic specific	3 (0)	3 (0)	4 (0.67)
Specialised topic	4 (0.67)	3 (0)	3 (0)
Specialised vocabulary	4 (0.67)	4 (0.67)	3 (0)

Table 9.9 Totals and WRAP statistics for the two 'Highly Specific' texts

	(LMS)Genes	*(LMS)Nitro*
Contextualisation:		
BSS	5 (0.67)	6 (0.67)
LMS	2 (0.67)	2 (0.67)
PST	4 (0.67)	4 (0.67)
Academic specific	4 (0.33)	6 (1.0)
Specialised topic	6 (1.0)	6 (1.0)
Specialised vocabulary	6 (1.0)	6 (1.0)

Although most of the facets in Table 9.8 show moderate agreement (0.67), it is interesting that there is total disagreement among the raters concerning the 'Specialised Topic' facet for two of the passages, (LMS)Child and (LMS)Fuel. Although this may be accounted for by a lack of clarity in the TMC Instrument it is more likely to be the result of the generality of the texts. In Table 9.9 it will be seen that there is total agreement as to the specificity of each topic.

It seems clear that however we approach those 'general' passages their properties are not as easily distinguishable as are those of the 'highly specific' ones. If we look, for example, at the contextualisation facets, we can see that for the 'highly specific' passages, the raters have judged them most contextualised for LMS students, and least for BSS ones, which is just as might be expected. However, for the 'general' texts there is no such clear cut delineation, and indeed (LMS)Child is considered to be equally contextualised for BSS, LMS and PST students.

This trend is to some extent reinforced if we look at how far the raters agreed over individual passages. Of course not too much should be made of these findings as there is so much room for error, but it does seem to be the case that the 'general' passages tend to have lower agreement among judges. The two which have the lowest agreement (Mean WRAP 0.60) are (PST)Fuel and (LMS)Child (see Table 9.7).

To conclude this section on the TMC Scale, it has to be said that I have not succeeded in finding a formula for identifying factors contributing to the specificity of texts. It may be that the passages are too similar to each other to be suitable for this kind of analysis, or that the training of raters was not sufficiently detailed, or that the modified TMC Instrument is ambiguous in parts, or that the three point scale is too limited. On the other hand it may be that it would be very difficult to get more agreement on some of these facets under any circumstances. Although it should surely be possible to achieve total agreement on the facets relating to culture, and those requiring simple counts such as 'cultural' and 'figurative references', and high agreement on those concerning linguistic complexity, as indeed has been shown in the various Bachman studies, agreement on those relating to specialised topics may be more elusive. We may still not know enough about academic and subject specificity for the raters to be able to agree. However, this does not wholly invalidate the modified TMC instrument. The very process of trying to assign a rating forces raters to think about aspects of the test which might not otherwise have occurred to them. Were it not for the length of even the modified TMC instrument I would recommend that it be used as a standard tool for the content validation of new tests.

Conclusion

The present study has identified some factors which appear to affect the specificity of ESP reading tests. By comparing various features of the 'highly specific' subtests with those of the 'general' ones it has been possible to show the following:

(1) The reading subtests' subject specificity partially depends on students' familiarity or lack of familiarity with the subject area of the reading passages.

(2) Some of the passages are either too general or too specialised for students in the intended subject areas. This has led to the poor subject specificity of some of the subtests.

(3) It is not clear how much effect source of text has on the specificity of a subtest. It is not the case that an extract from an academic journal is automatically specific to students in that subject area. Some extracts may be too general, and some too specific. Specificity may well depend on the rhetorical function of the passage. It may also depend not so much on the presence of subject specific vocabulary as the presence of unexplained subject specific concepts. There was not enough agreement among raters for the Bachman 'Degree of Contextualisation: Topic Specificity' facet to throw any light on this. It needs more research.

(4) According to the TMC ratings, linguistic complexity had no effect on subject specificity. However, it may be that the TMC three-point scale is insufficiently detailed to distinguish between texts of the complexity of the IELTS ones.

(5) There was some difference in the Cultural Content of the three modules but it is not clear whether this affected subject specificity. This needs to be considered further.

(6) An initial study of the TMC ratings of the test items showed no evidence that the items' content was affecting subject specificity, but the data need more thorough analysis.

It might of course be asked how much the specificity of an ESP test matters. In the case of a test such as IELTS, where the subject areas are so broad, it could be argued that as long as passages *look* appropriate superficially, and face validity is thus maintained, the reading tests will be suitable for their candidates. However, one of the purposes of providing subject specific modules is to ensure that students are not disadvantaged by test content, and as the above study has shown, it is possible to choose a passage which seems appropriate at first glance, but which is actually easier for students in disciplines outside the intended subject area. In this case the test is not appropriate for the designated students, and the test results are therefore invalidated.

As far as researchers into the effect of background knowledge on reading performance are concerned, specificity may be a key variable which should be considered during the design and analysis stages of any research project.

Finally, it is not possible to give a full answer to the question 'What Makes an ESP Reading Test Appropriate for Its Candidates?', but this paper has shown that appropriacy is not as simple a matter as might have been supposed.

Acknowlegements

Many thanks are due to Barbara Adams, Joan Allwright and Nicki McLeod for the time-consuming task of assessing the test method characteristics of the three reading modules.

References

Bachman, L. (1990) *Fundamental Considerations in Language Testing*. Oxford: Oxford University Press.

Bachman, L., Davidson, F., Lynch, B. and Ryan, K. (1989) Content analysis and statistical modelling of EFL proficiency tests. Paper presented at the 11th Annual Language Testing Research Colloquium, San Antonio, Texas.

Bachman, L., Davidson, F. and Milanovic, M. (1991) The use of test method characteristics in the content analysis and design of English proficiency tests. Paper presented at the 13th Annual Language Testing Research Colloquium at Princeton, New Jersey.

Bachman, L., Davidson, F., Ryan, K. and Choi, I. (1995) *The Cambridge Comparability Study*. Cambridge: Cambridge University Press.

Bazerman, C. (1988) *Shaping Written Knowledge*. London: The University of Wisconsin Press.

Clapham, C. M. (1991) The effect of academic discipline on reading test performance. Paper presented at the 13th Annual Language Testing Research Colloquium, Princeton, New Jersey.

— (1993) Is ESP testing justified? In D. Douglas and C. Chapelle (eds) *A New Decade of Language Testing Research*. Alexandria, VA: TESOL.

Dudley-Evans, T. and Henderson, W. (1990) *The Language of Economics: The Analysis of Economics Discourse*. ELT Documents 134, London: Modern English Publications.

Fahnestock, J. (1986) Accommodating science: The rhetorical life of scientific facts. *Written Communication* 3, 275–96.

Myers, G. (1991) Lexical cohesion and specialized knowledge in science and popular science tests. *Discourse Processes* 14, 1–26.

Swales, J. (1990) *Genre Analysis*. Cambridge: Cambridge University Press.

Appendix 1. Test method characteristics of the IELTS reading modules

(This is an abbreviated version of the notes given to raters. Instructions have been shortened and item TMCs omitted.)

Adapted from Bachman's Test Method Rating Instrument (4 March 1991)

In general, all scales are intended to be directional, so that a larger value would be expected to make an item more difficult. However, it should be remembered that these are not direct ratings of difficulty, but ratings of the content of the test itself in terms of the specific facets. That is, the ratings on these facets will enable us to look at how these characteristics of test tasks and content relate to difficulty, but they are not in themselves ratings of difficulty.

Propositional content

Vocabulary (Bachman (1990) p. 131)

Answer this in relation to the specific group of test takers for whom the test is intended. In the case of IELTS the test takers are ESL students who are attending or are hoping to attend undergraduate or postgraduate courses at English medium universities.

NB: These facets apply not only to words but also to fixed phrases and idiomatic expressions that may be relatively infrequent, specialised or ambiguous.

INFREQUENT	(Frequent) 0	1	2 (Infrequent)
SPECIALISED (e.g. technical, jargon, slang)	(General) 0	1	2 (Specialised)
AMBIGUOUS	(Clear) 0	1	2 (Ambiguous)

(Ambiguity refers to the possibility of more than one reading, or interpretation, of a phrase, sentence or text.)

Degree of contextualisation (Bachman (1990) p. 131)

In rating this facet, consider the relative proportion of 'new' to 'contextual' information. 'New information' (which includes new vocabulary) is that which is not known to the test taker and cannot be predicted from the context. 'Contextual information' is that which is developed in the passage itself. Thus, a passage is 'not at all contextualised' if there is a lot of new information in the passage that is not explained through definition, example, paraphrase, etc. The passage is 'highly contextualised' if there is no new information, or if the new information is explained. If the reader has prior knowledge that will help comprehension, then the text is contextualised. If the reader does not have relevant prior knowledge, the discourse is context reduced.

Input can be contextualised in terms of two types of information: cultural and that which is topic specific. Cultural Content relates to national (general) culture such as national habits, customs and beliefs (see over).

Ratings on this facet should be as follows:

	Highly contextualised		Not at all contextualised
With respect to CULTURAL CONTENT	0	1	2
With respect to TOPIC SPECIFICITY	0	1	2

(Give separate ratings for ASS [Arts and Social Science], LMS [Life and Medical Science], and PST [Physical Science and Technology] students.)

Example of rating:
0 = No new information, or new information is explained in text
1 = Little new information, not explained in the text
2 = New information that may be unfamiliar and is not explained in text

---

Topic (Bachman (1990) p. 137)

This facet has to do with the topic, or 'subject', of the text, and not whether the test taker is British, or an academic, or in a specialised area. Thus, for example, a text that has a great deal of specific American, Australian, British or Canadian cultural content is highly specific to this category, and would be rated '2', irrespective of whether a given test taker is of that background or orientation.

Note, therefore, that for this facet the test taker should *not* be taken into account.

	Not at all specific		Highly specific
CULTURE SPECIFIC	0	1	2
ACADEMIC SPECIFIC	0	1	2
SPECIALISED TOPIC	0	1	2

Organisational characteristics (Bachman (1990) p. 139)

Grammar

This relates to the complexity of sentence types and embeddings, and the frequency of the passive voice.

	Very simple		Very complex
GRAMMAR	0	1	2

Cohesion

This relates to the use of cohesive devices such as Reference, Substitution, Adversatives, Causals, Temporals and Lexical Cohesion as in M. A. K. Halliday & Ruqaiya Hasan, *Cohesion in English*, Longman, 1976.

	Not at all complex		Highly complex
COMPLEXITY OF COHESIVE DEVICES	0	1	2

Rhetorical complexity

This facet should be rated in terms of how complex the rhetorical organisation is, not on how familiar test takers are with it. RHETORICAL ORGANISATION should be rated according to how complex the text is in the classical rhetorical sense, e.g. instruction < description < comparison & contrast < argumentation. In general, instruction and description should be rated 0, comparison and contrast 1, and argumentation 2.

	Very simple		Very complex
RHETORICAL ORGANISATION	0	1	2

	One	Two	Three or more
NUMBER OF SPECIFIC TYPES OF RHETORICAL ORGANISATION	0	1	2

Sociolinguistic characteristics (Bachman (1990) p. 97)

	No occurrences	One occurrence	Two or more occurrences
CULTURAL REFERENCES (Passages only)	0	1	2
FIGURATIVE LANGUAGE (Clichés, metaphors etc.) (Passages only)	0	1	2

10 Examining Washback: The Sri Lankan Impact Study[1]

DIANNE WALL and J. CHARLES ALDERSON

Language tests are frequently criticised for having negative impact on teaching – so-called 'negative washback'. Some writers believe that it is possible to bring about positive change in language teaching by changing tests. However, neither positive nor negative washback on classrooms has been established empirically by observation of classrooms. This chapter seeks to redress this situation by reporting on an innovative study of the impact of a new English examination in Sri Lanka on language teaching. Although impact is demonstrated on the content of teaching, no evidence was found for any influence of the test on how teachers taught. It is argued that studies of washback need to relate teachers' attitudes to and understanding of exams to observations of classrooms in order to understand why teachers teach the way they do, and why tests might not have the impact that is frequently asserted. It is concluded that the supposition of washback as currently formulated is an oversimplified account of the relationship between tests and teaching and it is suggested that the complexity of that relationship, and of curricular innovation more generally, needs further exploration.

Introduction

It is common to claim the existence of washback (the impact of a test on teaching) and to declare that tests can be powerful determiners, both positively and negatively, of what happens in classrooms. Some (Morrow, 1986; Frederiksen & Collins, 1989) have even suggested that a test's validity should be measured by the degree to which it has a beneficial impact on teaching. However, in a recent article, Alderson & Wall (1993) have questioned these claims, and have pointed out that very little empirical research has been conducted to establish the influence of a language test on language teaching. They explore the concept of washback, and suggest that the Washback Hypothesis (in its simplest form, that tests influence teaching) is in need of considerable refinement. They suggest a number of possible alternative formulations, critically review the few studies that have been conducted to date, and make a series of suggestions for further research.

The purpose of this chapter is to describe research in Sri Lanka investigating the impact of a new examination on English language teaching in secondary schools. Unlike the previous attempts to describe examination washback in language education reviewed by Alderson & Wall (1993) (Wesdorp, 1982; Hughes, 1988; Khaniya, 1990), which were based on questionnaire and interview results and on test scores rather than on direct observation of classrooms, the study we describe takes into account not only what teachers report about the effect of an examination on their classroom practice, but what their teaching looks like in reality. We present a description of the educational context, a discussion of what examination washback might look like in this setting, a description of a two-year examination impact study, findings from the investigation, and a discussion of the nature of washback and the implications for the Washback Hypothesis.

The Context

The educational context

English is a second language in Sri Lanka, and one on which the country depends for various internal trade and social purposes and for conducting business with the outside world. Students study English from Year 3 to Year 11, and, as with most other subjects in the curriculum, they must sit an examination ('the O-Level') at the end of their 11th year. Their grades on the complete set of O-Levels will determine whether they will be allowed to enter higher education or whether, if they leave schooling, they will be eligible for desirable employment. Competition is intense for the few places available in higher education and for the limited number of good jobs a school-leaver can aspire to, so a student's O-Level grades, particularly in English, are among the most important in his or her academic career.

In the 1960s and 1970s very few students managed to pass the O-Level English exam (the passing mark of 35/100 was usually attained by only 20% of the population). Even those who did pass were usually not adequately prepared for the situations in which they needed English. The teaching programme that they had followed was structurally based and emphasized the development of general reading abilities. Students had little opportunity to engage in everyday communication, either orally or in writing.

The 1980s brought many changes to English teaching in Sri Lanka. In response to a need for more practical English, the Ministry of Education, with the help of the British Overseas Development Administration, launched several textbook and teacher-training initiatives. A new textbook series was written for secondary schools, which was meant to emphasize reading and

writing for a purpose and oral skills. Preservice and in-service training programmes were established to help teachers to cope with the demands of the
new materials. There was, however, a recognition that these innovations
might not be taken seriously unless they were accompanied by an examination which reflected the nature of the new textbooks. Plans were drawn up
to introduce a new O-Level English examination in 1988, when the first cohort
of students to go through Years 9, 10 and 11 of the textbook series were
reaching the end of their studies.

The O-Level examination and the textbook

The relationship between the O-Level exam and the textbook series was
quite explicit: the exam was intended to reinforce the textbook. To this end,
the examination designers inspected the textbooks and drew up a set of test
specifications in consultation with the textbook writers. The original plan
had been to produce an examination which covered all four language skills
(the written skills were to be tested in a 'final paper' at the end of Year 11,
and the oral skills would be tested by means of continuous assessment tasks
throughout Years 9 to 11) but this plan soon proved practically and politi-
cally impossible. The continuous assessment idea was dropped, leaving an
examination which would test only the written skills. Nevertheless, at least
for reading and writing, the exam is closely based on the textbook.

The specifications for reading and writing, which included the types of
texts that students would be expected to cope with, the types of reading skills
they were expected to master, and the types of writing they would be expected
to produce, were printed in the official introduction to the exam (National
Institute of Education, 1988). Naturally, even this reduced 'syllabus' was
much broader than could be covered in a single year's exam. The exam team
therefore deliberately adopted the policy of changing the exam with each
new administration: any one year's exam would sample only some of the text
types and reading and writing skills, but over a number of years the whole
syllabus would (ideally) be covered. This meant that teachers could not rely
on the same topics and types of questionss appearing each year, which, at
least in theory, would oblige them to cover the whole textbook series in their
classes rather than engage in 'question spotting' and coaching.

The Sri Lankan O-Level Evaluation Project

Lancaster University was commissioned to carry out an evaluation of the new
examination and its impact on classrooms. Our terms of reference included
investigating the validity and the reliability of the examination itself, and
measuring its washback on classroom teaching. The evaluation project was
to run from mid-1988 to the end of 1991.

Our evaluation of the first administration of the examination is reported elsewhere (Alderson & Wall, 1989), and so will not be discussed in detail in this chapter. Suffice it to say that we considered the first year's exam to be a valid and fairly reliable means of assessing what students were supposed to have learned in their last few years of English study. We concluded that, with one or two exceptions, the examination was an accurate reflection of the reading and writing activities in the textbook, and thus had content validity. There were a number of 'teething problems', but our research enabled the examination team to address problems in content and procedures before the second administration. The examination team took over some of the evaluation work during the second year and by the third year had sole responsibility for carrying out observations of administration and marking, conducting qualitative and statistical analyses of results, and making recommendations for further improvements of the exam.

The task of measuring the washback of the exam began even before we began working on the project, with baseline studies carried out by the examination team. Our own responsibilities included analysing baseline data, and conducting a long-term impact study, which would consist of questionnaires, interviews, materials analysis, and most importantly, observations of classroom teaching.

The Impact Study

What would washback look like?

The first challenge facing the Impact Study was to decide what washback from the exam might look like. This meant examining all the official statements about the goals of the examination and of the textbook series it was meant to reinforce. The textbook series introduced a number of new ideas into Sri Lankan ELT, both in terms of content and methodology. The series aimed to introduce a more communicative approach to language teaching, through a focus on texts and topics relevant to Sri Lankan schoolchildren, many of these authentic in nature, tasks that reflected the sorts of purposes such pupils might have for reading such texts, and innovations in content through a focus on language skills rather than just grammar. The reading skills that were to be developed included skimming and scanning, deducing the meaning of unknown words, picking out the main idea from supporting detail, understanding the communicative function or value of sentences, etc. (National Institute of Education, 1988: 1). The writing skills included planning and organising information, giving information explicitly, transferring information from pictures to reports, and so on. The texts that were to be dealt with ranged from short messages to informative academic texts in the case of reading, and application forms to quite lengthy reports in the case of writing. Grammar was also taught but it was meant to be down-played: while its importance was recognised by the textbook designers and teachers its treatment in the textbook series was neither frequent nor systematic.

Finally, there were many exercises to develop listening and speaking abilities: role plays, dialogues, picture descriptions, and discussion tasks. It is this attention to oral skills that most distinguishes these textbooks from earlier materials.

The textbook writers also hoped to encourage innovations in metho-dology. Their main aim was to convince teachers to be less dominant. Teachers were to encourage students to take more risks and to engage in pair and group work instead of depending on their teachers to supply them with all the answers. The *Teacher's Guide* which accompanied the first textbook in the series (Year 7) laid down the essentials of the approach that teachers were to follow and gave suggestions about how the new material should be dealt with in the classroom. It was hoped that these suggestions, along with the teacher training efforts that accompanied the introduction of the series, would change the traditional classroom into a more active learning place, where students would have sufficient opportunity to practise the skills the textbook writers hoped to encourage.

As stated above, the new examination was meant to reinforce the ideas introduced in the textbooks, both in terms of content and methodology. The exam was to provide a 'lever for change' (Pearson, 1988), which would persuade teachers to take seriously innovations which they might otherwise acknowledge but then ignore. The Impact Study was to investigate whether the exam was having the washback it was intended to have. Were teachers teaching the way the textbook designers and exam team wanted them to? If so, was the exam playing any role in this? If not, was the exam in any way responsible?

It should be clear by now that one of the main problems the Impact Study would face would be disentangling the influence of the exam from that of the textbook. If we discovered that teachers were using the materials and methodology that they were supposed to, it would be difficult to say whether they were merely doing what the textbook asked them to do or whether the exam was compelling them to do something they would not ordinarily have done. Either way, though, the results would be positive, in that the goals of the textbook designers (which for the purposes of the study were taken to be worthwhile) would have been achieved.

Positive washback

If there were no conflicts in the aims, activities or the marking criteria of the textbook and the exam, and if teachers accepted these and worked towards them, then a form of positive washback could be assumed to have occurred.

This positive washback, or co-operation between textbook and exam, would presumably produce results like the following:

(1) *Content of teaching.* Teachers would be 'teaching the textbook', because they would realise that any of the text types or tasks therein might appear on the final exam. They would not be giving more emphasis to any one skill than the textbook gave, because the weighting of the exam would reflect the weighting of the textbook.

(2) *Method of teaching.* Teachers would be using the general approach and the methods suggested by the *Teacher's Guides*, as they would recognise these to be efficient means of developing the skills that would be assessed on the exam.

(3) *Ways of assessing.* Teachers would be writing tests that would mirror the content of the textbook, because this would also be the content that would appear on the exam. They would mark their students' work using the criteria laid down in the textbook, which would also be the criteria used by examiners when marking the O-Level exam.

When teachers were asked why they were teaching and marking the way they were they would reply that they were guided by both the textbook and the exam.

Negative washback

There was always a possibility that the exam and the textbook would be pulling in different directions: where the exam, in spite of the good intentions surrounding its introduction, might have a restraining or distorting influence on what was being taught and how. In the case of this exam, the most obvious danger was that teachers might concentrate more on reading and writing rather than listening and speaking, since the oral skills were not to be tested. There were several other ways in which the examination could work against the textbook if it did not reflect the textbook as fully as it should have. This would constitute 'negative washback', which in its extreme form might look like the following:

(1) *Content of teaching.* Teachers would not teach the whole textbook because they would realise that some skills, namely listening and speaking, were not assessed and that it was more useful to spend limited class time practising reading and writing.

Even when teaching these skills teachers might neglect some text types or activities, feeling that these never appeared on the exam and were therefore not worth spending time on.

Teachers might abandon the use of the textbook altogether, and begin to use other materials which were more obviously related to the exam. These might include teacher-designed materials, past examination papers, or publications designed to help students to prepare for the exam, and might result in a 'narrowing of the curriculum' to match the exam (Smith, 1991).

(2) *Methodology*. Teachers would use whatever methodology they felt most expedient to help them to prepare their students for the exam. Some aspects of the new textbook's approach might be sacrificed if the teachers felt that these were not efficient means of preparing the students.

(3) *Assessing the students*. Teachers would write tests which would mirror the content of past examination papers rather than the content of the textbook. They would adapt questions, or would simply 'lift' them, either from past papers or from publications designed to prepare students for the exam.

Teachers would adopt the marking criteria used by the exam and would ignore advice in the textbook which went against this way of marking.

When teachers were asked why they were teaching and marking the way they were they would reply that they were driven by the exam rather than by the textbook.

Expectations

We did not expect to find either totally positive or totally negative washback, given that reality is bound to be more complicated than either of the above scenarios would suggest. What we did not know at the time, though, was just how difficult it would be to determine whether washback had occurred at all, and to decide, if there were no evidence for it, whether this was because there was no such thing or because there were conditions in the educational setting that were preventing it from 'getting through'.

The Washback Hypothesis, in most of the forms suggested (Alderson & Wall, 1993), implies that a test on its own makes all the difference. If it is a 'good' test (i.e. if it reflects the aims of the syllabus, and its content and method) then it will produce positive washback; if it is a 'bad' test (if it does not) then it will produce negative washback.

Alderson & Wall (1993) discuss possible refinements to the basic Wash-back Hypothesis by distinguishing content of teaching from the methodology used, and teaching from learning, as well as addressing the need to consider the impact of a test not only on teaching and learning but also on attitudes, materials and effort. We were to come to understand, through our attempts to establish washback and understand its nature, that what is not mentioned in any of the formulations of the Washback Hypothesis are the other factors that might also contribute to what teaching will look like: Do the teachers understand the approach of the textbook? Are they prepared to accept this? Are they able to implement the new ideas? Are they aware of the nature of the exam? Are they willing to go along with its demands? Are they able to prepare their students for what is to come? We return to these important points in the concluding section of this chapter.

Method

The baseline studies

Before we could determine whether the new O-Level examination was having an effect on teaching, it was necessary to find out what teaching was like before the introduction of the exam. The examination team carried out a series of baseline studies in 1988, about six months before the exam was to be held for the first time. In one of these studies members of the examination team observed teaching in 14 schools in five different areas of Sri Lanka. They were interested in seeing how teachers handled the textbooks, and in finding out how they viewed their own teaching and the influences upon it.

In general, teachers claimed that they had begun using a 'communica-tive methodology' once they had received the new textbooks, but the obser-vations indicated that this was not the case. Most classes were very formal, students spent much time listening to the teacher or practising language form rather than using the language, and many teachers did not seem to have clear objectives. Although the teachers were using the new materials, the methods that they were employing were not noticeably different from the traditional 'teacher dominant' methods which the textbook writers had tried to get them to leave behind.

There was no chance that the exam could have affected their teaching at that time. Although the first administration was supposed to occur soon, the official description of what the exam would cover and the types of tech-niques it might contain had only just been developed and had barely begun to be distributed to schools. Those teachers who claimed to have knowledge of the exam could only give vague or confused explanations of what they expected, which showed that in reality they had no such knowledge; most teachers readily declared that they knew nothing.

The baseline observations showed that teachers had begun to teach the content of the new textbooks but that their methodology resembled the type of teaching that the textbook designers had hoped to discourage. The new ideas about methodology had not yet taken hold. Whatever teachers were doing was guided by their understanding or lack of understanding of the text-book series alone, since they could not yet know what the exam would look like. This provided a reasonable baseline from which to measure whether either agent, the textbook or, more importantly for us, the exam, would have any influence on teaching in years to come.

Observation programme: 1990–91

At the core of this programme were seven Sri Lankan teachers, based in five different parts of the country, who had agreed to act as observers for the Impact Study. These teachers attended a three-month training programme which included discussions about the new teaching materials and the philo-sophy behind them, discussions and analysis of the new examination, dis-cussions about examination washback and how they would recognise this in classrooms, and practise in classroom observations. Each observer agreed to monitor seven schools in his or her own area, making a total of 49 schools across the country. The observers would visit each school six times, once a term for two academic years. They would fill in observation schedules for each classroom they visited, conduct interviews with the teachers they had observed, and record their own opinions about what they had seen and heard. They would then send their completed schedules to Lancaster, where a member of the Lancaster team would analyse their data (using SPSS-X for the most part) and would draw conclusions about the data and the means of collecting it. The analyst would then send feedback to the observers and instructions for the next round of observations.

Round 1, which took place in the first term of the 1990 academic year (the year had started four months late as a result of political difficulties throughout the country) served as a pilot round, which gave us useful infor-mation but also revealed problems in the instruments and procedures that we had designed for the study. We revised these in time for Round 2. This second round, held four months later and about three months before the 1990 exam was to be given, yielded important information and gave us further insights into what we should be looking for.

Round 3, however, produced data for only a few schools. This round took place a month before the exam, but observers found that many of the classrooms they visited had 'dissolved': schools had stopped giving classes so that students could study on their own. The fact that so many schools had stopped teaching so early was a strong indication of how much influence any examination was bound to have in this particular setting. Unfortunately, though, it left us with too little data to indicate how classes might have been affected by the exam when they were in session.

In December 1990 the UK team members held discussions with each of the Impact Study observers, which resulted in further revisions in the instruments and procedures before the next sets of observations.

Rounds 4, 5 and 6 took place in 1991, the first 'normal' academic year that much of Sri Lanka had experienced since before the introduction of the exam. Schools had been closed during much of 1988 and parts of 1989, because of civil disturbances, and this had a 'knock-on' effect into 1990. In 1991, however, many areas of the country, including those covered by our study, were able to enjoy a full three terms of teaching before the O-Level exam was given. The Impact Study sample size fluctuated during this year, due to the departure of one of the original observers, the arrival of several new team members, and the difficulties that all observers had in being released from their regular teaching duties to carry out the research. At its largest the sample contained 64 schools; at its smallest (excluding Round 3) it contained 36. There were 18 schools that were observed during all the rounds that were eventually used for the final analyses.

We do not propose in this chapter to present the findings of the earlier rounds, except to say that our analyses of all the data led us to believe that there were no important differences between the data gathered in Rounds 1, 2 and 4, and the data to be reported here from Rounds 5 and 6. The chapter will be based on the last two sets of observations: Round 5, the largest round and, we believe, a 'typical' one, and Round 6, when much formal 'exam preparation' was taking place, and reference will also be made, where appropriate, to the baseline data. There will also be references to interviews with many of the teachers who were observed during the two years, to see if they could help us to understand better what they had been doing and why.

Results: What did classes look like?

Round 5: A 'typical' round

In Round 5 (June–July 1991, five months before the exam) observers visited 64 Year 11 classrooms. They wrote detailed descriptions of each lesson and filled in checklists recording the types of texts and the types of activities that they observed. They also recorded their views of the effectiveness of each lesson, and whether the teaching in the lesson might have been influenced by the examination. They then sent their descriptions to Lancaster, where a member of the UK team analysed the data and tried to decide whether there was likely to have been examination impact on the content or methodology of each lesson.

When deciding whether there might be exam impact on the content (the passages, exercises and/or tasks) of the lesson, the analyst first looked at whether teachers were using the prescribed textbook or whether they were using materials from other sources. If they were using the textbook it was necessary to check whether they were working on content which resembled the exam, whether they were modifying this content in any way, and whether they were paying the same amount of attention to each of the four skills as the textbook did. If teachers were not using the textbook it was necessary to find out why they had chosen the content they were using, which skills they had chosen to emphasise, and how similar their material was to what had appeared in previous exams.

To investigate the effect of the exam on methodology it would first be necessary to see if the methodology that the teachers used matched the suggested methods given in the *Teacher's Guides* to the textbooks. If there was a difference between what the textbooks suggested and what the teachers did, then the teachers' explanations of why they did what they did would be examined. Of the 64 classes observed, 75% were using the textbook, and 25% were not.

Lessons where the textbook was used (75%): In Round 5, approximately 75% of the teachers were using the textbook on the day of the observation. It was felt that there was no exam impact on the content of 30% of these lessons, since the material being used did not resemble the exam in any way (e.g. exercises which focused on decontextualised grammar, or on developing listening or speaking skills). In the other 70% of the lessons there was some resemblance between the content of the class and the exam; however, this did not mean there was exam impact. In almost half these classes the teachers were taking the content (text and exercises) straight from the textbook. They had added no content of their own to the lesson so there was no reason to believe that they were doing anything more than what they were 'supposed to be doing'. In fact all but two teachers stated that they had chosen their content for the day because it was 'next in line' in the textbook.

In the other half of these classes the teachers were using the texts that appeared in the textbook but adding questions or other tasks. These questions/tasks were of the sort that might appear on the exam. However, this did not necessarily mean that the teachers had been influenced by the exam.

Their desire to check their students' comprehension is understandable, and the fact that they used certain question types more than others (mainly short-answer questions) might simply have been because they did not know how to use any others. Indeed, only a quarter of these teachers reported that they were preparing their students for the exam on the day of the observation; the others, with one or two exceptions, reported that they were using the material that was 'next in line'. The fact that so many teachers claimed to be teaching what came next in the textbook suggests that there was no exam impact on content. While it is always possible that the teachers would not have been teaching the next lesson if they had not believed it relevant to the exam, the observations offered no evidence to prove this. (See, however, information from group interviews, discussed in the section headed 'The need for complementary data' below.)

The second factor to be considered was how much attention teachers using the textbook paid to each skill area. As predicted, teachers seemed to be spending more time on written skills than on oral skills. Table 10.1 shows that the percentage of classes paying attention to reading was far greater than the percentage for any other skill, especially listening. This might have supported the idea of examination impact since roughly half the examination is devoted to reading; however, it does not explain why writing, which also accounts for about half of the examination, was the focus of so few classes. An analysis of the textbook units the teachers were covering provided a possible explanation for this discrepancy. The first column of Table 10.1 presents the percentage of textbook exercises that were devoted to each skill.

Table 10.1 Comparison of textbook and observed classes by skill, Round 5

Skill	% of textbook exercises devoted to this skill	% of classes devoted to this skill
Reading	40	52
Writing	20	17
Listening	10	5
Speaking	25	17
Language form	5	10

The minor attention paid to writing does not seem surprising given the emphasis in the textbook itself, nor does the minimal attention given to listening. There is also a suggestion that the amount of attention that teachers were devoting to reading only reflected the amount of attention the textbook devoted to this skill. The fact that the classroom figure for reading is about 10% higher than the textbook figure may indicate some impact though, as two or three teachers reported that they were preparing their students for the exam rather than simply teaching what was next in line. Overall, however, there does not seem to be very much independent impact from the exam.

There is little evidence from the observations, then, that teachers were modifying the content of the textbook on account of the exam or that they were emphasising any skills much more than the textbook itself would have suggested, with the possible exception of reading.

The Impact Study also looked into whether the exam was having any effect on teachers' methodology. There was no evidence in Round 5 (or any of the earlier rounds) that the exam was affecting the approach or techniques that teachers who were using the textbook used for teaching reading. Their methodology was very like the methodology that appeared in the baseline classrooms, which in turn resembled the way of teaching that the textbook designers had originally wished to discourage. It was hoped that specifying skills like 'skimming to obtain the gist' and 'finding specific information' in the official exam support documents and including fairly long passages in the exam itself would convince teachers to give their students training in reading quickly and disregarding irrelevant detail. However, the observers' reports indicated that such activities were not taking place in Round 5. Teachers were not giving their students practice in reading selectively; in fact, many teachers seemed to expect their students to understand all the words and the grammar in every passage, regardless of the types of questions they might be given to test their comprehension.

The *Teacher's Guides* to the textbook might be partly to blame for this state of affairs as they do not provide clear alternatives to a word-by-word approach to reading. The guide for Years 10/11 often provides 'prereading' and 'scanning' questions, but it does not explain how to use these questions to their best advantage (timing students, giving them hints as to how to find key information, etc.). It refers occasionally to a procedure called 'Finding Out', but this procedure, explained in the guide to Year 7, encourages teachers to develop reading by giving background to the topic, clarifying difficult structures or vocabulary, reading the passage aloud, having the students read it silently for five minutes, reading it aloud again, and getting the students to read it aloud – all before asking the students to answer any content questions! Although this method *might* be suitable for students at the start of their secondary school studies, it does not seem appropriate for O-Level students, who must read longer and more complex passages quite quickly.

What is ironic, however, is that many teachers provided even more support than is recommended in the earlier *Teacher's Guide*, to the point of 'spoon-feeding'. Teachers in all the rounds were observed explaining *all* the difficult words of the passage (see the *Teacher's Guide*: 'The pupil's own skill of guessing intelligently from context and relating mutually explanatory parts of the passage MUST be given scope'), dissecting passages sentence by sentence ('They must learn to focus their attention on the GENERAL message in the first instance and not on minor details'), and doing considerable amounts of explaining in the first language ('Don't kill their interest by giving them everything "on a plate" in advance'). Students were often required to read at the pace of the group rather than at their own pace. It is worth emphasising that the teachers who were teaching in this way were not only not being influenced by the exam, but not by the textbook either.

Nor was there evidence of exam impact on the methodology used in teaching writing. An inspection of the tasks given in the exam and the criteria for judging students' performance indicates that relevance of ideas and a certain sensitivity to audience are important factors, but these are matters of content and do not suggest or demand any particular methodology. What was hoped, however, was that the exam might reinforce suggestions given in the *Teacher's Guides* to get students to work together and help each other in deciding what should go into a piece of writing. The observers' reports showed that in general writing teachers did not give students the chance to work things out for themselves: like teachers of reading they tended to give far more guidance, even to the point of interference, than the *Teacher's Guides* recommended.

To summarise, then, there was no evidence that the exam was having any impact on methodology in classes where teachers were using the textbooks. In fact, the observations suggested that the way that teachers presented their content and got students to practise may not have been appropriate for the exam or the textbook and may have run contrary to some of the basic principles of the textbook series. There are many reasons why this might have been happening, but the most obvious one that emerged from later interviews was that many teachers did not really understand what the exam was testing or what the textbook was teaching in the first place. (See the section headed 'The need for complementary data' below for further discussion of this point.)

Lessons where the textbook was not used (25%): There were 17 classes where the textbook was not being used and it was felt that there was exam impact on the *content* of all of them. The first indicator of this was the teachers' own admission that they had chosen the content of their classes in order to prepare their students for examinations or tests: two-thirds referred specifically to the O-Level examination, and one-third referred to teacher-made tests. We know from other studies (Wall, 1991) that these often resemble the O-Level examination.

The second indicator was the emphasis that the teachers placed on written skills: seven classes focused on reading, seven on writing, and three on language form. None of the classes focused on listening or speaking. In fact, there was almost no oral work to be seen, apart from the students listening to the teacher and answering the teacher's questions.

The third indicator was the type and source of materials that were being used in the classrooms. In the case of reading classes nearly all the passages and tasks were taken straight from past examination papers or from commercial exam preparation books. In the case of writing classes, with only two exceptions, the tasks were taken from past papers, official exam support material, or commercial examination preparation books. In the case of classes concentrating on language form, the tasks were designed by teachers but the task types had all appeared on past exams.

However, the *methodology* of these lessons showed no impact from the exam, and showed little relation to suggestions in the *Teacher's Guides* to the textbooks. This was especially true in the case of reading. All of the reading classes followed roughly the same pattern:

Teacher writes passage on board.
Students copy passage into copybooks.
Teacher and/or student reads passage aloud.

Teacher writes (occasionally dictates) questions.
Students copy questions into copybooks.

Teacher dwells on instructions, often using L1.

Students take much time to answer questions on own (although occasionally they work in lockstep, question by question).

Teacher asks for answers and students give them.
Teacher and students discuss incorrect answers (sometimes).

Teacher asks how many students have got all the questions right, all but one, all but two, etc.

Teachers occasionally dissected texts before they asked students to answer the questions – explaining or translating the difficult words, paraphrasing or translating difficult sentences. Interestingly, though, this explaining or translating process was often lacking when it would have been most useful: when students had given incorrect answers and needed help to find out how they had gone wrong. Students' answers were discussed in about 60% of the lessons, but in the remainder they were merely accepted by the teacher or rejected.

This methodology obviously eliminated any possibility of skimming or scanning. Students usually read through the passage several times (as the teacher was writing it on the board, as they were copying it into their copybooks, and as they heard it read aloud or read it aloud themselves) before they read and copied the questions. This meant that there was no opportunity for them to practise selective reading. When the students were allowed to work on their own they often worked with no strict time limit, so they did not get used to the idea of having to read quickly. When they worked in lockstep, some did not have a chance to practise reading at all as others who worked more quickly were often requested by the teacher to supply answers to the whole group.

The pattern for writing lessons was less rigid but still visible:

Teacher writes rubric on blackboard.
Students copy rubric into copybooks.
Teachers spends some time explaining instructions, often using L1.

Teacher asks students questions about the task.
Teacher either puts key words or full sentences on blackboard. (On one occasion teacher dictated full sentences.)

Students write individually.

Correction: Students read what they have written to rest of the group. Teacher corrects the student who is reading and the other students try to correct themselves *or* teacher walks around correcting as he or she goes *or* students take copybooks to teacher for correction.

In only one class were students allowed to brainstorm within a small group. In several classes no correction was done because the writing itself took up the whole period. In no class were the criteria that were being used to correct written work made explicit to the students.

Although the content of the writing lessons matched the content of past examination papers, the methodology bore little resemblance to what students would have to do when sitting the exam. The biggest difference was in the amount of support the teachers gave the students, including writing out models for them to copy. There was no evidence that students were made aware of the criteria that would be used to judge them on the O-Level examination.

In summary, then, the Round 5 observations suggested the following:

(1) If teachers were using the textbooks in their lessons, their choice of content was not obviously influenced by the exam. Many took their content (texts and exercises) straight from the textbook, which did not necessarily involve thinking about the exam. Others added comprehension questions or tasks, but there was no evidence that they made these additions because of the exam.

(2) If the teachers were not using the textbook the content of their lessons was very much influenced by the exam.

(3) The methodology that the teachers were using, whether they were teaching from the textbook or not, showed no impact from the exam. Indeed, it often showed little impact from the *Teacher's Guides* to the textbooks.

Round 6: 'Exam preparation'

In Round 6 (October–November 1991, approximately one month before the examination), observers visited 41 Year 11 classrooms. Of these, only 29% were using the textbook and 71% were using other sorts of materials in classes. As in Round 5, the most evident examination impact seemed to be in classes where the teachers were supplying their own material.

Classes where the textbook was being used (29%): There was a resemblance between the content of the classes and the content of the examination in 11 out of 12 classes. In only two cases, however, did teachers change the content of the textbook lesson they were working from, and, as in Round 5, this meant adding exercises. The fact that teachers added exercises to a lesson does not necessarily indicate that they are influenced by the exam.

Most of the teachers who were teaching from the textbook were working on one of the last three units of Book 11. Table 10.2 shows the relative amount of attention paid to each skill in these three chapters and the proportion of the teachers who were working on exercises which were supposed to develop these skills.

Table 10.2 Comparison of textbook and observed classes by skill, Round 6

Skill	% of textbook exercises devoted to this skill	% of classes devoted to this skill
Reading	32	58
Writing	27	33
Listening	7	0
Speaking	27	8

These figures show that teachers were paying far less attention to the oral skills than the textbook itself would have had them do, and far more attention to reading. This emphasis on reading might have indicated examination impact; however, this was difficult to prove given that all but two of the teachers reported that they were teaching the lesson which came next in line in their textbooks rather than doing exam preparation.

As with Round 5, there seemed to be little evidence that the exam was having any independent impact on the content of lessons where the textbook was being used. The methodology was very much the same as that found in Round 5, in earlier rounds, and in the baseline data, and the comments made earlier about the inappropriateness of the methodology when compared to the goals of the exam and the textbook also apply here.

Lessons where the textbook was not used (71%): As in Round 5 it was easier to find exam impact when teachers were not using the official textbook. All of the teachers who responded to a question concerning the purpose of the day's lesson reported that they were doing 'exam preparation', and all but one of these referred specifically to the O-Level exam rather than to internal year-end tests.

The teachers either used teacher-designed materials (about a quarter of the sample) or commercial publications designed to help teachers and students to prepare for the exam (about half the sample). Only 13% were using past examination papers, and only one teacher was using official exam support material. It is interesting to note the large difference between the number of teachers using commercial materials and the number using official exam support materials. Although the latter are well written and informative, they are not used very often in classrooms. This may be a problem of distribution (only half the teachers owned or had access to either of the two official booklets) or it may be that the commercial materials (which are available in the urban areas, for a price which is equivalent to half the daily earnings of the typical secondary school teacher) hold some other attraction which we have not yet discovered.

The skills that the teachers were concentrating on during Round 6 were:

Reading	52% of sample
Writing	31%
Language form	17%

There was no attention paid to either listening or speaking. The students listened only to their teachers reading aloud or explaining lessons. The most common form of 'speaking' was answering questions asked by the teacher, although occasionally some students were asked to read aloud.

The text types and exercise or task types being used were clearly related to the exam. The two most commonly used text types had appeared frequently on the exam, and all of the question types had appeared on past papers. In the writing classes students were practising the filling in of application forms in all the classes but two. This is a type of writing that had appeared on every version of the new exam. In the language form classes students were practising grammar transformation exercises in all classes but one. Again, this type of exercise had appeared on every version of the new exam.

It was clear then that the exam was having an impact on the content of classes where the textbook was not being used, with the most obvious effect being the virtual disappearance of listening and speaking – attention being given to text types and exercise or task types which had appeared frequently on past exams.

With regard to methodology, the Round 6 classes where the textbook was not being used followed the same general patterns as in Round 5. In approximately half the reading classes the students did not have copies of the passages they were supposed to study. This meant that large amounts of class time were spent on writing: the teacher transferring a text and questions from a past paper or a commercial publication onto the blackboard, and the students copying from the board into their exercise books. Sometimes the students spent so much time copying that there was little time left for answering the questions or for checking whether the answers were correct. An observer wrote the following description of one such lesson:

Time
8.35 Teacher started writing the text on the blackboard: an advertisement calling for applications for trainee accounts clerks.
8.45 Teacher and students still writing or copying the text.
8.50 Teacher wrote comprehension questions on the blackboard. Six questions, e.g.
      (1) When is the closing date?
      (2) Can you forward typewritten applications?
8.55 Teacher asked students to answer the questions in their exercise books.
9.00 Students still writing.
9.10 The period over.

In the other half of the reading classes the teachers had either borrowed class sets of books which came earlier in the textbook series (students have to return their books to the school at the end of each year), or collected money from the students to pay for the duplication of past papers, or asked the students to buy copies of the commercial publications. Duplicating is less expensive than getting students to buy books; however, both options are beyond the means of most families. The observers reported only one teacher who had found a way around the problem of providing supplementary texts in poor areas: she brought in authentic texts from newspapers and distributed different texts to each of the students, allowing them to read and answer questions at their own pace and then providing answers for each student individually. This is the kind of activity that the *Teacher's Guides* to the textbook and the examination support materials should be suggesting, but unfortunately are not.

In classes where the students were concentrating on shorter texts or where they had their own copies of texts, the teachers might set three or four 'model questions' in a single period. Here the pattern was very tedious: students copied the text, answered the questions, gave their answers to the teacher, found out whether they are wright or wrong, and then passed on to the next exercise. There seemed to be less attention paid to clarifying instructions and to discussing the answers in Round 6 than in Round 5.

The methodology for writing classes and for language form classes was much the same as for Round 5. Again, if texts and questions were short some groups could manage to get through more than one exercise in a period. However, it would be difficult to try to deal with any of the longer tasks that are found toward the middle and the end of the O-Level exam because there would be too much to copy. This meant that students from poorer families and in schools with fewer resources were not always able to engage in certain types of exam practice because it took too much time to copy texts from one place to another.

Discussion

What are the observations showing us?

These two rounds of observations, in combination with previous ones, seem to suggest the following:

(1) Most teachers follow the textbook during the first two terms of the year. They work their way through the materials, unit by unit, exercise by exercise. This may be because they believe they have to 'cover the book' so that their students will do well on the exam, but there is no evidence from the observations to prove this.

(2) Less attention is paid in Year 11 to the development of oral skills than to written skills, even in normal teaching terms. This may be the effect of the exam; however, it may also be due to the fact that the textbook pays

less attention to these skills, or that teachers do not know how to teach listening and speaking.

(3) There is little visible exam impact on the content of reading, writing and grammar lessons if teachers are using the textbook. Teachers occasionally add questions or tasks to the day's lesson, but this may be to compensate for a lack of suitable exercises in the textbooks and not because of the exam. It is important to note, however, that the changes they do make are always changes in the direction of the exam.

(4) The third term of the academic year is very different from the first two terms. It is clear that there is a 'narrowing of the curriculum' as teachers finish or abandon their textbooks and begin intensive work with past papers and commercial publications to prepare their students for the exam. At this point there is obvious exam impact on the content of the teaching.

(5) There is no relationship between the methodology that teachers use, whatever the time of year, and the methodology that might be most suitable for students to apply when sitting the exam. (It is worth noting here that when the observers were asked to judge the effectiveness of the classes they had visited they judged them 'effective' in fewer than half the cases. They were not convinced that many teachers understood the basic principles of the textbook they were using or that they were in command of communicative teaching techniques.)

These findings are useful, but what they do not tell us is *why* teachers do what they do, what they understand about the underlying principles of the textbook and the examination, and what they believe to be effective means of teaching and learning. Observations on their own cannot give a full account of what is happening in classrooms. It was necessary to employ additional means of data collection.

The need for complementary data

Although the observations provided us with many insights into the relationship between teaching and the examination, they also left us with questions like the following:

(1) Many teachers reported that they were teaching the lesson that was next in line, even in Round 6. Why were they doing this?

(2) Some teachers reported that they had selected certain material in the textbook in order to prepare their students for the exam. What kinds of material had they skipped over, and why?

(3) Were there any kinds of material that teachers consistently and deliberately missed out?

(4) If teachers brought in supplementary material, what skills did they hope to develop?

(5) What was the attraction of the commercial publications that so many teachers were using in Rounds 5 and 6?

(6) How much did the teachers really understand of the aims of the textbook series?

(7) How much did they really know about the exam?

(8) How much influence did they feel the exam had had on the way they chose their content and methodology, and the way they designed and marked their tests?

(9) Did they believe the exam influenced their teaching in Years 9 and 10, when the exam was still a long way off?

It was important for us to complement the classroom observations with teacher interviews, questionnaires to teachers and teacher advisors, and analyses of materials (especially tests) that teachers had prepared for classes. It is not possible in this chapter to report the findings of these studies (see Wall, 1991; Alderson & Wall, 1992 for more details); however, it is relevant to record insights gained like the following:

(1) Many teachers believe they have to follow the textbook faithfully because the exam may test any of the content therein. Many teachers give extra classes to their students after normal school hours, on weekends and during holidays – not to work on special exam preparation material but simply to cover as many units as possible in their textbook. This implies exam impact on how teachers choose their content. (Data gathered from group interviews.)

(2) Many teachers believe that they have to cover the earlier textbooks in the series equally thoroughly, especially the Year-10 book. An important factor contributing to this belief is that past exams have taken some passages straight from earlier books in the textbook series. The teachers call these 'seen passages' and believe that if their students have studied every passage in every book they have a better chance of recognising any passage which appears on the exam – even though the questions/tasks accompanying the passages may be different. This implies exam impact on how teachers choose their content. (Group interviews.)

(3) A number of teachers, however, consistently skip over the listening lessons in their textbooks, because they know that listening will not be tested in the exam. Other teachers may 'do listening', but in a way that does not resemble the textbook designers' intentions. One teacher, for example, admitted that he only covers the listening lessons if the type of

question that students have to answer resembles an item type that might appear in the examination for reading. Other teachers use the listening comprehension texts, which are printed in the back of the student book, as passages for reading practice. This implies exam impact on lesson content. (Group interviews.)

(4) Many teachers report that they continue to teach listening and speaking; however, they admit that they do not test oral skills in their classrooms. The testing of listening and speaking seems to have died out with the dropping of continuous assessment. This implies examination impact on the way teachers assess their students. (Group interviews, analysis of tests.)

(5) Examination preparation takes up a large amount of the teaching year. Some teachers begin giving exam preparation classes halfway through the year; most teachers report that by late October or early November they are spending much of their class time and often extra time (again, after school, weekends, public holidays) helping their students to prepare for the exam. This implies exam impact on content. (Group interviews.)

(6) Many teachers know less about the exam than they realise. Most teachers can list the types of passages that might appear or the types of writing tasks, but they may not understand what is really being tested. Some teachers report that they teach the 'content' of the reading passages in their students' textbooks or in exam preparation books, because they believe their students will need to know facts such as the names of parts of a computer, the characteristics of certain animals, the number of radio transmitters in the USA and so on. If their students learn these facts then they will more easily be able to understand 'seen passages', or will be able to use this information in the writing subtests. The notion of reading in order to get new information rather than confirm old information is not widely understood. Many teachers are also unfamiliar with the criteria that will be used to mark student writing. (Group interviews.)

(7) A quarter of the teachers have not received any training on how to use the textbooks, and as many as 40% do not have access to some of the *Teacher's Guides*. This ignorance could prevent examination impact. (Individual interviews.)

(8) Only one-third have received any training on how to prepare students for the exam and only half have access to copies of official examination support materials. Again, this ignorance could prevent exam impact. (Individual interviews.)

The value of observations

The sceptic might ask why, if we were able to find out so much from individual and group interviews and from other forms of data collection, it was necessary to go to all the expense and trouble of observing classrooms. There are three answers to this question:

(1) If there had been no classroom observations, we would not have known that certain questions needed to be asked. For example, it might not have occurred to us to ask about the teachers' training and access to *Teacher's Guides* if we had not observed that many teachers did not seem to understand what it was they were meant to be teaching. We might not have asked about commercial publications had we not seen how often teachers use them rather than official exam support material. The list of such questions is long.

(2) If there had been no observations, we might not have been able to understand some of the answers that teachers gave us in the questionnaires and interviews, especially when they referred to local factors (e.g. classroom conditions, staff shortages, lack of resources) that helped to determine what they taught and how.

(3) If we had not analysed what goes on in classrooms we would have had no choice but to believe what the teachers told us. We might not have so readily doubted the claim that 85% of the teachers made in Round 5 and 90% of the teachers in Round 6: that the examination had influenced their methodology. Classroom observations reveal that this is definitely not the case, and they have helped us to appreciate that the exam can have no impact on methodology unless the teachers understand correctly what it is the exam is testing. Interviews or questionnaires on their own would have painted a more positive picture of washback than observations allowed us to accept.

Above all, we would not have known that the exam had virtually no impact on methodology if we had not observed classes. However, we would not have been able to understand *why* the exam had no impact on how teachers taught without discussions with teachers *after* having observed their classes. Thus observations and interviews/questionnaires/discussions necessarily complement each other in studies of this type. Observations on their own can only reveal part of what is happening within any educational setting: the observers can see what is going on, but they may not understand all they see. The other forms of data-gathering, though, will be equally uninformative if not accompanied by an analysis of teaching. Without observations the researchers are unlikely to know all the questions they should be asking and may not understand (or be sufficiently critical of) the answers they are given.

Conclusions

We conclude by returning to our expectations about positive and negative washback (see section headed 'The Impact Study' above) and listing our findings, from observations and other forms of data collection.

Content of teaching

There is evidence of washback on the content of teaching. Some of this is positive and some negative.

Evidence: Teachers' determination to cover the textbooks (mostly positive, but negative if the motivation is to memorise texts which may become 'seen passages'), more attention being paid to reading than textbook provides for (negative), less attention paid to oral skills than textbook provides for (negative), claims from teachers that they skip listening lessons because the exam does not test this skill (negative), long examination preparation period with materials reflecting content of exam and abandonment of listening and speaking (negative).

Methodology

There is no evidence of washback on methodology.

Evidence: Teachers teach in the same way in all six rounds of the Impact Study, and this is essentially the same as the methodology observed in the baseline studies. The way teachers teach before an exam is essentially the way they teach for the rest of the year, and the same as they taught before the new examination was introduced.

Teachers cannot tell by looking at the exam how they should teach reading or writing, and the official exam support materials do not help them to understand. The *Teacher's Guide* to Years 10–11 offers little advice on methodology, and the advice which is given in earlier *Teacher's Guides* seems to contradict the type of methodology that would be suitable for the aims of the syllabus that were agreed between textbook writers and exam design team.

Ways of assessing

There is evidence of washback on the way teachers and local education offices design tests. Some of this is positive and some negative.

Evidence: More attention to reading and writing than to grammar (positive), much use of item types which have appeared on the exam (positive when these have also appeared in the textbook, but negative when they have not and when certain types are over-used), much copying of passages and questions straight from past papers (negative).

There is no evidence of washback on the way that teachers mark their students' class tests and assignments. Few teachers have served as markers or received any training concerning the exam. Many have not received official exam support materials which explain the marking system. *Teacher's Guides* to the textbook also lack advice in this area.

Our conclusions are that the exam has had impact on the content of the teaching in that teachers are anxious to cover those parts of the textbook which they feel are most likely to be tested. This means that listening and speaking are not receiving the attention they should receive, because of the attention that teachers feel they must pay to reading. There is no indication that the exam is affecting the methodology of the classroom or that teachers have yet understood or been able to implement the methodology of the textbooks.

Earlier in this chapter (see section headed 'Expectations') we indicated that during the course of this study we came to question whether an exam on its own could make a difference in teaching and we referred to other factors that might contribute to what teaching looks like.

Although they seem obvious to us now they were not so apparent when our research began and it has only been by combining observations with other types of studies that we have been able to see the following:

(1) A considerable number of teachers do not understand the philosophy/ approach of the textbook. Many have not received adequate training and do not find that the *Teacher's Guides* on their own give enough guidance.
(2) Many teachers are unable, or feel unable, to implement the recommended methodology. They either lack the skills or feel that factors in their teaching situation prevent them from teaching the way they understood they should.
(3) Many teachers are not aware of the nature of the exam – what is really being tested. They may never have received the official exam support documents or attended training sessions which would explain the skills that students need to succeed at various exam tasks.
(4) All teachers seem willing to go along with the demands of the exam (if only they knew what they were).
(5) Many teachers are unable, or feel unable, to prepare their students for everything that might appear on future exams.

We now believe that an exam on its own cannot reinforce an approach to teaching that the educational system has not adequately prepared its teachers for. Factors which may prevent the implementation of the new approach, and which may make the task of reinforcement by an examination (washback) difficult include frequent turnover in teaching staff, lack of material resources, management practices within schools, insufficient exam-specific teacher training, inadequate communication between those responsible for the exam and its users, inadequate understanding of the philosophy of the textbook or the examination, teachers' beliefs that a particular method is more effective than those represented by the textbook or implicit in the examination, the degree of commitment of teachers to the profession, other obligations, including teaching commitments in other institutions or privately, and so on.

Until the educational system is able to coordinate the efforts of material designers, exam designers, teacher trainers, and those inspecting classes and advising teachers the mere setting into place of an examination will not reinforce materials and approaches to teaching which may not be well enough understood in the first place. By the same reasoning, the mere existence of an examination which is in conflict with textbook content, methodology or philosophy, or with teacher beliefs and practices, will not necessarily 'force' teachers into teaching a particular content, or using a particular methodology.

In short, if an exam is to have the impact intended, educationalists and education managers need to consider a range of factors that affect how innovations succeed or fail and that influence teacher (and pupil) behaviours. The exam is only one of these factors.

The study reported in this paper is an attempt to establish what impact an examination has, and by so doing, to investigate the frequently asserted but rarely researched belief that tests have washback – the Washback Hypothesis discussed in Alderson & Wall (1993). On the basis of our results, we believe the Washback Hypothesis to be overly simplistic and in need of considerable further discussion, refinement and investigation. We have produced convincing evidence, in the Sri Lankan context, that tests have impact on *what* teachers teach but not on *how* they teach. We have explored some of the factors that contribute to and inhibit washback, and have implied, at least, that the nature of curricular innovation is much more complex than the advocates or critics of washback seem to understand it to be. Testers need to pay much more attention to the washback of their tests, but they should also guard against oversimplified beliefs that 'good' tests will automatically have 'good' impact. Washback needs to be studied and understood, not asserted.

Note

1. Reproduced with permission from *Language Testing* Vol. 10.1, 1993, pp 41–69.

References

Alderson, J. C. and Wall, D. (1989) *The Sri Lankan O-Level Evaluation Project: First Interim Report.* Lancaster University.
— (1992) *The Sri Lankan O-Level Evaluation Project: Fourth and Final Report.* Lancaster University.
— (1993) Does washback exist? *Applied Linguistics* 14, June 1993.
Frederiksen, J. R. and Collins, A. (1989) A systems approach to educational testing. *Educational Researcher* 18, 27–32.
Hughes, A. (1988) Introducing a needs-based test of English Language proficiency into an English-medium university in Turkey. In A. Hughes (ed.) *Testing English for University Study.* ELT Documents 127 (pp. 134–53). London: Modern English Publications.
Khaniya, T. R. (1990b) Examinations as instruments for educational change: Investigating the washback effect of the Nepalese English exams. Unpublished PhD thesis, University of Edinburgh.
Morrow, K. (1986) The evaluation of tests of communicative performance. In M. Portal (ed.) *Innovations in Language Testing* (pp. 1–13). NFER/Nelson.
National Institute of Education, Ministry of Education, Sri Lanka (1987) *Teacher's Guides to Years 7 and 10/11.* English Every Day.
— (1988) *Guidelines to the O-Level Examination for 1988 and Beyond.*
Pearson, I. (1988) Tests as levers for change. In D. Chamberlain and R. Baumgardner (eds) *ESP in the Classroom: Practice and Evaluation.* ELT Documents 128 (pp. 98–107). Modern English Publications.
Smith, M. L. (1991) Put to the test: The effects of external testing on teachers. *Educational Researcher* 20, 5, June–July 1991, 8–11.
Wall, D. (1991) Measuring washback: The Sri Lankan Evaluation Project. Paper delivered at the International Association of Educational Assessment conference, Nairobi.
Wesdorp, H. (1982) Backwash effects of language testing in primary and secondary education. *Stichting Centrum voor onderwijsonderzoek van de Universiteit van Amsterdam.* Amsterdam.

11 The Role of the Segmental Dictionary in Professional Validation: Constructing a Dictionary of Language Testing

ALAN DAVIES

'He that undertakes to compile a Dictionary undertakes that which, if it comprehends the full extent of his design, he knows himself unable to perform.'

(Johnson, 1773)

The argument of this chapter is that professionalisation in the field of language testing is an important aspect of validation by virtue of its attempt to help establish the 'values, ideologies and broader theories related to the conceptual framework guiding the program of construct validation' (Messick, 1988). The chapter proposes that the writing of a specialist dictionary, also called a segmental dictionary (Opitz, 1983), can foster agreement among a profession of language testers on goals, procedures, methods of evaluating innovations, and terminology and norms, fulfilling a similar role to dictionaries in language standardization.

Professionalisation

Two of the stages in the formation of a new profession are, according to Elliott (1972), the establishment of training and selection procedures and the formation of a professional association. It is our contention that the preparation of a specific purpose glossary or dictionary of language testing is a necessary part of the continuing process of setting the standards and norms which a new profession requires. But it is not only public agreement on standards and norms that is required; it is also the need in a profession to make available to everyday use among new entrants and trainees the accepted and understood vocabularies of expertise (Atkinson, 1981: 20–1).

It is not so much that a profession needs a terminological dictionary, providing both the vocabulary and the concepts in use in the profession, as that the consensus allowing one to be constructed must be in place. As an institutional icon of value implications, a dictionary of language testing meets Messick's construct validity demands by marrying test consequences to test interpretation.

Means of Professional Education

The present discussion of writing a dictionary of language testing must first be viewed within the context of the educational role of an organisation such as the National Languages and Literacy Institute of Australia (NLLIA) of which the Language Testing Research Centre (LTRC) at the University of Melbourne forms part. Very properly the NLLIA sees its task as wider than the improvement of language teaching throughout Australia. Or to put that another way, the improvement of language teaching requires work at many levels, theoretical and practical. One aspect of that work is educational, making skills, techniques, methodologies, and knowledge about language and about languages widely known. A serious commitment to this educational responsibility means that the various Research and Development Centres of the NLLIA within their own areas of expertise need to concern themselves with the provision of information both for practitioners and for the public at large.

Such provision includes (in the case of the LTRC) training courses in methods of test construction and in assessment techniques (at the narrowest in the operating of a particular test instrument or procedure). The Language Testing and Curriculum Centre (LTACC) at Griffith University and the LTRC have discussed the setting up of the first type of training kind, perhaps a modular certificate course; and the LTACC itself is involved in training of the second kind.

Other types of educational activity range from the essential (and internal) training of research assistants to reading papers at conferences and to lecturing for outside groups. There is textbook writing, one aspect of which, for example, is represented by a series of videos on language testing for use by postgraduate students in Applied Linguistics, currently being prepared by the LTRC. There is writing about the work of the Centre, this time not so much for the profession as for a more public audience.

What a professional dictionary does in this context is to bring together the functions of training and of establishing norms and standards. What I will show in this description of our first attempts to compile a specialist dictionary of standard terminology used in language testing is what logical steps are necessary to prepare definitions for key terms. Further, I will argue that a transparent consensus on such terms is necessary to achieve a broad construct validation for language testing practices among cooperating professionals. Indeed I would maintain that unless it is possible to reach such consensus (and make it explicit in a dictionary) then it becomes supererogatory to speak of there being a profession of language testing. This argument raises such questions as: how does one determine what count as fundamental concepts informing constructs of language testing? What does the training of language testers involve? How are the specialized techniques and practices of language testing best conveyed to other professionals in language education?

The Role of a Dictionary

The idea for a dictionary was an attempt to provide a solution to such questions. Centre members need one, a kind of in-house set of glosses so that they all know what is being talked about, their own register; then, as with textbooks, there is a possible compromise between the profession (in this case, those working in Applied Linguistics and language testing) and the public. Typically this targets those with general rather than specialist knowledge, such as MA students of the relevant disciplines. Very much, in fact, like the audience targeted by Richards, Platt & Weber in their *Longman Dictionary of Applied Linguistics* (1985). Centre staff have found that working together on this dictionary is a felicitous way of sharing and educating one another, precisely because it helps define, explore and create the very register they need for their work. Those working on the dictionary, all very much on a part-time basis, are aware that this is a long term task for a small team. (This group includes Annie Brown, Chris Corbel, Alan Davies, Cathie Elder, Tom Lumley, Tim McNamara and Yap Soon Hock, all of the NLLIA Language Testing Centre, University of Melbourne.)

In the task of writing a dictionary, care must obviously be taken that the definitions or explanations can be understood by the reader, attributing to the dictionary a pedagogic role. This raises the questions of just what a dictionary is and in particular what sort of word-book is needed for a professional–academic audience. Some views by dictionary makers will be of interest.

Abercrombie, Hill & Turner, authors of a *Dictionary of Sociology* (1984) claims that 'A dictionary of sociology is not just a collection of definitions, but inevitably a statement of what the discipline is. It is also prescriptive in suggesting lines of development and consolidation' (p. vii). '. . . *a statement of what the discipline is.*': a tall order indeed but nevertheless inevitably what all dictionary making assumes in its normative role.

Angeles (1981: ix) states that his dictionary (of philosophy) 'is intended as an at-hand reference for students, laypersons, and teachers. It can be used as a supplement to texts and philosophy readings; it can also be consulted for philosophy's own enjoyment and enlightenment'. Even the '*laypersons*' Angeles referred to must surely be informed, interested, educated and so on. Audience is critical and when it includes students necessarily demands some measure of simplification, if not of language, certainly of substance.

Terms listed in a professional dictionary are typically (Illingworth *et al.*, 1985), those of use to students, and teachers of (the subject) and (sometimes) of all related subjects. It should also be of some use to the interested layman. A professional dictionary needs to be distinguished from an ideological one, for example, *The Feminist Dictionary* (Kramarae & Treichler, 1985), which asserts itself as a feminist dictionary, not a dictionary of feminism.

The problems encountered in preparing the dictionary have to do with audience and definition; equally important are selection and coverage, scope and format of entry. In attempting to reach agreement themselves over these matters LTRC staff have been helped by the realisation that such concerns are not at all new in lexicography.

Types of Dictionary

Kipfer (1984: 1), writing for trainee lexicographers, notes that a dictionary may be more than a reference book about words, 'it can contain biographical and geographical knowledge as well as information on pronunciations, meanings, grammar and usage and even the kind of information an encyclopedia gives about the thing the word names'. In other words, the term dictionary has many interpretations.

There are indeed many terms for the LTRC's dictionary ambition: but is it for a dictionary, an encyclopedia, a word list, a glossary, a reference list? Opitz writes of a 'segmental dictionary', but is that what it is or is it a glossary, that is, a list of technical terms rather than an attempt 'to isolate a distinct register', which is what Opitz meant by a segmental dictionary (1983: 58).

A glossary is defined by Hartmann (1983: 223) as a 'word-list with explanation of meanings'. Moulin describes a glossary as a list of glosses appended to text, often specialised, and details two techniques of ordering, by areas of interest and by alphabet: 'most authors [of specialist dictionaries] are neither linguists nor professional lexicographers, but specialists in the particular discipline . . . these glossaries are commissioned . . . to try and introduce a measure of normalisation in the use of specialist terms and thus facilitate the exchange of information' (Moulin, 1983: 146). I shall return to that concern for a 'measure of normalisation'.

Is it an encyclopedia? Hartmann tells us that encyclopedic information has to do with 'practical knowledge of things versus lexical information' (1983: 223). A more elaborate distinction is made by Read (1976: 713ff), quoted in McArthur (1986): 'The distinction between a dictionary and an encyclopedia is easy to state but difficult to carry out in a practical way: a dictionary explains words, whereas an encyclopedia explains things.' He points out that because words achieve their usefulness by referring to things, a dictionary cannot be constructed without considerable attention to the objects and abstractions designated.

McArthur reminds us that the *Encyclopedia Britannica* had as its original title: 'The Encyclopedia Britannica or a Dictionary of Arts and Sciences, compiled upon a New Plan' (Edinburgh, 1768–71, sponsored by the Society of Gentlemen in Scotland). The Britannica was a very obvious product (no doubt influenced by the French *philosophes*) of the Scottish Enlightenment, that high point in Scottish history. From that high point we are brought down to earth by the comment of William Smellie, one of the original Britannica authors: 'with pastepot and scissors I composed it' (W. Smellie in Kogan, 1956: 14, quoted in McArthur, 1986: 106–7).

McArthur (1986: 104) suggests as a way of resolving the overlap in the uses of the terms dictionary and encyclopedia that it is probably best not to bother proposing a continuum between the two. At one end of McArthur's continuum is the dictionary, at the other the encyclopedia and in between the *encyclopedic dictionary*. Malkiel (1962: 15) refers to this as a 'hybrid genre' which has been tolerated by publishing centres 'in defiance of common sense'.

Undismayed, McArthur suggests as a way of relating dictionaries and encyclopedias (which in the USA and France have always been linked) the terms micro- and macro-lexicography. The first deals with words, producing in most instances an alphabetic dictionary. The second (macro-lexicography) shades out into the world of things and subjects, and centres on compendia of knowledge. In most instances this leads to an encyclopedia, which, nowadays is usually also alphabetic (McArthur, 1986: 109).

When we look at attempts within the field of Applied Linguistics two well-known products are the *Longman Dictionary of Applied Linguistics* and the *First Dictionary of Linguistics and Phonetics*. In the Introduction to their *Longman Dictionary of Applied Linguistics*, Richards, Platt & Weber asked who their dictionary was intended for and concludes that it was intended for students of Applied Linguistics and General Linguistics and for language teachers both in training and in the field. Richards, Platt & Weber (1985: v) explains that their aim was to produce clear and simple definitions which communicate the basic and essential meanings of a term in non-technical language. As far as possible their definitions were self-contained, but cross-referencing was used where necessary.

Crystal, on the other hand, finds it necessary in the *First Dictionary of Linguistics and Phonetics* (1980: 5) to introduce a discursive approach to the definitions: 'Most entries accordingly contain encyclopedic information about such matters as the historical context in which a term was used, or the relationship between a term and others from associated fields'. Crystal uses no obligatory cross-referencing in his dictionary, each entry being self-contained. He points out that this leads to some repetition: 'This repetition', he says, 'would be a weakness, if the book were read from cover to cover; but a dictionary should not be used as a text-book, and while the result has been a somewhat longer volume than would have been the case if the "See . . ." convention had been used, I remain convinced of the greater benefits of look-up convenience and entry coherence' (Crystal, 1980: 5).

The LTRC Language Testing Dictionary Project

After some preliminary trials, pilot entry writing and a small-scale survey of the entries among teachers and MA students, we agreed upon the following guidelines:

(1) the entries should be on the encyclopedia side of McArthur's continuum, explaining where appropriate;

(2) they should where possible (and appropriate) give examples so as to situate the explanations;

(3) they should accept overlap, in Crystal's sense, so that referring to other entries for necessary explanation would be avoided, except where necessary for informative purposes;

(4) citations would be minimised except in the sense of the informative purpose above;

(5) where possible one clear definition should be attempted, in other words coming down on the side of being normative rather than descriptive. The

view has been taken that unlike a truly descriptive dictionary (such as the OED) it is this dictionary's role to contain and confine to 'try and introduce a measure of normalisation in the use of specialist terms and thus facilitate the exchange of information'. (Moulin, 1983: 146)

These guidelines have recently received support by a further small-scale probe. A small group of Masters' students attending a Language Testing course were invited to consider four graded versions of a definition of 'Face Validity' A B C D (see Appendix 1). D is the full version (contributed by Cathie Elder); C removes the Further Reading and Citations from the D version, B removes the alternative definitions from version C, and A removes the remaining examples from version B. A question was also asked about cross-referencing, following Crystal (1980) quoted above. The results suggested that while some simplification of the D version was preferred, there was a clear distinction between two types of simplification. The inclusion of the features: Further Reading, Citations and Examples is more desirable than provision for cross-referencing and offering one single clear definition. This suggests that the view taken by users of such a dictionary is more that of a text-book than of a word-list.

Whether this project therefore should be called a dictionary or an encyclopedia is really beside the point. However, while it does veer towards the encyclopedia side of the McArthur continuum it retains important aspects of dictionary-ness. It does attempt definitions, it avoids essays (so it is not strictly a Glossary: 'I have retained the procedure of organizing the Glossary as a series of essays' [Abrams, 1981: v]) but unlike many dictionaries it has no information of a pronunciation kind (though obviously it would not eschew this where it seemed relevant) nor does it systematically contain historical material about derivations. So it probably is what McArthur calls an encyclopedic dictionary.

The distinction made by Landau (1974) between extracted and imposed meanings relates directly to the value bearing and norm imposing characteristics of a professional dictionary and therefore reinforces our claim that the construction of a segmental dictionary is an act of construct validation.

At the same time Landau's distinction between extracted and imposed meanings is relevant:

General words are defined on the basis of citations illustrating actual usage: the meanings are EXTRACTED from a body of evidence . . . The meanings of scientific entries, on the other hand, are IMPOSED on the basis of expert advice. The experts may have sources apart from their own knowledge and experience, but their sources are informative and encyclopedic rather than lexical, that is, they are likely to consist of authoritative definitions composed by other experts whose concern is maintaining the internal coherence of their discipline rather than faithfully recording how terms are used. Their goal is ease and accuracy of communication between those versed in the language of science. (Landau, 1974: 242)

Survey

The plan for the Language Testing Dictionary is to establish a uniform style of entry and at the same time to ensure adequate coverage. To illustrate these questions and through them the importance of being more encyclopedic than dictionary-like, I turn now to a comparison of alternative entries.

The LTRC language testing dictionary team of writers (TW) anticipate that the final version will contain somewhere between 500 and 1,000 entries. Given the choice between the B versions and the A versions (Appendix 2 below) below, TW's present view is very much in favour of the B versions, even though use of the A versions would permit a larger number of entries. In each case the A version is much shorter than the B version, in some sense therefore the B version is more encyclopedia like and the A version more dictionary-like.

In making the comparisons reported below TW's hypothesis was that because of their perceived nature of this dictionary the B versions were more likely to be readable than the A versions. A class of MA students ($N = 21$) were asked to read three sets of alternative dictionary entries (see Appendix 2) and comment on (1) their length – were they too long, too short or about right; and (2) on their difficulty – were they too difficult, too easy or about right. With hindsight it is apparent that these were unsatisfactory choices to have to make. What after all does 'too easy' mean? Nevertheless the responses do provide some indication of the readability of the contrasting versions TW had provided.

Next a comparison was made between the (a) and (b) versions on the basis of their lexical density (Halliday, 1985). Lexical density is an indication of the ratio of lexical to grammatical loading clause by clause. Halliday reports that in informal spoken English lexical density is about two; in adult written language it is typically more dense, say about six per clause. In scientific writing it can be as high as 10–13 per clause. That is one reason why scientific writing is often so difficult except to the expert. (It is also an explanation of why newspaper headlines can be almost uninterpretable, unless the reader knows exactly what is currently at issue.)

Here are the summed responses of the Masters' students alongside the lexical density finding for each entry:

Table 11.1 Draft entries: Responses and lexical density

	1A	1B	2A	2B	3Ai	3A2	3B
Too long	0	9	0	7	0	0	16
Too short	14	0	17	0	19	8	0
About right	7	12	3	14	2	13	4
No response	0	0	1	0	0	0	1
Difficult	5	10	6	3	6	2	9
Easy	7	1	9	0	13	4	1
About right	9	10	4	18	2	14	9
No response	0	0	2	0	0	1	2
Lexical density	7	7	12	5.8	11	6.5	6.8

Note: $N = 21$; see Appendix 2 for draft entries.

As a rule of thumb I suggest that 50+% approval for an entry indicates acceptability (with an N of 21, to reach 50% requires a raw score of at least 11 on both 'about right' entries, i.e. for Length and for Difficulty). On that basis, two entries, 2B and 3A2 may be labelled acceptable. That judgement is supported by the lexical density comparison for these two entries. Note that 2B has a much lower lexical density than 2A (less than half) and that 3A2, while much lower on lexical density than 3A1, is also marginally lower than 3B. The problem with 3B, which TW had predicted would be rated as more acceptable by the class, seems to be sheer length. It is interesting that (see Table 11.1) there is substantial agreement (16/21) that this entry is too long and yet at the same time as many as 9/21 accorded it 'about right' for difficulty. A similar result emerges for Entry 1 where there is no separation between the A and the B versions in terms of lexical density ($= 7$). At the same time (and here is the similarity with entry 3B), there were nine responses in the 'about right' response for 1A and 10 for 1B. It might therefore be suggested that acceptability as indicated by being accorded 'about right' for difficulty is in part a function of lexical density. Where lexical density does not discriminate (as in the 1A and 1B entries) neither choice is regarded as being more acceptable. Where there may be little to choose in terms of lexical density (as between Entries 3A2 and 3B) length of an entry may militate against the choice of an entry (as with Entry 3B).

Concluding Remarks

Of course it may be queried whether a response of 'about right' is appropriate, whether indeed (as with the figure quoted above for scientific writing, a lexical density of between 10 and 13) specialists – as opposed to lay people – tolerate a high density, a 'more difficult' entry. But that is after all a comment on the sampling of the Survey's responses and it is indeed TW's contention that the class whose responses are reported here are the appropriate audience for this Dictionary of Language Testing, students on Masters' programmes who are in the process of being introduced to courses in Applied Linguistics, including Language Testing. Specialists in the field (*pace* Abercrombie *et al.*, 1984) are not TW's concern in this task. We distinguish the consensus of the specialists as to what the key terms are and how they are commonly used and the learning needs of the trainees (MA students for example). Both groups are needed to validate our dictionary since agreement on norms of a profession (or indeed of a society) is achieved both by consensus and by learnability. Consensus and learnability together are recognised signs of the value implications of construct validity. In my view dictionaries (and here I would agree with Abercrombie *et al.*, 1984) are always normative in the sense that they are drawing boundaries with a pedagogic intent. No dictionary, certainly not a segmental dictionary, can ever satisfy the specialist! And that is what TW have decided to term their effusion, a segmental dictionary: as such it retains its professional/vocational/registral association and at the same time its normative/pedagogical purpose.

References

Abercrombie, N., Hill, S. and Turner, B. S. (eds) (1984) *The Penguin Dictionary of Sociology*. London: Penguin.

Abrams, M. H. (1981) *A Glossary of Literary Terms* (4th ed.). Japan: Holt-Saunder.

Angeles, P. A. (1981) *Dictionary of Philosophy*. New York: Barnes & Noble/Harper & Row.

Atkinson, P. (1981) *The Clinical Experience: The Construction and Reconstruction of Medical Reality*. Farnborough: Gower.

Crystal, D. (1980) *A First Dictionary of Linguistics and Phonetics*. London: Andre Deutsch.

Elliott, P. (1972) *The Sociology of the Professions*. London: Macmillan.

Halliday, M. A. K. (1985) *Spoken and Written Language*. Deakin University, Australia: Deakin University Press.

Hartmann, R. R. K. (ed.) (1983) *Lexicography: Principles and Practice*. London: Academic Press.

Illingworth, V., Glaser, E. L. and Pyle, I. C. (1985) *Dictionary of Computing*. Oxford: Oxford University Press.

Johnson, S. (1955) *The Dictionary, with a Grammar and History of the English Language* (Preface to 4th ed., 1773). London.

Kipfer, B. (1984) *Workbook of Lexicography*. Exeter: University of Exeter Linguistics Series.

Kramarae, C. and Treichler, P. (1985) *A Feminist Dictionary*. London: Pandora (Routledge, Kegan, Paul).

Landau, S. I. (1974) Of matters lexicographical: Scientific and technical entries in American dictionaries. *American Speech* 49, 242.

Malkiel, Y. (1962) A typological classification of dictionaries on the basis of distinctive features. In F. Householder and S. Saporta (eds) *Problems in Lexicography* (pp. 3–24). Bloomington, IN: Indiana University Research Center in Anthropology, Folklore and Linguistics.

McArthur, T. (1986) *Worlds of Reference: Lexicography, Learning and Language from the Clay Tablet to the Computer*. Cambridge: Cambridge University Press.

Messick, S. (1988) The once and future uses of validity: Assessing the meaning and consequences of measurement. In H. Wainer and H. Braun (eds) *Test Validity* (pp. 33–45). Hillsdale, NJ: Erlbaum.

Moulin, A. (1983) L.S.P. dictionaries for E.F.L. learners. In R. R. K. Hartmann (ed.) *Lexicography: Principles and Practice* (pp. 144–52). London: Academic Press.

Opitz, K. (1983) On dictionaries for special registers. In R. R. K. Hartmann (ed.) *Lexicography: Principles and Practice* (pp. 53–64). London: Academic Press.

Read, A. W. (1976/1991). Dictionaries. *Encyclopedia Britannica* 15th ed. New York.

Richards, J., Platt, J. and Weber, H. (1985). *Longman Dictionary of Applied Linguistics*. London: Longman.

Appendix 1

FACE VALIDITY (A)

A type of VALIDITY referring to the degree to which a test appears to measure the knowledge or abilities it claims to measure, as judged by an untrained observer (such as the candidate taking the test, or the institution which plans to administer it).

FACE VALIDITY (B)

A type of VALIDITY referring to the degree to which a test appears to measure the knowledge or abilities it claims to measure, as judged by an untrained observer (such as the candidate taking the test, or the institution which plans to administer it).

For example, a gate-keeping test administered prior to entry to a particular profession (e.g. dentistry) which simulates actual work-place conditions can be said to have high face validity (even though the skills measured may not in fact be reliable predictors of future performance).

FACE VALIDITY (C)

A type of VALIDITY referring to the degree to which a test appears to measure the knowledge or abilities it claims to measure, as judged by an untrained observer (such as the candidate taking the test, or the institution which plans to administer it).

Appendix 1 *continued*

For example, a gate-keeping test administered prior to entry to a particular profession (e.g. dentistry) which simulates actual work-place conditions can be said to have high face validity (even though the skills measured may not in fact be reliable predictors of future performance).

Conversely, if a test of listening comprehension uses a speaker with a strong regional accent which is unfamiliar to the majority of candidates, the test may be judged as lacking face validity. A more obvious example of poor face validity is the use of a dictation activity to measure an apparently unrelated skill such as speaking ability (although there may be empirical evidence of a high correlation between the two skills). The term is often used in a pejorative sense.

However, failure to take issues of face validity into account may jeopardize the public credibility of a test (and indeed the curriculum on which the test may be based) and the notion of 'test appeal', insofar as it is achievable, is a practical consideration which test designers cannot afford to overlook. DIRECT TESTS are in fact often produced out of a concern for face validity.

See also CONTENT VALIDITY (a clear distinction is not always made between the two terms).

FACE VALIDITY (D)

A type of VALIDITY referring to the degree to which a test appears to measure the knowledge or abilities it claims to measure, as judged by an untrained observer (such as the candidate taking the test, or the institution which plans to administer it).

For example, a gate-keeping test administered prior to entry to a particular profession (e.g. dentistry) which simulates actual work-place conditions can be said to have high face validity (even though the skills measured may not in fact be reliable predictors of future performance).

Conversely, if a test of listening comprehension uses a speaker with a strong regional accent which is unfamiliar to the majority of candidates, the test may be judged as lacking face validity. A more obvious example of poor face validity is the use of a dictation activity to measure an apparently unrelated skill such as speaking ability (although there may be empirical evidence of a high correlation between the two skills).

The term is often used in a pejorative sense:

'in some trivial sense face or faith validity perhaps still has a role, but in diplomacy rather than psychology'. (Cattell, 1964: 8)

'the term face validity is . . . used to imply that the appearance of a relationship between the test and the external criterion is sufficient evidence of pragmatic validity'. (Mosier, 1947)

Appendix 1 *continued*

> 'validity of interpretations should not be compromised for the sake of face validity'. (Cronbach, 1984: 182–3)

However, Davies (1977) and Alderson (1981) argue that failure to take issues of face validity into account may jeopardize the public credibility of a test (and indeed the curriculum on which the test may be based) and that the notion of 'test appeal' insofar as it is achievable is a practical consideration which test designers cannot afford to overlook. DIRECT TESTS are in fact often produced out of a concern for face validity.

See also CONTENT VALIDITY (a clear distinction is not always made between the two terms).

Further reading Bachman (1990: 285–9).

Appendix 2

Entry 1A

Variance: (in testing and statistics) a measure of the DISPERSION of a SAMPLE. The variance of a set of scores, on a test for example, would be based on how much the scores obtained differ from the MEAN. and is itself the square of the STANDARD DEVIATION.

Entry 1B

Variance: a statistical measure of the DISPERSION of a SAMPLE which can be expressed in a standardised square root form as a STANDARD DEVIATION, that is to say that the variance of a sample is the standard deviation squared.

The dispersion of a sample on one measure (or test) may be compared with its dispersion on another; this comparison is referred to as the shared variance. Such a comparison is achieved by means of a CORRELATION and further comparisons of dispersion on other measures are carried out by means of ANALYSIS OF VARIANCE. The square of the correlation indicates in percentage terms the shared variance between two measures. Two tests which correlate 0.7 would have a shared variance of 49%, while a higher correlation of 0.9 would still indicate a shared variance of only 81%, leaving 19% of the variance unexplained by the overlap between the two tests.

Entry 2A

Analysis of variance: a statistical procedure used for estimating the relative effects of different sources of variance on test scores (ANOVA) (Bachman, 1990: 193).

Entry 2B

Analysis of variance: a statistical procedure which combines correlations of several variables with one another and against a common criterion, with the

Appendix 2 *continued*

intention of determining the influence (if any) of one variable upon another. Analysis of Variance (or Anova as it is often called) helps observers to avoid simplistic conclusions assuming causality between one variable and a criterion. Anova is commonly available on computer statistical packages.

Example: success at the end of an intermediate language course is shown to be significantly correlated with scores on an entry language test; when two other variables, age and motivation, are added to the study, it might turn out that entry scores no longer predict or do so only in relation to age and/or motivation; or that age is now so important a predictor that, when the 'variance' due to age is removed from the analysis, what remains for entry scores is trivial (see: *variance, correlation, criterion, variable, predict*)

Entry 3Ai

Bias: 'systematic error associated with any type of group membership, sex and age group membership included' (Jensen, 1980)

Entry 3A2

Bias: 'systematic differences in test performance that are the result of differences in individual characteristics, other than the ability being tested, of test takers'. (Bachman, 1990: 271)

Entry 3B

Bias: bias is defined by Jensen (1980) as 'systematic error associated with any type of group membership, sex and age group membership included'. The terms *systematic error* and *group* are important in this definition. In a trivial way all tests are biased against individuals who lack knowledge or skill. But since that is what tests are designed to do, such 'bias' or, better, discrimination is not systematic error, that is to say there will be random error as in all measurement but it is not systematic or deliberate. The *group* issue is more problematic in situations of norm conflict such as recent migrant communities. Should children from such communities with only a few years of schooling in the target language (e.g. English) take the same language tests as first language speaking children? In conflict are (1) the general educational norms and standards of the host community and (2) what it is reasonable to expect in terms of English language proficiency of the migrant children. In situations where the first consideration weighs more heavily, migrant children will take the same English test as first language children. In situations where the second consideration is more important, a more specialised test of ESL may be used.

12 Language Testing Courses: What Are They?

KATHLEEN M. BAILEY and JAMES DEAN BROWN

In recent years, language testing courses have been offered as part of language teacher training programs around the world. As a result, the ideologies, value systems, and normative practices of language testing are increasingly informing language teaching, and vice versa. The purpose of this study was to investigate the structure, content, and student attitudes toward introductory language testing courses so as to better understand the interaction of language teaching and testing. To those ends, we designed a questionnaire to cover a variety of topics about language testing courses, including instructors' backgrounds, the topics covered in these courses, and the types of students in the classes, as well as students' attitudes toward language testing before and after the courses. Although the items were predominantly Likert-scale in format, we also included a number of open-ended questions. Results from 84 respondents in various parts of the world describe the attributes of those who teach language testing courses, the features of the courses, and the attitudes of students toward such courses.

A certain amount of self-scrutiny is inherent in developing professionalism in any field. Applied Linguistics is no exception. In recent years applied linguists have begun to examine their own preparation and the professional training they offer language teachers. As suggested by the introductory chapter to this volume, as well as Davies' chapter, such inquiry forms a necessary basis for the validation of the social consequences of language testing, broadly conceived. For example, Lazarton, Riggenbach & Ediger (1987: 263) surveyed 121 applied linguists, 'about their knowledge of and attitudes toward statistics and empirical research'. The authors concluded that there was a wide range of familiarity among the respondents with regard to empirical research methods.

In another investigation, Richards & Crookes (1988) surveyed 120 US-based MA programs offering degrees in TESOL and related fields. Their work followed that of Richards & Hino (1983), which was a survey of American TESOL MA-holders working in Japan. Richards and Crookes focused specifically on the practicum component of MA programs, in order to determine its goals and contents in the 78 MA programs whose representatives responded to the survey.

There is a need for similar work in language testing. Jones (1985: 16) pointed out that:

> there is really a sub-profession within language teaching that is dedicated to the science of language proficiency measurement. The level of sophistication has become so great that an understanding gap has emerged between the testing specialists and their colleagues in other areas of language teaching.

We believe that the 'understanding gap' that Jones referred to can be bridged, in part, by language teachers learning more about language testing in specialized courses such as those examined in the present study. (Of course, language testers must also be knowledgeable about language teaching.) Two recent papers have discussed the education of language teachers with regard to language assessment: Brindley (1991) has discussed the issues and problems associated with developing professional development programs in assessment for teachers in the Australian Adult Migrant English Program. And Peirce (1990) has discussed a model for collaborative work on language testing by inservice teachers at the Ontario Institute for Studies in Education.

In education generally, problems have been noted which are similar to the situation in language teaching and testing: 'few teachers receive adequate training in effective assessment techniques' (Assessment Standards, 1990: 2). Seven standards for teacher development in this area have been written by the American Federation of Teachers, the National Council on Measurement in Education, and the National Education Association:

(1) Teachers should be skilled in choosing assessment methods appropriate for instructional decisions.
(2) Teachers should be skilled in developing assessment methods appropriate for instructional decisions.
(3) Teachers should be skilled in administering, scoring, and interpreting the results of both externally produced and teacher-produced assessment methods.
(4) Teachers should be skilled in using assessment results when making decisions about individual students, planning teaching, developing curriculum, and improving schools.
(5) Teachers should be skilled in developing valid pupil grading procedures which use pupil assessment.

(6) Teachers should be skilled in communicating assessment results to students, parents, other lay audiences, and other educators.
(7) Teachers should be skilled in recognizing unethical, illegal, and otherwise inappropriate assessment methods and uses of assessment information.

We will return to these standards in discussing the results of the present study.

Brown, Knowles, Murray, Neu & Violand-Hainer (1992) recently surveyed TESOL members regarding ESL and EFL teachers' preparation in statistics courses and/or courses in testing. The respondents represented the general membership as well as four particular interest sections (ISs). A majority of the respondents in each group had, in fact, taken a course in statistics: 60.4% of the general membership group ($n = 334$), 77.3% from the Applied Linguistics IS ($n = 66$), 58.1% from the ESL in Higher Education IS ($n = 62$), 95.1% from the Research IS ($n = 82$) and 71.4% of the respondents in the Teacher Education IS ($n = 63$). Although the percentages are not quite as high, a majority of the respondents in these same categories had also taken a course in language testing: 56.1% of the TESOL general membership, 57.8% from the Applied Linguistics IS, 50.8% from the ESL in Higher Education IS, 66.2% from the Research IS, and 63.9% from the Teacher Education IS. (These data were taken from Brown *et al.*, 1992, Table 5.) It is encouraging that regardless of the subgroup sampled in each case, over half of the respondents had taken a course in language testing. We assume that, as the theoretical, practical and legal importance of language testing increases, teacher preparation in this area must also increase and, indeed, develop.

The purpose of the present study was to investigate the existing teacher training courses in language testing so that we can eventually understand how the ideologies, value systems, and normative practices of language testing (i.e. the consequential bases, especially the social consequences, of construct validation) are informing language teaching and vice versa. To that end, the focus of this study was on the structure, content, and student attitudes toward introductory language testing courses.

Method

Materials

The questionnaire used in this study (see Appendix 1) was developed by the researchers in order to gather relevant biodata information on the respondents as well as data on their various language testing courses. It consisted of four pages of open-ended, yes/no, and Likert type questions. To make the response process as efficient as possible, a question near the top of the first page asked whether the respondents had 'ever taught a language testing course'. If the respondents answered NO, they were asked to 'please stop and mail the questionnaire'. Otherwise they were to continue answering the questions.

The questionnaire contained groups of items designed to gather information about the instructor of the course, about the students who take the course, and about the course itself. The questions about the course were further subdivided into questions about different topics that might be covered: validity, item analysis, descriptive statistics, test consistency, and general topics.

Procedures

Questionnaires were sent to all of the 'active' members on the mailing list of the Language Testing Research Colloquium (LTRC) in 1990. A total of 396 questionnaires were mailed out in fall 1990. Two months later, a second mailing was sent out to those active members who had not responded to the first request for information. Three questionnaires were returned because they were 'undeliverable'. Five other people were contacted at the suggestion of respondents to the first round of questionnaires. (These people were not on the LTRC mailing list, but were known to LTRC participants as having some responsibility for training language teachers about testing.)

Finally, the questionnaires obtained though this process were matched with the programs listed in the directory of professional preparation programs published by the TESOL organization (Kornblum with Gilligan, 1989). We then sent a questionnaire to the department head of any program listed in the directory but not already represented in our data base. We asked that the survey be routed to any faculty member having responsibility for language teacher preparation in assessment.

Respondents

Of the approximately 400 people who received this survey, a total of 177 questionnaires were returned, for an overall response rate of about 44%. Of those who responded, 84 had taught a language testing course. It was these 84 language testing teachers who served as the basis for the results which are reported in this study.

Respondents to the survey were language testers (a group more accustomed to being researchers than subjects). Those who had recently taught a language testing course were about evenly split between females (48.2%) and males (51.2%). On average, the respondents were 45.25 years old but ranged in age from 31 to 74 (with nine rather sensitive abstentions). As for nationality, 67.6% were from the United States, 8.4% from Britain, 7.2% from Canada, 4.8% from The Netherlands, 2.4% each from Australia and Thailand, and 1.2% each from Chile, Finland, Germany, Hong Kong, Israel, and New Zealand. (This geographic distribution was probably influenced by our use of the TESOL directory of programs, which has a North American focus.)

Results

The survey data will be described in terms of the structure of the question-naire. The main sections elicited information about the instructors, about the courses, and about the students.

Information about the instructors

Some information about the instructors (sex, age, and nationality) was presented above. However, other information was also gathered on the questionnaire, allowing us to describe the language testing teachers in our sample in terms of their highest degree, major field of study, number of statistics courses taken, and other non-course testing experience.

The highest degrees attained by the respondents included 16.7% MA degrees, 76.2% PhD degrees, and 7.1% 'all but dissertation'. Of these degrees, 36.1% were in Applied Linguistics or a closely related field, 26.5% were in Education or Educational Psychology, 16.9% were in Linguistics, 7.2% were in a particular foreign language, 4.8% were in Psychology, and 3.6% were in Bilingual Education. An additional 4.8% were in other disci-plines.

In response to a question about the number of statistics/testing courses taken by these teacher-trainers, it turned out that the respondents had taken an average of 4.14 courses, but there was considerable variation in this type of experience, as indicated by a standard deviation of 3.01 courses and a range of 0 courses to 12. There were eight respondents who wrote that they had taken no such courses, and eight who had taken ten or more. It is impor-tant to remember, however, that higher education in the form of 'courses' is not universal – particularly at the MA and PhD levels.

In response to a question about other non-course testing experience, a wide variety of responses were given, including the following: classroom test development, committees for ETS (and other) testing programs, consult-ing, dissertation research, extensive reading, Language Testing Research Colloquiums, program evaluation, rater training, research grants, survey research, TESOL Conferences, test scoring, test analysis, test development, test administration, testing research, working as a testing program director, working with individual (named) language testers, giving and taking on testing, and writing TOEFL preparation materials. Thus, not surprisingly, the survey respondents reported having background in both formal education and practical experience related to language assessment.

Information about courses

A number of the items in the Likert-scale format were designed to elicit the responding language testers' estimates of the amount of coverage given to a large number of potential topics that could be covered in such a course. The Likert scale offered respondents a choice as follows:

	Amount of time				
Type of experience:	*None*	*Some*	*Moderate*	*Extensive*	
item writing	0	1	2	3	4	5
test administration	0	1	2	3	4	5
test scoring	0	1	2	3	4	5
etc . . .						

The results were analyzed in terms of the mean and standard deviation for the ratings as well as for the percent of respondents choosing each of the points along the Likert scale.

The results for the *Course Structure* questions are shown in Table 12.1. The percent of negative responses is given (indicating the percent of respondents who said that they do not teach the particular topic) and the percent of respondents who selected *Some, Moderate*, or *Extensive* coverage or some point in between. All of the positive responses and the negative responses taken together should add up to approximately 100% (with some rounding error, of course).

As shown in Table 12.1, Test Critiquing had the highest mean Likert rating and generally seems to have received more extensive coverage than the other topics. In contrast, Test Taking was the topic which received the lowest mean Likert rating and had the lowest levels of coverage. Nonetheless, the topics in Table 12.1 were generally rated higher in terms of means and coverage than many of the topics in the tables that follow.

Other relationships may prove interesting to readers depending on whether they wish to think in terms of what the average language testing course contains or in terms of how their own language testing course compares to what is taught by others. The remaining discussion will point out the topics that are outstanding in one way or another, i.e. those which receive especially high, or low, Likert ratings and coverage.

Table 12.1 Responses for course structure

Topic	Likert Mean	SD	Percent negative responses 0	Percent positive responses Some 1	Moderate 2	3	Extensive 4	5
Item writing	3.24	1.46	2.4	14.3	13.1	29.8	20.2	26.2
Test admin.	2.06	1.34	15.7	20.5	22.9	26.5	12.0	2.4
Test scoring	2.42	1.32	6.0	21.7	24.1	26.5	15.7	6.0
Test score interp.	3.10	1.26	1.2	10.7	21.4	23.8	29.8	13.1
Test revision	2.45	1.42	8.5	20.7	22.0	22.0	19.5	7.3
Test critiquing	3.38	1.35	4.8	4.8	11.9	28.6	26.2	23.8
Test taking	1.89	1.28	9.8	36.6	25.6	14.6	9.8	3.7

Table 12.2 Responses for general topics

Topic	Likert Mean	SD	Percent negative responses 0	Percent positive responses Some 1	Moderate 2	3	Extensive 4	5
Norm-referenced testing	2.60	1.24	1.2	24.1	18.1	32.5	18.1	6.0
Criterion-referenced testing	2.84	1.28	0.0	20.5	18.1	28.9	21.7	10.8
Achievement testing	2.92	1.23	2.4	13.3	16.9	33.7	25.3	8.4
Aptitude testing	1.28	1.09	23.2	47.6	11.0	14.6	3.7	0.0
Diagnostic testing	2.15	1.29	8.5	26.8	25.6	23.2	12.2	3.7
Placement testing	2.37	1.18	7.2	14.5	31.3	28.9	16.9	1.2
Proficiency testing	3.31	1.10	0.0	8.6	9.9	37.0	30.9	13.6
Measuring attitudes	1.17	1.19	37.0	28.4	19.8	11.1	2.5	1.2
Measuring the different skills	3.37	1.21	0.0	9.6	12.0	28.9	30.1	19.3
Assessment at different levels	2.68	1.20	0.0	18.3	29.3	25.6	19.5	7.3
Critiquing published tests	2.45	1.48	9.8	19.5	23.2	20.7	17.1	9.8

For example, other *General Topics* were rated as shown in Table 12.2. Notice that fairly large percentages of respondents do not cover the topics of Aptitude Testing or Measuring Attitudes (23.2 and 37.0%, respectively) and that these issues receive correspondingly low mean ratings and coverage. In contrast, all the respondents reported covering Criterion-referenced Testing, Proficiency Testing, Measuring the Different Skills, and Assessment at Different Levels, although they do so with different degrees of coverage.

The analysis of topics related to *Item Analysis* is presented in Table 12.3: Item Writing, Item Writing for Different Skills, Item Content Analysis, and Item Quality Analysis are covered by 90% or more of the respondents

Table 12.3 Responses for item analysis

Topic	Likert Mean SD	Percent negative responses 0	Some 1	Moderate 2	3	Extensive 4	5
Item writing	3.08 1.44	3.6	14.5	13.3	27.7	20.5	20.5
Item writing for diff. skills	3.02 1.41	3.6	14.5	14.5	28.9	20.5	18.1
Item content analysis	2.85 1.30	2.5	12.3	27.2	27.2	17.3	13.6
Item quality analysis	2.94 1.35	5.1	11.4	17.7	27.8	26.6	11.4
Item facility	2.90 1.40	6.1	14.6	11.0	30.5	26.8	11.0
Item discrimination (trad.)	2.57 1.47	12.2	14.6	13.4	30.5	22.0	7.3
Biserial correlation	1.49 1.33	30.4	22.8	22.8	17.7	3.8	2.5
Item agreement	0.95 1.16	51.4	18.9	14.9	13.5	1.4	0.0
Item beta	0.51 0.94	73.0	9.5	10.8	6.8	0.0	0.0
Distractor efficiency analysis	1.81 1.69	32.5	18.8	13.7	11.2	17.5	6.3
One-parameter IRT	0.63 1.11	63.3	24.1	5.1	3.8	1.3	2.5
Two-parameter IRT	0.33 0.73	77.2	16.5	3.8	1.3	1.3	0.0
Three-parameter IRT	0.27 0.52	77.2	19.0	3.8	0.0	0.0	0.0

(though to varying degrees). Traditional Item Discrimination, Biserial Correlation, and Distractor Efficiency Analysis are covered to some degree in more than two-thirds of the courses. In contrast, criterion-referenced item statistics (Item Agreement and Item Beta) and item response theory (One-parameter, Two-parameter and Three-parameter IRT) are only covered in 22.8 to 48.6% of the courses.

Table 12.4 indicates that the topic of basic *Descriptive Statistics* for central tendency (Mean, Mode, Median and Midpoint) and dispersion (Range, Standard Deviation and Variance) receives coverage in most language testing courses. Statistics for reporting standardized scores (stanines, z scores, T scores and CEEB scores) get less attention in general and that attention is focused in fewer courses. In some instances, respondents indicated that statistics were dealt with in another (often prerequisite) course.

Table 12.4 Responses for descriptive statistics

| | Likert | Percent negative responses | Percent positive responses | | | | |
| | | | Some | Moderate | | Extensive | |
Topic	Mean SD	0	1	2	3	4	5
Mean	2.68 1.32	3.7	17.5	22.5	30.0	16.2	10.0
Mode	2.33 1.32	6.3	25.3	21.5	29.1	11.4	6.3
Median	2.44 1.27	5.0	21.2	23.7	31.3	12.5	6.3
Midpoint	2.22 1.44	14.5	19.7	18.4	30.3	10.5	6.6
Range	2.43 1.34	6.3	23.7	18.8	30.0	15.0	6.3
Standard deviation	2.61 1.36	7.5	15.0	20.0	32.5	16.2	8.7
Variance	2.29 1.42	11.2	22.5	17.5	31.3	10.0	7.5
Stanines	1.20 1.29	39.2	27.8	12.7	16.5	1.3	2.5
Z scores	1.81 1.44	21.2	28.7	13.7	25.0	6.3	5.0
T scores	1.66 1.39	23.7	30.0	15.0	22.5	5.0	3.7
CEEB scores	0.97 1.25	50.6	23.4	7.8	15.6	1.3	1.3

Similarly, in the results for *Test Consistency* shown in Table 12.5, theoretical issues are covered in 80 to 90% of the courses in varying degrees. These topics include those involved with reliability (Sources of Testing Error, Reliability and Test Length, and Reliability and Ranges of Talent) as well as the general strategies for estimating test reliability (Test-retest Reliability, Parallel Forms Reliability, Internal Consistency Reliability, Standard Error

Table 12.5 Responses for test consistency

Topic	Likert Mean SD	Percent negative responses 0	Some 1	Moderate 2	3	Extensive 4	5
Sources of testing error	2.65 1.33	6.1	14.6	22.0	31.7	17.1	8.5
Reliability and test length	2.65 1.34	6.1	14.6	23.2	29.3	18.3	8.5
Reliability and ranges of talent	2.16 1.40	15.9	18.3	19.5	31.7	9.8	4.9
Test-retest reliability	2.35 1.37	9.6	22.9	14.5	34.9	12.0	6.0
Parallel forms reliability	2.23 1.38	10.8	25.3	15.7	32.5.	9.6	6.0
Internal consistency reliability	2.57 1.42	6.1	22.0	17.1	29.3	14.6	11.0
Standard error of measurement	2.20 1.45	15.9	18.3	20.7	26.8	12.2	6.1
Split-half adjusted method	1.80 1.44	26.8	18.3	15.9	26.8	11.0	1.2
Spearman-Brown prophecy formula	1.60 1.44	34.1	14.6	19.5	23.2	6.1	2.4
K-R 20	1.54 1.47	32.9	20.7	20.7	17.1	2.4	6.1
K-R 21	1.57 1.52	34.1	19.5	17.1	19.5	3.7	6.1
Cronbach alpha	1.30 1.52	43.9	19.5	14.6	12.2	3.7	6.1
Rulon	0.13 0.37	88.7	10.0	1.2	0.0	0.0	0.0
Flanagan	0.15 0.56	89.9	7.6	1.3	0.0	1.3	0.0
Guttman	0.45 0.89	73.5	13.3	10.8	1.2	0.0	1.2
Interrater	2.25 1.55	18.1	16.9	19.3	19.3	20.5	6.0
Intrarater	2.05 1.56	21.0	21.0	18.5	16.0	18.5	4.9
Phi coefficient	0.47 0.92	71.6	18.5	3.7	3.7	2.5	0.0
Phi (lambda)	0.32 0.74	79.0	13.6	4.9	1.2	1.2	0.0
Agreement coefficient	0.51 1.04	73.7	12.5	6.3	5.0	1.2	1.2
Kappa	0.26 0.71	83.7	10.0	3.7	1.2	1.2	0.0
Generalizability coefficient	0.44 0.85	72.8	16.0	4.9	6.2	0.0	0.0

Table 12.6 Responses for test validity

Topic	Likert Mean SD	Percent negative responses 0	Percent positive responses Some 1	Moderate 2	3	Extensive 4	5
Content validity	3.17 1.26	1.2	9.5	19.0	28.6	25.0	16.7
Item-objective congruence	2.15 1.42	15.9	18.3	24.4	22.0	15.9	3.7
Item-specification congruence	2.10 1.45	18.3	17.1	24.4	20.7	15.9	3.7
Construct validity	3.01 1.37	2.4	13.3	20.5	25.3	21.7	16.9
Criterion-related validity	2.75 1.40	6.0	15.7	19.3	26.5	21.7	10.8
Correlational analysis	2.33 1.60	17.3	18.5	13.6	23.5	18.5	8.6
Simple regression analysis	1.11 1.29	47.6	17.1	17.1	14.6	2.4	1.2
Standard error of estimate	1.22 1.30	41.5	20.7	18.3	14.6	3.7	1.2
Principle components analysis	0.48 0.82	67.5	21.7	6.0	4.8	0.0	0.0
Rotated factor analysis	0.40 0.75	72.3	19.3	4.8	3.6	0.0	0.0
Confirmatory factor analysis	0.39 0.71	71.1	22.9	2.4	3.6	0.0	0.0
Multi-trait/multi-measure	0.73 0.98	53.0	30.1	8.4	7.2	1.2	0.0

of Measurement, and Interrater and Intrarater Reliability). Some of the more detailed methods that are used for calculating internal consistency reliability (Split-half Adjusted Method, Spearman-Brown Prophecy Formula, K-R 20, K-R 21 and Cronbach Alpha) are taught to some degree in 65 to 75% of the courses. Other less familiar methods for calculating internal consistency reliability (Rulon, Flanagan & Guttman) and other statistics for criterion-referenced test dependability (Phi Coefficient, Phi [lambda], Agreement Coefficient, Kappa and Generalizability Coefficient) had much lower average Likert ratings and were covered in many fewer courses (no more than 28.4%).

Table 12.6 shows the results for topics related to test validity. Again, the overall strategies for establishing test validity (Content Validity, Item-objective Congruence, Item-Specification Congruence, Construct Validity, Criterion-related Validity and Simple Correlational analysis) all appeared to be relatively common and received relatively more coverage in language testing courses, while regression analysis (Simple Regression Analysis and Standard Error of Estimate) received less attention and was covered in fewer courses. In addition, more complex forms of correlational analysis (Principle Components Analysis, Rotated Factor Analysis, Confirmatory Factor Analysis and Multi-trait/Multi-method analysis) received far less coverage and were less taught less frequently.

There was also a question about the percent of the course that was devoted to criterion-referenced and norm-referenced testing issues. The respondents apparently found this question to be ambiguous and interpreted it in two ways: 50% of the respondents answered as though criterion-referenced and norm-referenced testing were overall organizing principles for the entire course with other topics being subordinate (i.e. the percents added up to 100%). On average, these respondents reported that criterion-referenced testing made up 48.28% of their course, while norm-referenced testing accounted for 51.72%. The other 50% of the respondents answered as though criterion-referenced and norm-referenced testing were topics like any other topic on the Likert scale questions discussed above (i.e. they added up to something less than 100%). On average, these respondents reported that criterion-referenced testing made up 15.44% of their course, while norm-referenced testing accounted for 17.62%.

In response to a question on whether their institutions offered an advanced language testing course, 83.3% of the respondents answered NO. Only 16.7% indicated that an advanced testing course was available.

Respondents were asked to send a copy of their syllabus or course outline with the completed surveys. Fifty out of the 84 respondents did so. These materials varied widely in terms of the extent to which goals and assignments were specified. However, we were able to ascertain which textbooks are commonly used by the language testing instructors. Table 12.7 lists the author and title of each text mentioned, and whether or not it was required or optional. From these titles one can infer that there is a wide range of emphasis, from the very theoretical to the very practical, in the assessment preparation language teachers receive.

Table 12.7 Textbooks listed in language testing course syllabuses (n = 50)

Author	Title	Required/optional
Henning:	*A Guide to Language Testing*	10 / 2
Madsen:	*Techniques in Testing*	10 / 2
Hughes:	*Testing for Language Teachers*	9 / 0
Bachman:	*Fundamental Considerations in Language Testing*	8 / 1
Oller:	*Language Tests at School*	7 / 0
Shohamy:	*A Practical Handbook in Language Testing for the Second Language Teacher*	6 / 0
Cohen:	*Testing Language Ability in the Classroom*	4 / 4
Gronlund:	*Measurement and Evaluation in Teaching*	3 / 0
Harris:	*Testing English as a Second Language*	3 / 0
Valette:	*Modern Language Testing*	3 / 0
Brown:	*Understanding Research in Second Language Learning*	2 / 0
Brown:	*Language Testing: A Practical Guide to . . . Testing* (ms.)	2 / 0
Carroll & Hall:	*Make Your Own Language Tests*	2 / 0
Gronlund:	*How to Construct Achievement Tests*	2 / 0
Heaton:	*Classroom Testing*	2 / 0
E.T.S.:	*TOEFL Test and Score Manual*	2 / 0
Alderson et al.:	*Reviews of English Language Proficiency Tests*	1 / 3
Hatch & Farhady:	*Research Design and Statistics for Applied Linguistics*	1 / 2
Carroll:	*Testing Communicative Performance*	1 / 1
Oller:	*Issues in Language Testing*	1 / 1
Baker:	*Language Testing: A Critical Survey & Practical Guide*	1 / 0
Douglas:	*English Language Testing in US Colleges & Universities*	1 / 0
Heaton:	*Writing English Language Tests*	1 / 0

Table 12.7 *continued*

Author	Title	Required/ optional
Hudson:	*L2 Testing: Forms and Functions of Test Content* (ms.)	1/0
Huff:	*How to Lie with Statistics*	1/0
Jacobs *et al.*:	*Testing ESL Composition: A Practical Approach*	1/0
Joint Committee on Testing Practices:	*Code of Fair Testing Practices in Education*	1/0
Kerlinger:	*Foundations of Behavioral Research*	1/0
	TOEFL Research Report #7 (Communicative Viewpoint . . .)	1/0
Woods, Fletcher & Hughes:	*Statistics in Language Studies*	1/0
de Jong & Stevenson	*Individualizing the Assessment of Language Abilities*	1/0
Underhill:	*Testing Spoken Language*	0/1
Lado:	*Language Testing – The Construction & Use of F.L. Tests*	0/1

Information about students

According to this sample, 77.1% of the courses described were intended for graduate students, 7.2% for undergraduates and 15.7% for both graduate and undergraduate students. It also appears that 39.8% of the students take the program's testing course as an elective, while it is a required course for 60.2%. In addition, 97.6% of the respondents indicated that the course provided credit toward the students' degrees, while 2.4% answered that the course did not count toward the academic degrees.

In selecting from a list of eight adjective phrases describing how their students reacted to their language testing courses, 80% of the respondents indicated that their students found the courses *interesting*, 80% selected *useful*, 68% chose *challenging*, 60% selected *nice balance between theory and practice*, 46% choose *difficult*, 33% selected *too theoretical*, and only 7% and 4% selected *easy* and *too practical*, respectively.

Discussion and Conclusions

At the beginning of this chapter we listed seven standards for teacher development regarding assessment in general education. Although the items in the present questionnaire were not developed with these standards in mind, it behooves us, as a profession to consider drafting or adapting a similar set of standards dealing specifically with language assessment.

At this time, given the results of the present survey, it is clear that there is a great deal of diversity in the sorts of language testing preparation provided to teachers. This diversity is revealed in the quantitative data on testing course emphases (reported in Tables 12.1 through 12.6) and the list of required and optional textbooks (Table 12.7).

Possibly as an artifact of our sampling procedures, over 67% of the respondents in this particular survey were from programs in the United States. Thus the trends reported probably reflect a US-bias in terms of the contents of such courses, the characteristics of the students, and the background of the instructors. Further research is needed, including investigations in more teacher preparation programs outside the United States.

In addition, given the membership of the LTRC and our use of the TESOL program directory to increase the pool of respondents, the respondents in this study were largely concerned with the assessment of learners' English (whether in a second-language context or a foreign-language context). Although we did not exclude other languages from our data base, teachers (and teacher educators) from the foreign language field are underrepresented in this study. Further research is needed to examine the assessment preparation for teachers of languages other than English. Such research might well be conducted by professional organizations such as the American Council of Teachers of Foreign Languages (ACTFL).

As a group, we are just beginning to examine the ways in which we prepare language teachers for their testing responsibilities. The results of this survey have been reported in hopes that language testers (particularly those responsible for teacher education with regard to assessment) may benefit from an initial description of the language testing 'sub-profession' discussed by Jones (1985: 16).

Acknowledgements

The authors wish to thank Donna Ilyin for providing the mailing list for the LTRC, Thom Hudson for his help in developing the questionnaire, and Ally Joye and Lisa Patnoe for their assistance with the word processing and the qualitative data analysis.

References

Assessment Standards (1990) *The Northwest Report*, October, p. 2.

Brindley, G. (1991) Language assessment and teacher development. Paper presented at the International Conference on Teacher Education, City Polytechnic of Hong Kong, 17–19 April.

Brown, J. D., Knowles, M., Murray, D., Neu, J. and Violand-Hainer, E. (1992) TESOL research task force survey. Paper presented at the TESOL Convention, Vancouver, British Columbia.

Jones, R. L. (1985) Second language performance testing: An overview. In P. C. Hauptman, R. Le Blanc and M. B. Wesche, (eds) *Second Language Performance Testing*. Ottawa: University of Ottawa Press.

Kornblum, H. with Gilligan, M. (1989) *Directory of Professional Preparation Programs in TESOL in the United States, 1989–1991*. Alexandria, VA: TESOL.

Lazarton, A., Riggenbach, H. and Ediger, A. (1987) Forming a discipline: Applied linguists' literacy in research methodology and statistics. *TESOL Quarterly* 21, 263–77.

Peirce, B. (1990) Demystifying language assessment. Paper presented at the Language Testing Research Colloquium, San Francisco.

Richards, J. C. and Crookes, G. (1988) The practicum in TESOL. *TESOL Quarterly* 22, 9–27.

Richards, J. C. and Hino, N. (1983) Training TESOL teachers: The need for needs assessment. In J. E. Alatis, P. Strevens and H. H. Stern (eds) *Applied Linguistics and the Preparation of Second Language Teachers: Toward a Rationale* (pp. 312–26). Washington, DC: Georgetown University Press.

Appendix 1: Language testing course description questionnaire

Name .... Sex .... Age ....

Nationality .... Office Phone: (........)...............

Institution ....

Address ....

....

(1) Have you ever taught an INTRODUCTORY level
    language testing course of any kind (Circle one)?   YES   NO

If your answer to question 1 is NO, please stop and mail the questionnaire in the self-addressed envelope provided. Remember, it is important that we hear from those of you not teaching testing courses, too. If your answer was YES, please continue!

About the instructor:

What degrees do you hold (include the field of study for each)?

....

....

....

....

How many testing/statistics courses have you taken? And, what were they?

....

....

....

....

What other types of non-course testing experiences/preparation have you had?

....

....

....

....

About the course:

How much time do the students spend actually getting hands-on experience with the following in your course (circle number)?

	Amount of time				
Type of experience:	*None*	*Some*	*Moderate*		*Extensive*
item writing	0	1	2	3	4	5
test administration	0	1	2	3	4	5
test scoring	0	1	2	3	4	5
test score interpretation	0	1	2	3	4	5
test revision	0	1	2	3	4	5
test critiquing	0	1	2	3	4	5
test taking	0	1	2	3	4	5

How much time do you spend on the following topics (circle number)?

General:	None	Some	Moderate		Extensive	
			Amount of time			
norm-referenced testing	0	1	2	3	4	5
criterion-referenced testing	0	1	2	3	4	5
achievement testing	0	1	2	3	4	5
aptitude testing	0	1	2	3	4	5
diagnostic testing	0	1	2	3	4	5
placement testing	0	1	2	3	4	5
proficiency testing	0	1	2	3	4	5
measuring attitudes	0	1	2	3	4	5
measuring the different skills	0	1	2	3	4	5
assessment at different levels	0	1	2	3	4	5
critiquing published tests	0	1	2	3	4	5
others?	0	1	2	3	4	5
....	0	1	2	3	4	5
....	0	1	2	3	4	5

Item analysis:						
item writing	0	1	2	3	4	5
item writing for different skills	0	1	2	3	4	5
item content analysis	0	1	2	3	4	5
item quality analysis	0	1	2	3	4	5
item facility (a.k.a. item difficulty or easiness)	0	1	2	3	4	5
item discrimination (traditional)	0	1	2	3	4	5
biserial correlation	0	1	2	3	4	5
item agreement	0	1	2	3	4	5
item beta	0	1	2	3	4	5
distractor efficiency analysis	0	1	2	3	4	5
one-parameter IRT	0	1	2	3	4	5
two-parameter IRT	0	1	2	3	4	5
three-parameter IRT	0	1	2	3	4	5
others?	0	1	2	3	4	5
....	0	1	2	3	4	5
....	0	1	2	3	4	5

	Amount of time				
Descriptive statistics:	*None*	*Some*	*Moderate*		*Extensive*	
mean	0	1	2	3	4	5
mode	0	1	2	3	4	5
median	0	1	2	3	4	5
midpoint	0	1	2	3	4	5
range	0	1	2	3	4	5
standard deviation	0	1	2	3	4	5
variance	0	1	2	3	4	5
stanines	0	1	2	3	4	5
z scores	0	1	2	3	4	5
T scores	0	1	2	3	4	5
CEEB scores	0	1	2	3	4	5
others?	0	1	2	3	4	5
....	0	1	2	3	4	5
....	0	1	2	3	4	5
Test consistency:						
reliability and test length	0	1	2	3	4	5
reliability and ranges of talent	0	1	2	3	4	5
test-retest reliability	0	1	2	3	4	5
parallel forms reliability	0	1	2	3	4	5
internal consistency reliability	0	1	2	3	4	5
standard error of measurement	0	1	2	3	4	5
split-half adjusted method	0	1	2	3	4	5
Spearman-Brown Prophecy Formula	0	1	2	3	4	5
K-R 20	0	1	2	3	4	5
K-R 21	0	1	2	3	4	5
Cronbach alpha	0	1	2	3	4	5
Rulon	0	1	2	3	4	5
Flanagan	0	1	2	3	4	5
Guttman	0	1	2	3	4	5
interrater	0	1	2	3	4	5
intrarater	0	1	2	3	4	5
phi coefficient	0	1	2	3	4	5
phi (lambda)	0	1	2	3	4	5
agreement coefficient	0	1	2	3	4	5
kappa	0	1	2	3	4	5
generalizability coefficient	0	1	2	3	4	5
others?	0	1	2	3	4	5
....	0	1	2	3	4	5
....	0	1	2	3	4	5

	None	*Some*	*Moderate*		*Extensive*	
			Amount of time			
Validity:						
content validity	0	1	2	3	4	5
item-objective congruence	0	1	2	3	4	5
item-specification congruence	0	1	2	3	4	5
construct validity	0	1	2	3	4	5
criterion-related validity	0	1	2	3	4	5
correlational analysis	0	1	2	3	4	5
simple regression analysis	0	1	2	3	4	5
standard error of estimate	0	1	2	3	4	5
principle components analysis	0	1	2	3	4	5
rotated factor analysis	0	1	2	3	4	5
confirmatory factor analysis	0	1	2	3	4	5
multi-trait/multi-measure	0	1	2	3	4	5
others?	0	1	2	3	4	5
....	0	1	2	3	4	5
....	0	1	2	3	4	5

What percentage of the course do you devote to these general areas:

Criterion-referenced testing issues? ....

Norm-referenced testing issues? ....

The students:

What type(s) of students take your course (graduate/undergraduate, majors, etc.)?

....

....

Does the course count toward a degree or other certification?

....

....

Is the course required or optional (circle one)?   required   optional

How do your students feel about language testing before the course?

....

....

How do your students feel about language testing after having taken the course?

....

....

In general, do you think that your students find your course (check all of those which you think apply):

.... interesting

.... too theoretical

.... easy

.... useful

.... too practical

.... difficult

.... a nice balance between theory and practice

.... challenging

.... others?

Do you teach any other more advanced courses in language testing at your institution (briefly describe course and level)?

....

....

What other questions do you think should have been on this questionnaire, and how would you answer them?

....

....

Other comments of any kind (use back of page if you need more space):

....

....

Please remember to attach a copy of a recent course syllabus or other material describing your course. And check the box below if you would like a copy of our final report on this project.

Thank you in advance for your help with this project!

Subject Index

analysis of variance, 85-88, 173, 234-235

catalytic validity, 4
classroom observation, 201-217
communicative competence or strategies, 7, 15-17, 19, 59, 60, 75, 114, 124-153, 154-170, 197
computer-adaptive assessment, 10, 111-123
concurrent validity, 2, 8-9, 10, 11, 94-95, 102-110, 111-122
consequential basis of validity, 5-7, 10, 11-12, 194-220, 223, 236, 238
construct validity, 2, 5-9, 10, 39, 49, 53, 58-71, 72-90, 111-112, 125, 222-223, 246-247
content validity, 3, 8, 11, 16, 60, 73-75, 80-82, 125-142, 155, 159-162, 175-193, 197, 233-234, 246-247
convergent validity, 3, 104, 117-121, 171-193
criterion-related validity, 3, 10, 76, 246-247

discriminant validity, 3
distractors, 98, 105, 115, 244

ecological validity, 3, 201-213
evidential basis of validity, 6, 10, 113, 218-219
expert judgments, 11, 20, 42-51, 75, 124-142, 159, 176, 180-184

face validity, 3, 4, 20, 94, 101-102, 155-156, 228, 232-234
factorial validity, 3, 58, 71, 113, 247

grammar, 16-24, 32, 35, 60-70, 72-90, 182-183, 185, 198

hypothesis-testing, 10, 59-71, 82-89

instrinsic validity, 3
interviews, 17-20, 83, 124
item response theory, 112, 117, 120, 122, 244

languages tested:
— English, 15-38, 39-58, 58-71, 72-90, 94-110, 124-153, 171-193, 194-220
— French, 111-123, 124-153, 154-170
— Spanish, 124-153
listening comprehension, 60-70, 198, 205

Messick's progressive matrix, 6-7, 10
multivariate analyses, 62-69, 104

operational validity, 3

partial credit analysis, 25
placement testing, 40-43, 58-60, 70, 83, 94, 96, 111-113, 242
population validity, 3, 87-88, 127, 132-142
predictive validity, 3, 8-9, 113
professional training and standards, 222-235, 236-256

Rasch analysis, 9, 25-30, 39, 43-53, 115, 125-142
rater training, 20, 49-51, 78-79, 180-181
rating scales, 9, 18-30, 41-53, 60-70, 72, 74, 101, 124-142, 179-180
reading comprehension, 11, 60-70, 94-110, 113-114, 154-170, 171-193, 195-198, 205-208
reliability, 9, 20-24, 42, 44-49, 77-79, 84, 95, 97, 100-101, 105-106, 115-117, 121-122, 127-142, 157, 181-184, 244-246

reflexive validity, 4

self-assessment, 95-96, 98, 101-102, 106
spoken (oral) discourse production, 15-
    38, 124-153, 198

task validity or variability, 3, 18, 47-49,
    74-76, 86-87, 90, 97, 100-101, 104,
    105, 111, 116, 122, 140-141, 155-169,
    171-193
temporal validity, 3
test development, 17, 20, 41-42, 60, 98,
    115, 120, 126, 154-156, 196-198

test use, 6, 10, 156-163, 197-201, 213-216
think-aloud protocols, 157-170

validity generalization, 3, 7-8, 73, 158,
    162-163
vocabulary, 16-29, 32, 72, 75, 77, 82-
    88, 114, 170, 178, 183, 185, 191,
    223-231

washback, 7, 11, 155, 194-220
written discourse production, 39-57,
    60-70, 72-90, 97-98, 196-198, 205,
    207, 209